CLASSIC

DEER CAMPS

ROBERT WEGNER

©2008 Robert Wegner

Published by

krause publications
An Imprint of F+W Publications

700 East State Street • Iola, WI 54990-0001
715-445-2214 • 888-457-2873
www.krausebooks.com

Our toll-free number to place an order or obtain
a free catalog is (800) 258-0929.

Library of Congress Control Number: 2007942608

ISBN-13: 978-0-89689-655-0
ISBN-10: 0-89689-655-2

Designed by Paul Birling
Edited by Dan Shideler

Printed in China

DEDICATION

For the memory of Fred Bear,
the "Natty Bumppo" of my youth,
who instilled in me
a life-long passion
for romancing deer camp, wood smoke
and the whitetail.

Robert Wegner, Ph.D.
Deer Valley, Wisconsin – March, 2008

Opening day. Better give it our best shot.

Twelve after four. Undercooked bacon, overcooked eggs and coffee that would ordinarily get more attention than respect.

You didn't notice. Everything tasted great on this greatest of all days—opening day. And, when you're getting ready to go after that big buck, remember this: once you're lined up on him, the success or failure of the whole hunt could depend on one shot.

When you squeeze the trigger, the bullet must go right where you aim it. And it's got to have plenty of stopping power when it gets there.

Now remember this: Remington cartridges with "Core-Lokt" bullets are known throughout the hunt-ing world for their excellent mushrooming qualities.

The metal jacket and lead core of a "Core-Lokt" bullet are locked together by the jacket's heavy mid-section. So the bullet stays in one piece for uniform expansion and all the one-shot power you need at any range.

Remington cartridges with "Core-Lokt" bullets. In 24 big game calibers. Give it your best shot with our best shot.

Remington. ⊙DUPONT

"Remington" and "Core-Lokt" are trademarks registered in the United States Patent Office.

PREFACE

Historically, the name REMINGTON has remained virtually synonymous with white-tailed deer hunting and deer camps ever since its inception in 1816, as this 1977 "Opening Day. Better give it our best shot" ad well indicates. This unique and striking image will live on in the minds of white-tailed deer hunters forever. It first caught my attention in the fall issues of Outdoor Life as I prepared for the opening day of deer season that year and headed for the deer shack – "The Jackson County Copa Cabana" – in the hills of central Wisconsin near the small town of Levis with my favorite Remington firearms: the 12-gauge Model 1100 slug shotgun and the Remington Model 700 .30-06 rifle – and, of course, the famous Remington cartridges with their "Core Lokt" bullets.

I came of age with this standard equipment at the deer shack in the heart of Remington Country. At twelve after four on opening day it didn't really matter whether Pa undercooked the bacon and overcooked the eggs; what did indeed matter, as the folks at Remington always insisted, was that I would give that buck my best shot. And Remington always supplied us with the traditionally splendid equipment to do just that.

In looking at this classic Remington deer hunting ad we immediately realize that the deer hunter in the plaid bathrobe receiving his over-cooked eggs doesn't seem to really care about the quality of his cuisine, for his mind remains riveted on white-tailed bucks and putting the final touches to his Remington Model 700 .30-06. For it's opening day, and he better give it his best shot! I grew up in Remington Country, where lots of Remington 700s appeared in the window racks of Chevy pickups, so much so that the Model 700 over time acquired the historic reputation as "Everyman's Deer Rifle" and today lies at the very heart of many legendary deer camps nationwide.

When I think of white-tailed deer and deer hunting I see red coats, plaid shirts, Remington guns and cartridges, classic deer camps, the current issues of *Deer & Deer Hunting* magazine, and of course white-tailed flags waving in the breeze and the sweet smell of venison tenderloins frying in onions and bacon in a cast iron pan. Opening day reminds me of "Holy Week" with all the religiosity that implies, a time when the deer camp becomes the Church in the Wildwood; where wood smoke and Old Number 7 make us dream and stay young. Come join me as I journey into the world of legendary deer camps, whitetail romance, adventure, nostalgia and Americana – all highlighted with great images from the Remington Art Collection.

Robert Wegner
Deer Valley – March, 2008

FOREWORD

by Art Wheaton

The woodstove has finally turned cold, when just a few hours ago it glowed with such warmth that it permeated even the peeled spruce logs that were chinked with oakum to keep out most of the frosty fall air. Sports and guides snore in chorus, interrupted only by an occasional snort or a hasty trip outside to restore personal comfort. The camp is cold now and the wool blankets are pulled snug around the neck. Sleep fast, deer hunters, as a head guide or cook will be rousting you out well before daylight.

Whether it be in those early lean-tos with fir and spruce bows for bedding or the low slung trappers cabins where one could hardly stand up, or later the old abandoned lumber camps with then "luxurious accommodations" like a mattress, deer hunters across the northeast traveled for days by train, buckboard or stage, then canoe, to those special places where the whitetail deer roamed free in the big woods.

Bucks searched along the hardwood ridges as the cold weather signaled a time for love; later, the shed antlers gave evidence of new racks and new beginnings. Deer often used the old logging trails for ease of travel, as did their pursuers, who followed in hopes of catching one unaware. A track in the snow testified to a wily old buck in search of courtship. Later these hardy whitetails yarded in cedar swamps during the deep snows, reaching for browse – a poorer quality food, yet it sustained life through the bitter cold long winter months.

They came from far and wide! The lore of giant big-bodied deer; the call of the wild; the woodsman-turned-guide who got his training cutting pine, spruce or fir logs and put on his cork boots to run the booms in spring, using the axe, crosscut, bucksaw then paddle, pole and canoe to penetrate the deep woods – all these caught the attention of America. Returning sports talked about a special breed of guide who knew his way with compass or dead reckoning to find the way home, who was a special friend in the wilderness, and who these greenhorns trusted with their lives.

The romance of these backwoods guides and the abundance of game as reported by a host of contemporary publications captured the imagination of sportsman across the country, and a deer hunting culture arose that became the foundation of a great American tradition. In the following pages, the storied past is researched and recreated by Rob Wegner, a deer hunter in his own right. Rob brings back these days gone by so that we might better understand why we do what we do each fall. His insatiable appetite to gather the black and white images of our past, his enthusiastic search for yellowing log books, and his endless passion for interviewing third generations of hunters before it is to late – all these are part and parcel of his love for the lore of classic American deer camps.

GREETINGS FROM NORTHERN MAINE.

CONTENTS

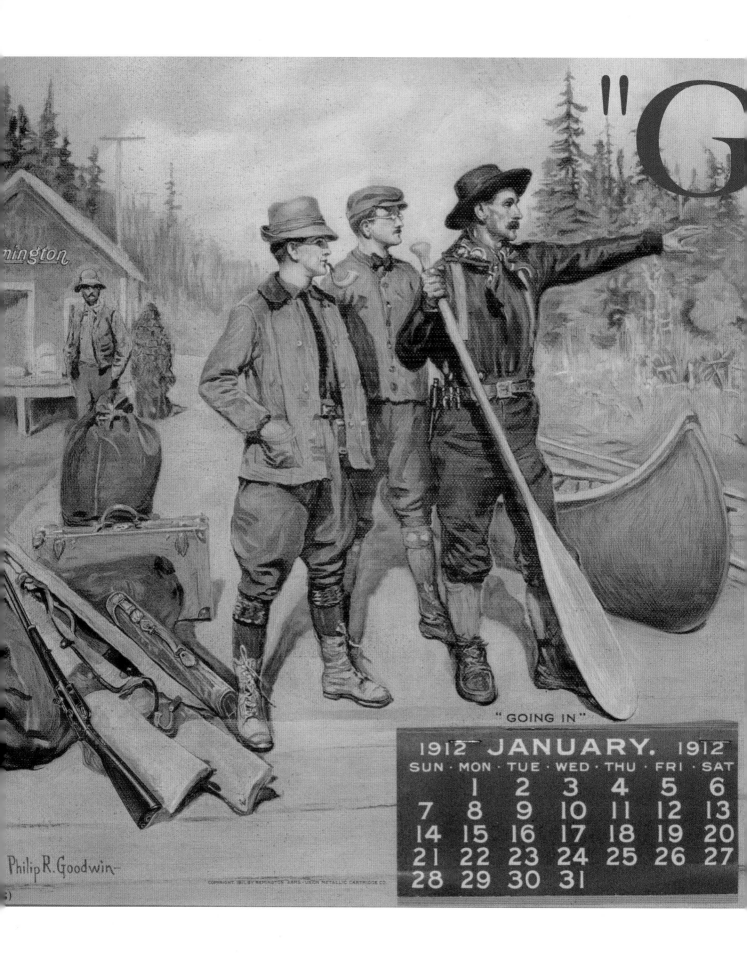

"GOING IN"

1912 **JANUARY.** 1912

SUN	MON	TUE	WED	THU	FRI	SAT
	1	2	3	4	5	6
7	8	9	10	11	12	13
14	15	16	17	18	19	20
21	22	23	24	25	26	27
28	29	30	31			

Philip R. Goodwin

OING IN"
BY ART WHEATON

The Hunters' Lament

In Maine when autumn rolls around
And leaves and frost are on the ground
We make our plans and check our gear,
For this is the time of year –
We head up north to try our luck
And see if we can shoot a buck.

– Bill Robson

P hilip R. Goodwin, in his 1912 calendar for Remington Arms Company, captured the essence of the Maine deer hunt at the turn of the last century with his "Going In" to the interior of this vast, game-rich wilderness via railroad and canoe. Goodwin's romantic train station scene of "sports," guide and luggage – as well as the very transportation system that brought thousands to chase mighty Maine bucks in this remote region opened from wood cutting operations – sets the tone for a look at some of America's classic, legendary deer camps.

My grandfather and later my father guided "sports" in these exciting times, when abundant game could be sold and transported to market; when the Great Depression of our country gave license to living off the land for survival; and when lenient enforcement

NGTON ARMS-UNION METALLIC CARTRIDGE CO.
299 Broadway.
NEW YORK

REMINGTON
UMC
TRADE MARK

Courtesy Art Wheaton.

"Going In." Oil on canvas. Philip R. Goodwin, 1912.

gave way to the Downeast Game War around Crawford and Wesley, Maine.

Maine became a state on March 15, 1820. Shortly thereafter Aroostook County incorporated in 1839 and enlarged in 1843, becoming the largest county in Maine. Aroostook County alone, with its approximately 6800 square miles, is nearly as large as Massachusetts and about 500 square miles larger than Connecticut. In perspective, if we drew a line across the state at Bangor, the area to the north would be greater than the area of the states of Vermont and New Hampshire combined.

The wild lands of northern Maine, while sparsely settled, were dotted with an endless chain of lakes and scores of rivers and streams, representing approximately 15,000 square miles of rich hunting and fishing territory – a true sporting paradise indeed. Private landowners from Massachusetts bought vast townships in Maine for a song and produced more timber than anyplace in the world from 1820 until after the Civil War. By the 1850s, these landowners cut most of the tall first-growth softwood trees within hauling distance of the rivers.

As a result, Bangor became the boom town lumber capital of the world, and by the 1870s logging railroads and portable steam powered sawmills enabled timber companies to reach deeper into previously inaccessible areas. Although these supposedly infinite supplies of virgin wood were showing their limits, railroads, logging roads and trails increased accessibility to game-rich, remote destinations.

With the big pine and spruce gone, the wood pulp and paper mills emerged by the 1880s and by 1910 large paper companies acquired the huge land tracks from

As the twentieth century got underway, women deer hunters following the lead of "Fly Rod" Crosby not only appeared in the deer camps of Maine but in the deer hunting advertisements, sporting literature and postcards of the era, circa 1909.

WINCHESTER AUTOMATIC RIFLE

the departing logging companies. Railroad companies seeking fares to these remote locations greatly promoted white-tailed deer hunting. The lumber camps gradually gave way to deer camps. Indeed, the railroad companies became a basic component of early American deer hunting by promoting in their travel literature the chase of big, white-tailed bucks (big deer over 200 pounds). Sportsman quickly sought out previously unheard-of small towns and villages in the Northeast. The deer-hunting adventures in these areas soon became "the talk" among the well-to-do sportsman of Boston, New York and other metropolitan areas.

As sportsman exhibits and shows became extraordinarily popular in Boston and New York, Maine jumped on the bandwagon by setting up full-size white-tailed deer mounts and complete deer hunting camps on location.

Deer hunting and fishing emerged as regular themes in the popular press with Maine's very own lady marketer, "Fly Rod" Crosby, taking center stage at places such as Park Square Garden, Boston and in the press as well.

Such events were the backdrop of the turn of the twentieth century and "sports," as hunters were commonly and fondly called in Maine, began "Going In" to Maine's sportsman's paradise via the Boston & Maine, Maine Central and Bangor & Aroostook railroads. These railroads actively and aggressively promoted access to remote Maine points from Boston, New York, Portland and other centers of population. The railroad system played a central role in opening this vast wilderness to the emergence of sporting camps at all levels of accommodation from the very rustic to the luxurious, secluded, and sacred deer camps.

"Going In" typically commenced on a "Pullman" or sleeper car that left Boston's Union Station and arrived at Bangor early in the morning. Following breakfast, the deer hunters found themselves deep into B&A territory. Peak travel occurred during the week prior to October 1, the opening of the deer season, and a week prior to October 15, the opening of the moose season.

Arthur R. Wheaton (1866-1938), my grandfather, came to Maine as a young lad in the mid-1800s from Rhode Island to work in the Shaw Brothers Tannery and by 1900 turned to guiding sportsmen for an occupation in and around the hamlets of Grand Lake Stream and Waite, Maine.

The logging of pine, spruce, and hemlock opened more deer hunting and fishing opportunities. Deer thrived in the new browse and lived in the cedar swamps in winter, and fish accompanied the log booms for the bugs that fell off them. Fly Rod Crosby continued to promote and market Maine deer hunting and fishing though her writings and outdoor adventures. In Fly Rod's day bamboo from Bangor was transformed by Maine producers such as Payne, Thomas and Leonard into the preferred tools of fly fishermen.

On March 19, 1897, Maine passed the Guide Bill that Fly Rod Crosby enthusiastically promoted; the state awarded this legendary sportswoman the very first Maine guide's license for her work. The bill created a comprehensive list of who's who in the field of guiding and the area in which they specialized. The bill required guides to pay a fee of one dollar each year and file a one-page annual report form.

Although both history and folklore play an important part in our knowledge of our deer camp culture, we must remember the wildlife conservation movement also began in the late 1800s. Following the disastrous Maine deer kill in 1882, sportsmen initiated legislation in 1883 for tougher restrictions on the use of dogs to hunt deer, the elimination of Sunday hunting and broader enforcement coupled with a limit of one moose, two caribou and three deer. The Crawford and Wesley area, off Maine's Route 9 (locally called the "airline") became the scene of strong resistance to this change.

The illegal deer poaching escapades of George Magoon (1851-1929), Wilber Day (1864-1924), and Calvin Graves (1844-1924), so well documented in Edward Ives' *George Magoon and the Down East Game War,* brought a way of life into direct conflict with the law. Poaching, running deer with dogs, out of season hunting and other infractions were credited to folks such as Magoon and Day, who became folk legend and cult heroes in outwitting game wardens as well as for being caught for their many game violations.

Day operated a deer hunting camp of his own and accommodated sportsman from "away." A violent reaction to the dogging law occurred when Graves confronted Warden Lynn Hill and his deputy, who, against Graves' warnings, killed Graves' bird dogs for running deer. Calvin Graves turned his shotgun on Hill and killed him along with his deputy and went off to Thomaston prison.

My dad, Woodie Wheaton (1909-1990), remembered the incident and many local stories coming from that area while living in his hometown of Grand Lake Stream. He frequently recalled that when Warden "Darky" White attempted to investigate the deer poaching activities of folks on one side of town, poachers immediately started to shoot deer out of season on the other side of town.

Some of the best known "deer camps," along with their proprietors, became legendary in this Maine woods Mecca; while many "hunting camps" run by guides themselves were also a part of the landscape. My family roots of Registered Maine Guides, born and/or raised in the Pine Tree State, lay deep in this outdoor tradition for more than 125 years; my grandfather guided for 38 years and my father held a Master Guide License for 68 years and I myself have been licensed since the 1950s.

Arthur Rutledge Wheaton (1866-1938), circa 1930.

Many of these guides left us with high-level prose about their deer camp adventures. Arthur Rutledge Wheaton left this classy, nostalgic prose about a stay on Wabash Stream:

Raleigh & Ralph & Rags & Me

The plot was ripe, the wind went down
At twilight, cool and clear.
The hunters started on their way
To stalk the foxy deer.
Away they went upon the lake.
Silently, side by side.

On, Sunday morn we slept quite late.
At half past ten we pulled our freight.
Canoes were full, don't tell the State,
I know a warden's heart would ache.

At last they came to their camping ground,
Which ended their dark long ride.
The camp was made, the night was spent.
Upon the ground they pitched their tent.

And as I dream of the mossy floor.
I seem to hear the same wind roar.
I seem to see the antlered buck
That gave us each our streak of luck.

At 4 A. M. I heard someone say,
"Come boys", don't sleep all day!"
Then we rolled out and scald the tea,
While Ralph made slugs for Raleigh and me.

The stately buck and the timid doe
Can never tell their tale of woe.
The handsome buck, the doe, the fawn,
They had their chance but some are gone,
And we will follow, soon or late.
Little it matters to the State,
Where it's graft, the rest is hate.

On each left arm laid a trusty gun,
And a lot of damage each had done.
With harness on and stars so bright,
We hit the trail before 'twas light.
With ears so keen and silent tread,

It could not be long 'til a deer was dead.
Now think it o'ver my trusty friend,
We'll be here once and then the end.
My pipes gone out but still I dream,
Of our little party at Wabash Stream.

The days sped on and every night,
We spun our yarns around camp fire bright.
The yarns were true, as blood did tell,
That many a buck his life did sell,
The hunt was o'ver, 'tis now a dream,
Our pleasant stay on Wabash Stream.

I'm getting old but my heart is young.
Worse songs than this are often sung.
My eyes are dim but still I see,
Raleigh and Ralph and Rags and me.

"Woodie" Wheaton's Grand Lake Brook Camp, 1945. Kneeling L-R: Ralph Beach, "Woodie" Wheaton. Back L-R: Archie Sparling, Bob White, Lewis Brown, Bill Sparling, Jack McKelvey, Jr.

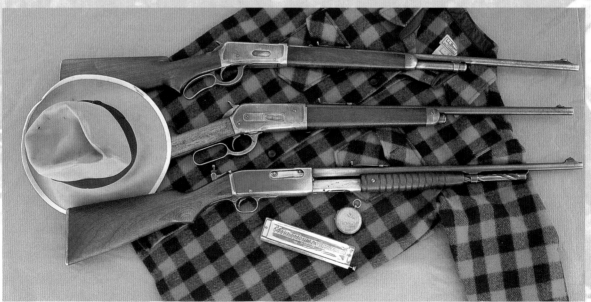

"Woodie" Wheaton's Remington Model 14 in .32 Remington Special; Winchester Model 1886 in .45-70 owned by his father, Arthur R. Wheaton; Winchester Model 1894 in .32 Winchester Special owned by Art Wheaton's other grandfather, Arthur H. Christie; and Woodie's Harmonica.

Buckboard driver Billy Brown taking the venison home from Woodie's deer camp, 1945.

"Woodie" Wheaton and guides at his Grand Lake Brook Camp, 1945. Front to back: "Woodie" Wheaton, guide; Archie Sparling; Bill Sparling; Bob White. Right side front to back: Jack McKelvy, guide; Ralph Beach, guide; Lewis Brown, guide; Howard Lilly. Camp photographer Frank Sparling not shown.

The game poles, rustic icons of the past, black and white images, the written word, legend and lore shape our past and give foundation to our deer camp traditions and heritage. White-tailed deer hunters need to bask in our past to better understand and relish the future.

Camp Caribou on Treat's Island, Parmachenee Lake, in the Rangeley area of western Maine and Lake Umbagog, N.H. established by John S. Danforth (1847-1913) in the early 1870's, emerged as one of the earliest legendary deer camps of the time. He leased approximately 200,000 acres from the Berlin Mills Company and initially set up a floating camp that would eventually be pulled ashore and have a foundation added to it. Ultimately, Danforth constructed further additions as more deer hunters and fisherman learned about the great adventures and big bucks at Camp Caribou.

Danforth, distinguished by his tall frame, generous moustache and upturned hat on one side, became a legendary hunter, trapper, and guide and published his *Hunting and Trapping on the Upper Magalloway and Parmachenee Lake: A Winter in the Wilderness* in 1882. An ambitious outdoorsman with tremendous ingenuity and boundless energy, Danforth promoted his deer hunting and fishing aggressively and "may have accomplished more in his life than most men ever dream about in three lifetimes" says author Robert W. Cook in his book *Chasing Danforth*.

In his system at Camp Caribou, Danforth used numerous outlying camps such as Camp Beanhole, Camp Parmachenee along the Cupsuptic River, Beaver Pond Camp, Cupsuptic Camp, Camp Ding Dong, Lower and Upper Black Pond Camps, Moose Bog Camp, Arnold's Bog, Rump Pond, Billings Pond and Long Pond Camps, to name but a few, to accommodate many of his sports who would hunt whitetails and fish these remote areas. Each party occupied a part of the wilderness for themselves and rotated to another site depending on Danforth's plan.

Interestingly, John Danforth hunted Woodland Caribou that disappeared from

Camp Caribou on Treat's Island, Parmachenee Lake in the Rangeley area of western Maine and Lake Umbagog, N. H. established by John S. Danforth – seen here sitting on a chair with his guides and holding what appears to be a Remington or Parker underlever shotgun, circa 1890.

Maine by 1900 as well as moose, which would be so depleted by 1936 that the season closed for 44 years (until 1980). Of course, he also hunted those giant, heavy-bodied white-tailed deer of yesteryear and today.

The name "Aroostook" at the time seemed to apply to all lands in northern Maine and actually encompassed other counties as well. That name indeed became the deer hunter's ultimate destination and sacred Mecca. The famous Libby Hotel in Oxbow, Maine, became the focal point for hunters "going in" to Atkins Camps on the Island of Millinocket Lake and many out camps owned by Charles C. Libby. The Libby camps on the shore of Millinocket Lake are steeped in Maine deer hunting tradition. "Going In" from the rail stations at Oakfield and later, Marsadis, Maine, deer hunters traveled via buckboard and the stage to the stopping off accommodations at the Libby Hotel, and then on up the Aroostook River by canoe.

Libby's Sporting Camps, nearly 180 miles north of Bangor, claim one of richest histories in the state. From the late 1800s they originally existed as Atkins Camps and later became Libby's owned by C. C. Libby followed by sons Will and Ike. Allie (Ike's son) and his wife worked on Libby Island as head cook and head guide in the 1930s. The Libby name captured the imagination of the sporting world, associated as it was with stories of giant bucks, trophy deer and bear, and canoe trips all over the watersheds in the great Northwoods.

"Come on in, Mom," Matt Libby said when I interviewed him in August 2007, as his 89-year-young mother, Elsie, came and joined us to reminisce about the great Libby sporting tradition of the North Maine woods. "Yes," he said, "in the old days, our Libby Hotel was used by sports and loggers, that is, foresters, landowners, dam owners and the like. It was the stopping off spot when folks came to the area. Sports 'going in' for a two-week hunting trip came to the Masardis station by rail, then buckboard to the hotel. The only way to go any further was by canoe. Our out camps were in the Allagash starting in 1890 or we accommodated folks going to other camps."

The famous trapper Will Atkins built his own hotel in 1903 (much later to be called the Oxbow Lodge) but also used the Libby Hotel as a stopover spot for his sports who traveled 35 miles by buckboard to Oxbow. The Bangor and Aroostook Railroad ended in Oakfield at the time, then later in Masardis. The sports then traveled by canoe up the Aroostook drainage and across

Double-end canoes served as the major form of transportation for Maine deer hunters at the time.

The legendary Libby Hotel, which served as the stopover and social centerpiece of the Maine deer hunting experience.

into the Allagash. Atkins maintained 13 log guest camps and a dining lodge on Libby Island on Millinocket Lake with another outpost camp on the mainland for use in bad weather. Elsie remembers cooking on Libby Island for her uncle; she remembers well the self-sufficiency of fresh milk and eggs from the cow and chickens.

By 1907, Will Atkins had sold out to his Oxbow neighbor, C. C. Libby, and his sons, Will and Ike Libby, an uncle and father of Allie and great uncle and grandfather of Matt. At that time Atkins owned some 52 camps throughout the Aroostook River headwaters. Will took over the camps in the 1930s by himself with the help of Elsie and Allie, but when he died and left the business to his sisters, dissent occurred, and Elsie and Allie Libby moved to the mainland in 1938, purchasing the three camps on the shore of Millinocket Lake that were built and owned by Wilfred "Sleepy" Atkins, the son of the great trapper and businessman, Will Atkins. "Sleepy" went on to become a Maine game warden.

Jack Dempsey, a deer hunter when not in the ring, visited Libby Island. He was obviously attracted by the lore of giant bucks and game aplenty as advertised profusely by the railroads and sporting camps during the heyday of this deer hunting paradise.

The romantic charm of Libby's remains constant. Cabins still have that classic construction but with modern conveniences demanded by today's "sports." The 13-foot Old Town Canoe, Elsie's personal canoe, rests on the round rafters above your head while Philip Goodwin's scene of an early deer hunter is centered above Matt's desk. A trophy brook trout caught by Sam Glover and mounted by Herb Welsh graces the wall. Antlers abound, both deer and moose. The character, solitude and serenity of the woods camp intimately combine with the touch of modern conveniences. In the background the woodshed, cedar kindling scabbed from the round logs, the ice house (Matt still cuts and stores block ice from Millinocket Lake during the winter) and the rather secret shed for the generator – a must these days for the satellite computer and bath facilities – all add romance to the deer camp scene.

Matt and Ellen took over the camps in 1977. In an interview, Matt noted, "The Libbys never throw anything away, the dump exists as just another place to go get stuff." Not too far-fetched when you understand that Ace hardware is a two-hour drive now, but in the old days you fashioned what you needed from what you could find. As we prowled the premises, looking over the ten cabins, many being updated, freshened with new chinking, bath facilities and other appliances, we were watched by Sleepy Atkins' 20-foot Old Town guide canoe, perched over the woodshed rafters in perfect shape, purchased from an auction house when Matt could not believe the family would part with it. Then

to the boathouse where two 20-foot Gallup canoes hung on the rafters belonging to Matt's dad and E. B. White – the past talking to us on every step.

It's important to remember that the lakes and rivers were the highways in these thick north wilderness areas. The "out camps," streams, spring holes and special spots all had names, some honoring the guides, a sport, or a special happening. When Allie Libby died in 1959, Elsie, the family matriarch, brought up her four boys clearing a system of hunting trails and working around the camps. Every trail had a camp fire spot on it.

Here and in yet other parts of Maine in 1891, the "Rough Rider" himself, Theodore Roosevelt, befriended the Sewalls as guides and traveled to the Billy and Belle Lodge at Lambert Lake,

At Moxie, accessible only by the Somerset Branch of the Maine Central Railroad, lever-action rifles dominated the scene.

Four Days Hunt at Moxie, The Forks, Me.

All The Law Allows in Maine.

The legendary V. E. ("Wildcat") Lynch with his favorite deer camp rifle – the Remington Model 8.

Washington County, near the border town of Vanceboro. There he found good success with whitetails in this Canada-U.S. border country as Washington County was renowned for its great deer hunting. Access to the region by rail existed on the Canadian Pacific spur through Mattawaumkeag, Danforth, Forest Station, Lambert Lake and Vanceboro.

Other "sports" went to Princeton and many found their way to Grand Lake Stream. It was here at the outlet of Little River Lake that Arthur R. Wheaton took "sports" in his own camp called "WishCumTru." Its game pole successfully hung some of the great whitetails of the region to the happiness of many a visitor "from away."

By the time V. E. Lynch (1884-1953) arrived in Ashland, Maine, in 1917, an unbroken wilderness of nearly 15,000 square miles existed in Aroostook County, much of it untouched by rod or gun or navigated by compass. Much has been written about the man called Virgil Everett ("Wildcat") Lynch, a trapper, hunter, guide and author whose adventures at his camp on the Machias River live on in northern Maine's deer hunting history. Lynch – known as "V. E." – became a guide in July of 1918, and for the next 26 years he prowled the backwoods of this vast wilderness in pursuit of giant-racked bucks. In 1923 he became the editor of the *National Sportsman* magazine.

Lynch quickly became a crack shot with his favorite .35 Remington Model 8 – a special gun he considered his good luck charm. As an expert trapper, student of wildlife and a showman of sorts, Virgil Lynch realized early the need to advertise his sporting camp business. His ads and articles sometimes touched a nerve with his competitors but "Wildcat" could usually back up his claims. We see the character of "Wildcat" Lynch in his *Trails to Successful Trapping; Thrilling Adventures;* and in the wonderful, collectible book by Oscar Cronk, *They Called Him Wildcat.*

Bud and Waldo Brooks bringing home the bacon. Spednik Lake, 1947.

Courtesy Art Wheaton.

In 1923 Lynch bought out his partner and became sole owner of "Forks of the Machias" camps. He began to promote his business by writing exciting deer hunting tales that were published in *Hunter, Trader, Trapper* magazine and *In the Maine Woods.* He created a colorful booklet describing the game rich area, and soon sportsman from all over America began to patronize his business.

"Going in" from Ashland station to "Forks of the Machias" camps took 16 miles to the Machias River and then four miles up the Machias. Like John Danforth on Parmachenee Lake, Lynch maintained out camps for many of his "sports." One thinks of his popular Spectacle Camp, Center Camp, Owl's Roost and his Bear Mountain Camp. With his keen knowledge of the woods and game, the hiring of crack guides, good food and accommodation, "Forks of the Machais" became a well-known destination for sportsman all over the country.

By 1940 "Woodie" Wheaton, another legendary Maine guide, also maintained his own "Grand Lake Brook" hunting camp where crack guides like Ralph Beach, Lewis Brown, and Jack McKelvey cruised the cedar swamps, ridges and complex deer trails for white-tailed bucks. Outdoor writer Bud Leavitt of the *Bangor Daily News* called this distinguished gentleman of the outdoors "the grandest of old Maine guides."

During the early decades of the twentieth century, *In the Maine Woods* steadily promoted Maine as a national deer hunting hotspot while the legendary Bangor & Aroostook Railroad marked the opening of the Maine wilderness to sportsman "from away." Other publications such as *Hunting and Fishing, The National Sportsman, Outdoor Life, Field & Stream,* and *Forest & Stream* touted the Maine woods experience in addition to columns by writers such as Crosby, Lynch and later Edmund Ware Smith, among others.

A glimpse of these times, its history and heritage, its love and lore for American sportsman, and its rich tradition gathered in words and pictures by Rob Wegner, will stir deep emotions for the folks who came before us, in another time, in America's wild and remote regions that shaped our deep seated passion for the white-tailed deer. Big racks and giant deer of our northern forest and deer hunters of today can reflect on this storied past for great enjoyment of the sport. Rob Wegner's love for this past cultural heritage, brought to life by his great research, wonderful black and white photo collection and his knack for presenting material with excitement, thrills and fact will leap from these pages so that the reader wishes for a moment he had been there, in those classic deer camps of yesteryear.

FORE

CHAPTER 2

ST CITY
UNTING CLUB

The memories of these things will live in the minds of those who partook of them, for ever and ever and I believe even beyond the grave.

– U. J. "Eulogy" Smith, 1908

During the early years of the twentieth century, generations of deer hunters stopped at the famous Poland Spring Hotel just north of Sebago Lake in route to Aroostook County – "Eulogy" Smith was one of them. At this legendary hotel Smith and countless other deer hunters stood in awe before Alexander Pope's classic oil on canvas, "Poland Spring Trophies," which Pope displayed there for many years. Perhaps Eulogy had that classic work of sporting art in mind when he wrote the memorable lines quoted above.

The handsomely, massive antlered buck sporting a late vintage Kentucky rifle exemplifies Maine's robust whitetails – the inside spread of this eight-point Maine Monarch clearly exceeds two feet. In this manly "After the Hunt" deer-hunting painting, one can smell the genuine, authentic leather of the game bag, the sweet aroma of whiskey from the flask and burnt gunpowder from the Model 1860 .44 revolver which the hunter clearly sighted in. In commenting on this

"Poland Spring Trophies," 1899.
Oil on canvas by Alexander Pope.

classic piece of whitetail memorabilia one critic wrote: "The wood is wood, the iron is iron and the brass is brass . . . ."

Historically, the state of Maine, like Virginia, Pennsylvania, Michigan, Minnesota and Wisconsin, produced some of the greatest legendary deer camps, hotels and hunts in the history of North American white-tailed deer hunting. One thinks first and foremost of the famous and romantic Libby's sporting camps on the headwaters of the Aroostook River (in Township 8, Range 9) and the V. E. Lynch's chain of deer camps in the great virgin wilds of Aroostook County as well, with their classy deer shacks and massive meat poles heavily laden with white-tailed deer meat.

One also thinks of America's premier antler collector and Winchester rifle enthusiast, Fred Goodwin, and the annual gathering of his deer-hunting clan at his deer camp on Silver Ridge in Aroostook County and the tens of thousands of other deer camps that came before them.

All of these Maine deer camps have become an American institution as Edmund Ware Smith reminds us in one of his great stories from the Maine woods, "Jake's Rangers Hunt the Whitetail":

"Each fall, the phenomenon of the deer-hunting groups, grows deeper into the country's grass roots. In Pennsylvania, New York, the Virginias, the Carolinas, Michigan, Maine, and other states, there are groups that were first organized well over fifty years ago. Rich in tradition and ritual, this annual gathering of the deer-hunting clan has become an American institution."

One of these great American institutions came into existence on March 3, 1901, in Cleveland, Ohio, and without exception the members of the very celebrated Forest City Hunting Club spent three weeks every fall in the wilds of northern Maine hunting whitetails at the Nine Mile Brook Deer Camp, nine miles from Oxbow, Maine, in Aroostook County. This legendary deer camp consisted of three log buildings of an old lumber company, as we learn from reading the blue-chip deer hunting book, *The 1907 Hunt of the Forest City Hunting Club,* written by Arthur G. Potter, manager of Tiffany's Studio in New York City, and others, and edited by Narrow S. Doty: a stable, an office and tool room and a dinning and sleeping room. Nationwide, these old lumber camps – many of them leased by the hunters – turned into

"Some of the Bunch." Left to right standing: A. G. Potter, Dr. M. A. Albl, F. A. Pierce, C. H. Mann, H. E. Doty. Kneeling: U. J. Smith.

spiffy deer camps as the wildlife conservation movement took hold.

Beautifully situated on the south bank of the Aroostook River, a winding, twisting stream with deep black water and a current of about five miles per hour, the camp usually included 15 Buckeye deerslayers from every walk of life, plus three guides and the camp cook Joe Campbell all from Maine. In his essay "Deer Camp: Maine Hunting Tradition," published in *The Maine Sportsman Book of Deer Hunting,* David O'Connor tells us that "Moses Jackson, the late and great warden from Bradley, once told me that there were two kinds of Maine deer camps: the ones where you pay for someone else's know how and the ones where you earn your own." The Nine Mile Brook Deer Camp represented the former.

Why they called their deer hunting club the Forest Lake Hunting Club remains somewhat nebulous and unclear. In checking *The Encyclopedia of Cleveland History* under "Forest City" we learn the phrase has long been Cleveland's nickname but has very murky origins. Some say editor Timothy Smead gave that nickname to Cleveland in the *Plain Dealer* on January 4, 1890. Others claim Mayor William Case did so in 1850. In any event the nickname stuck and as late as 1994 30 large and small firms in the greater Cleveland area still used it.

The trip from Cleveland, Ohio, to Masardis, Maine, took 42 hours by train. On Saturday night, October 26, 1907, at 8:30 PM, a congenial lot of nine men left Cleveland via the Nickel Plate Railroad with a wild sense of enthusiasm en route to Masardis for their annual deer hunt.

They came down Euclid Avenue in great haste and pulled into the train depot with Dr. M. A. Albl's old Ford Model K touring car pulling a trailer with three-weeks of deer camp supplies. Barbarossa beer, billed as "The Finest Bottled Beer In The World" in ads appearing in *The Sportsmen's Review,* dominated their cargo. This high-octane, liquefied wheat brew – brewed by The Christian Moerlein Brewing Co. of Cincinnati, Ohio – gave the Forest Lake boys something to look forward to; they loved its purity and wholesomeness! No deer hunt in the wilds of Aroostook County Maine would have been complete without it.

As the hunters were avid readers of *The American Field* and *In the Maine Woods,* their supplies at the railroad depot closely reflected some of the ads found in these sporting journals. "Narrow S." Doty, the Secretary/Treasurer of the club, packed his new Winchester Model 1907 Self-Loading .351 rifle that Winchester labeled as "The Gun That Shoots Through Steel!" No member of the club, not even the distinguished Dr. Albl, President of the Club, doubted the veracity of that hyperbole. The high-powered Model 1907 Self-Loading .351 would finish the buck for sure.

With the 1907 edition of *In the Maine Woods* in hand – the great romantic deer hunter's travel guide for the deer hunting Mecca of Maine – C. H. Mann, a visitor on the hunt that year and still sitting in the black leather back seat on the '07 Ford Model K, put in the plug for his Marlin Model '93 by reciting verbatim the Marlin ad on page 171, of that highly-cherished deer hunting guide:

"When the crash of the fleeing buck and doe makes your heart jump and brings your gun with a jerk to your shoulder, and your eye follows those good Marlin sights as you lead the white flag for a shot, it is a comfort to know that the gun is going to do its part."

This old crowd of jolly friends consisted of nine deer camp regulars plus their invited guest Arthur G. Potter, a historian and author, who would arrive later from New York; Dr. M. A. Albl; Mark Hutchinson; H. C. Hutchinson; S. A. Hand; U. J. Smith; Dr. E. J. ("Molar") Kochmit; C. H. Mann; F. A. Pierce; and H. E. Doty. They all viewed Aroostook County, Maine, as "The Happy Hunting Ground" – the white-tailed deer hunter's Mecca and the land of the finest potatoes in the world.

With their very unique publication *In the Maine Woods,* the Bangor and Aroostook Railroad greatly popularized white-tailed deer hunting. Filled with anticipation, this Maine deer hunter totes his gear to the canoe where his companions including Lady Diana await him. Judging from his ammunition belt, this guy intends to burn the barrel hot! The threesome will either hunt the stream from the canoe or land at another location to still hunt inland from the waterway.

Upon settling down in their "private car," the men sang their new deer camp song composed by Nine Mile Brook Deer Camp member Eulogy Smith:

We're a good bunch of Gazaboes
Good fellows all,
Who go up to the Maine woods
Every Fall.
Cares of all kinds we banish,
When we get on the train,
Leaving dull worry behind us
Until we get home again.

Our crowd is led by Doc Albl
The Prince of men,
Captained by Harry Doty
With whiskers on his chin.
Then Mark the dandy butcher,
Who takes care of our hides,
The only one in the party
Who hunts without a guide.

Then there is Hub the banker,
Who wins the tin,
In every game of poker
That he sits in.
Unless Hub has a hand full,
And bets them good and hard,
Then he will scoop the jackpot
Without drawing a card.
In case we need Furniture
Fred Pierce we see,
And if we have the toothache
Kochmit for me.
Friend Potter makes our Jewelry,
He ought to make a pot,
That's a thing we always need,
And a thing we haven't got.

Mann owns the American Express
In his mind—
Promoter Smith will form your trust

Or your combine.
We can't pass by Joe Campbell,
Whose teeth are filled with gold,
Nor forget our old pal Bordie,
Nor his recipe for a cold.

Guide Fleming has a mighty growth
On his chin—
In color fair each separate hair
Resembles a brass pin—
Reed also had a dense black growth
And an eye that finds the deer—
And when they sing "There was a little hen"
He's never in the rear.

Deer camp member Eulogy Smith – "the maitre de hotel, the author of those sumptuous menus, the poet, the choir master, the organist, the sign painter and the promoter, who was everything to all men" – describes their arrival on the platform at Masardis:

"When we stepped out on the platform at Masardis, after our 42 hour trip, and breathed the fresh air of Maine, and like hounds of old, appeared to scent the royal game, it seemed like home again to crawl into Libby's old, lop-sided, hay-wire, repaired, worn-out, buckboard-fur-overcoat proposition, for the eleven mile ride to his royal palace at Oxbow, where we were to be joined by our three guides and cook."

Eulogy's reference to "his royal palace at Oxbow" refers of course to the Libby Brothers' famous hunting and fishing resort, the Libby Hotel in Oxbow, which included a circuit of splendidly equipped deer hunting camps in the wilderness of the Aroostook Headwaters. From the "Flats" – the end of wagon transportation – they then traveled six more miles west in canoes and a lumberman's tote boat on the Aroostook River before reaching their final destination late in the day, the Nine Mile Brook Deer Camp on the South Bank north of Sebois Lake and south of Chandler Mountains. Potter describes the first night in deer camp:

The Deer-Hunting

"It was a most beautiful night. The air was crisp and cold, and in a cloudless sky of deep black blue, myriads of stars scintillated like diamonds on a background of richest velvet. Across the canopy stretched the Milky Way like a soft film of gauze. The river below the camp whispered softly against the reeds and border-ing undergrowth and pines and spruce across the water were silhouetted against the sky like church spires rising majestically heavenward. A wonderful stillness reigned supreme, the stillness only known out in God's open where men live close to nature, and contemplate His wonders with an unspoken awe in their hearts.

The Forest City Hunting Club boys traveled around in snazzy stage coaches, primitive buckboards and crude, "water-going" rafts and stopped at such plush backwoods distilleries as "Camp Skenosus" to proudly display their deer antlers and get a shot-'n'-beer.

"That ten men could live together as we did for nearly three weeks in such harmony and with such perfect enjoyment is indeed a tribute to their manliness and character."

On the first night everyone went to bed early and arose on the opening day before the cook even yelled, "Come and get it," which meant on that particular morning bacon, eggs, hot biscuits, potatoes with jackets on and the finest coffee money could buy plus Borden's Condensed Milk. The 1907 Maine deer hunt was on. They had reached the Pine Tree State – the capital of American white-tailed deer hunting; they were in the happy deer hunting grounds of the Aroostook.

Members of the Nine Mile Brook Deer Camp maintained a strong preference for Winchester rifles. Narrow S. Doty, camp secretary-treasurer, who used his old Winchester 1873 for many years, now sported, as mentioned earlier, the new Winchester Model 1907, Self-Loading

.351 caliber, first introduced in the January 1907 catalogue of Winchester rifles, and widely used at the time by law enforcement personnel to wage war against such criminals as John Dillinger, Bonnie and Clyde and Machine-gun Kelly. By the end of the first day Narrow S. had downed a nice buck with his new Self-Loading Winchester.

Eulogy Smith also chose the new and popular .351 Winchester Self-Loader. Hubbard Hutchinson, a financier, shot a Winchester .33 Special. Both Arthur Potter and Dr. Kochmit equipped themselves with .30-30 Winchesters as well: Bordie Stone used a .45-90 Winchester, Will Fleming a .30 U. S. Army Winchester and Clarence Reed a .30-30 Winchester Carbine, while Sam Pelkey always relied on his .38-55 Winchester with a sawed-off barrel. Hutchinson remained in the minority with his eternal reverence for the Marlin Model '93.

On the second day of the 1907 deer hunt, Potter grabbed his Winchester and started

Courtesy: Wegner's Deer & Deer Hunting Postcard Collection.

off for a still-hunt alone. Indeed, being alone with others in the pristine wilderness of northern Maine and still-hunting deer by himself was Potter's preferred method of hunting. He explains why in the diary of the 1907 deer hunt:

"I walked on slowly lost in thought, looking back to my boyhood days and the adventures and incidents of my past life. How happy one is when alone with Nature. Now and then the song of a bird or the snapping of a twig, which startled me and made me think that some animal had just slipped away, broke the stillness; perhaps a deer had jumped from his resting place and darted away.

"Sometimes you will get a shot at a deer but nine times out of ten you will not. If you do, the chances are you miss. What do you care! You are not there to kill all the game, but because you love Nature and want to be alone."

Good Sport at Umcolcus Lake Camps, Rockaberna, Me.

B & A Series.
On The Moose River.

Like many deer hunters, members of the Nine Mile Brook Deer Camp kept in touch with family and friends by sending deer-hunting postcards. By 1907, the American postcard phenomenon became a public addiction.

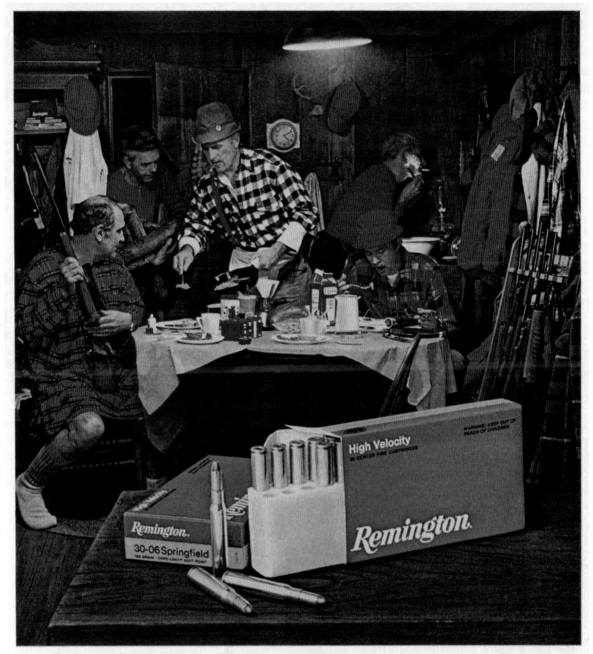

Opening day. Better give it our best shot.

Twelve after four. Undercooked bacon, overcooked eggs and coffee that would ordinarily get more attention than respect.

You didn't notice. Everything tasted great on this greatest of all days—opening day. And, when you're getting ready to go after that big buck, remember this: once you're lined up on him, the success or failure of the whole hunt could depend on one shot.

When you squeeze the trigger, the bullet must go right where you aim it. And it's got to have plenty of stopping power when it gets there.

Now remember this: Remington cartridges with "Core-Lokt" bullets are known throughout the hunt-ing world for their excellent mushrooming qualities.

The metal jacket and lead core of a "Core-Lokt" bullet are locked together by the jacket's heavy mid-section. So the bullet stays in one piece for uniform expansion and all the one-shot power you need at any range.

Remington cartridges with "Core-Lokt" bullets. In 24 big game calibers. Give it your best shot with our best shot.

Remington. DU PONT

DEDICATION

For the memory of Fred Bear,
the "Natty Bumppo" of my youth,
who instilled in me
a life-long passion
for romancing deer camp, wood smoke
and the whitetail.

Robert Wegner, Ph.D.
Deer Valley, Wisconsin – March, 2008

CONTENTS

"GOING IN"

Philip R. Goodwin

COPYRIGHT 1911 BY REMINGTON ARMS-UNION METALLIC CARTRIDGE CO.

1912	**JANUARY.**				1912	
SUN	MON	TUE	WED	THU	FRI	SAT
	1	2	3	4	5	6
7	8	9	10	11	12	13
14	15	16	17	18	19	20
21	22	23	24	25	26	27
28	29	30	31			

Waiting for the Wagon at Libby's Boat House. Left to right: Will Fleming (Guide), Bordie Stone (Guide), Dr. E. J. Kochmit, Joe Campbell (Cook), H. C. Hutchinson.

forest in their nightly quest for food."

In the background other camp members continued to play poker, test sundry libations and discuss the heroic deer poaching exploits of George Magoon from Crawford, Maine's most notorious deer poacher, and how he outwitted the wardens and distributed the venison to the poor. And the singing continued.

Another little drink
Wouldn't do us any harm,
Another little drink
Wouldn't do us any harm.

She ruffled up her feathers
To keep herself warm,
And another little drink
Wouldn't do us any harm.

Amidst the uproarious music and laughter, the in-house intellectual, author Potter, read the classic sporting literature of the day including the 1907 annual edition of *In the Maine Woods,* published by the Bangor & Aroostook Railroad, which contained photos

of the deer hunting adventures of the Forest City Hunt Club at such legendary deer camps as Reed's, Trafton's and Coffin's during the earlier years of the twentieth century. He was also reading the current issues of *The National Sportsman,* a sporting journal that billed itself in an ad *In the Maine Woods,* "as just a great big camp in the woods with 100,000 good fellows sitting around the fire, smoking and telling each other stories about their good times in the woods." It cost 15 cents per copy.

On the second day of this deer hunt, guide Will Fleming and Charlie Mann, king bee of the American Express Company so far as Cleveland was concerned, participated in this traditional Maine mode of chasing bucks on the run. After a very exhausting morning of running down a large-tracked deer without one sighting, they paused for their noon time luncheon: Limburger cheese and a tin can of Underwood's Original Deviled Ham, the famous can with the Little Red Devil on it made in Boston, Mass. No deer hunt was complete without it.

Arthur G. Potter. The 1907 Hunt of the Forest City Hunting Club, 1907.

A Merry Hunting Party from Ohio. Supper at Trafton's Camp, 1905 Hunt. Left to right: Front. F. A. Pierce, Mark Hutchinson, U. J. Smith, C. O Hawksley (Saw Filing Instructor), W. E. Kingzett. Rear: Sam Pelkey (Guide), Bordie Stone (Guide), Joe Campbell (Cook, standing), H. E. Doty, Dr. M. A. Albl.

After completing their luncheon they started to move up a ridge and to their utmost amazement soon jumped the buck they had been pursuing all morning – only 75 feet in front of them. Mann later admitted that it appeared as if by magic – the head of a beautiful 10-pointer with long wavy tines! The buck seemed to come out of nowhere. He was just there! And had been there while they ate their lunch. For a moment Mann forgot that he had been running all morning in pursuit of this old fellow. But he recovered himself in time to take careful aim with his popular Marlin Model '93. The first shot laid low this magnificent denizen of the Maine deer woods. This buck remained the finest ever taken by any member of the Forest City Hunting Club.

Despite the arguments over scarcity of deer in the pages of *The Maine Sportsman* – and despite the declining rail shipments of Aroostook County deer from a high in 1902,

Arthur G. Potter. The 1907 Hunt of the Forest City Hunting Club, 1907.

Potter's illustration of C. H. ("Case Hardened") Mann's ten-pointer, the finest white-tailed buck ever taken by a member of the Forest City Hunting Club in the deer woods of northern Maine, 1907.

as reported in Chester F. Banasiak's historic account *Deer in Maine* (1961) – when the 1907 deer hunt ended, two bucks, three spikes, five

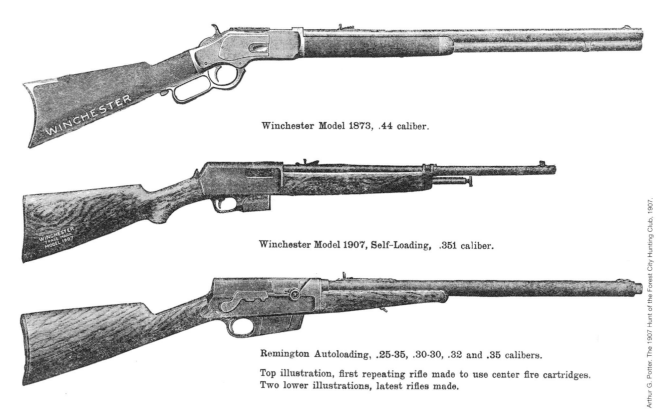

Winchester Model 1873, .44 caliber.

Winchester Model 1907, Self-Loading, .351 caliber.

Remington Autoloading, .25-35, .30-30, .32 and .35 calibers.

Top illustration, first repeating rifle made to use center fire cartridges.
Two lower illustrations, latest rifles made.

Arthur G. Potter. The 1907 Hunt of the Forest City Hunting Club, 1907.

Legendary rifles of the Forest City Hunting Club. Although many of the camp's members accepted the new Winchester Self Loading .351 caliber, old "J. Ashtabula" Hand still longed for the Kentucky Rifle and said so: "Ye Gods! Imagine, if you can, Daniel Boone shooting five shots from a self-loading rifle at a buck, so fast that you could hang your clothes on the stream of lead."

After walking for about four miles he came to the top of a high ridge where he could see the Chandler Mountains beyond the Aroostook River. A beautiful sight, he thought to himself, mountains and trees covered with snow and the sun in all its glory shining brightly on them. Later in the day it commenced to rain and he returned to camp wet, tired and hungry but just in time for dinner.

Their deer camp dinners were legendary and ceremonious events – venison feasts of great extravaganzas featuring venison liver and heart – "The Hunter's Dish." Every night developed into a major party in itself. These festive ceremonial feasts exuded and extended the spirit of the seasons – Thanksgiving and Christmas. Mark Hutchinson, the "dandy butcher" from Cleveland, kept up his reputation at the Nine Mile Brook Deer Camp by providing the camp with choice cuts of artistically designed venison and Joe Campbell the cook, made you feel like you never ate before. Eulogy Smith designed the menus:

Ma Albl's Pickles
Chow Chow
Olives
Catsup
Fried Venison Liver and Bacon
Baked Aroostook County Potatoes
Baked Sweet Potatoes
Canned Spinach
Ma Albl's Sauerkraut
Kingzetts' Corn Bread
Mince Pie
Stewed Prunes
Hot Crullers with Maple Syrup
Coffee with Evaporated Cream
Hand's Apples
York State Cheese
Ward's Crackers

Getting ready for Supper

Every night the Forest City deer camp boys turned supper into a major extravaganza and a special party ensued indeed!

After indulging in such high-order cuisine, members of the camp passed out the Liar's Medal to a winner who told the most preposterous falsehoods ever uttered in the realm of deer hunting stories, lies and misconceptions. Indeed, these classic, historic deer camps not only assembled for men to drink whisky and tell stories but as one modern day deer hunter reports to tell "tall tales, falsehoods, fibs, prevarications, exaggerations and just plain damn lies; concocted by men who spend a lot more of their lives occupying deer stands than they do in the House of the Lord!" Amen.

Deer camp ultimately means many things to many people but above all it represents the revival and transfer of memories, and no one in the Forest City Hunting Club did this better than Mark Hutchinson. According to Eulogy Smith, as a storyteller he was "simply beyond description, that is, in printing, – a printed description would probably put one of the representatives of the Society for the Suppression of Strong Language after him. It was his dashing, inimitable style of diction, his cuss punctuated imagination and his exalting manner of narration which always gave him the centre of the stage, and which held his audience spell-bound."

One can still almost hear the distinguished dentist Dr. E. J. Kochmit ("Molar Koc") singing an old club song to the tune of "Old Lang Syne" after he had too much to drink at the "Lemonade Crock":

> *It may be so*
> *But I don't know,*
> *It sounds to me*
> *Like a lie;*
> *It may be so*
> *But I don't know*
> *It sounds to me*
> *Like a lie.*

Music followed the issuance of the Liar's Medal at the Forest City Hunting Club. According to their deer camp diary, "Guide Fleming was induced to perform on the French harp to the accompaniment of Reed's deer rib bones with Uly at the Organ. Koch and 'Napoleon' improvised tambourines using tin pie plates, and music (?) filled the air . . . Indeed, bursts of music floated from cracks between the logs to startle the denizens of the

B.&A. Series. Camp on Schoodic Lake. Maine.

Waiting for the Freight at a Bangor & Aroostook Railroad Station. The Bangor & Aroostook Railroad used these two postcards to promote Maine as a great white-tailed deer hunting Mecca, 1906.

does and three fawns joined the mcat pole at the legendary Nine Mile Brook Deer Camp.

Historians of hunting generally label this period of time as "the good old days." In 1907, white-tailed deer populations were nearly at an all-time high and continued to soar. Henry Carson's classic picture of the legendary Libby's deer hunters' hotel in 1906 highlights a massive meat pole with more than 30 whitetails properly hanging with their white tails all pointing in the same direction.

On these November deer hunts, the Forest City Hunting Club usually shot between 15 to 20 deer. On November 18, 1907, the *Cleveland Leader* published a story entitled "Bring Back Many Deer" and reported that "The Forest City Hunting Club returned yesterday from northern Maine, where the members have spent three weeks hunting big game. They brought with them fourteen large deer. Others that were shot

Winchester ad for the popular .401 Caliber Self-Loading Rifle.

were eaten in camp." Maine's white-tailed deer hunting remained excellent in 1907. According to records kept by the Bangor and Aroostook Railroad, deer hunters shipped 3,153 white-tailed deer during the 1907 deer season (October 1 to December 1).

According to the *Cleveland Leader's* account, "They broke camp before daylight last Thursday morning, and floated down the Aroostook River in a blinding snowstorm in a lumberman's tote boat. The hunters had interesting experiences, running through several rapids and bumping on the rocks, but they finally landed twelve miles below camp,

where the boat was snubbed and everything reloaded in wagons and hauled eleven miles to a railroad."

As the first decade of the twentieth century came to a close the new Winchester .401 Caliber Self-Loading Rifle made its appearance in the Maine deer woods in 1910; it maintained the hitting power "Like the Hammer of Thor," as the folks at Winchester would have it. Several members of the club quickly purchased the new .401 including Narrow S. Doty and Eulogy Smith for the 1910 deer season.

On Friday, December 16, 1910, the *Bangor Daily News* reported that Maine deer hunters

Ernest Thompson Seton's illustration of the legendary Caesar Whitetail. "Eulogy" Smith, the great promoter of the Nine Mile Deer Camp, kept the memories alive of the Caesar Whitetail in his storytelling with the Forest City Hunting Club.

killed 3,401 deer that season – one of them a massive, non-typical buck shot with a .401 by Henry A. Caesar, a member of the New York Zoological Society and the Camp Fire Club, in the tradition of Maine's "Pure Men or Runners."

The September 1911 issue of the *Zoological Society Bulletin* called Caesar's buck "the world-record white-tailed head" and characterized it as a 42-pointer with 6-inch basal circumference and an outside spread of 27-3/4 inches. "These measurements," the Bulletin reported, "taken all in all, seem to make this splendid head No. 1 in the world's list of the greatest heads of this species." It became the hot talk of the Nine Mile Deer Camp's late night conversations. Potter attached newspaper clippings and stories about this buck from the sporting journals to the official diary of their club.

Henry Caesar gave this buck – the so-called Caesar Whitetail – to the New York Zoological Society. Mounted by the S. L. Crosby Company of Bangor, Maine, it became part of the National Collection of Heads and Horns. As late as 1929, Ernest Thompson Seton characterized it as the world record of the time and created an illustration of it for his *Lives of Game Animals* (1929), based on the photo in the September 1911 issue of the *Zoological Society Bulletin*.

The Caesar whitetail, first officially measured in 1953, entered into the Boone and Crockett Club's Records of North American Big Game in 1958, with a non-typical score of 228-1/8. At some time after its official measurement, the Caesar whitetail disappeared from the National Collection of Heads and Horns, never to be seen again. Nevertheless, Eulogy Smith kept the memories of this noble monarch alive in the minds of the Forest City Hunting Club's membership during the early years of the twentieth century.

WILBURN
BAL
O

"Burnie" Waters (1812-1875). An artist's rendering of Waters based on David Lowry Clark's portrait of him in the Historical Society of Washington County, Virginia.

489. "W

"BURNIE" WATERS: LADEER BUCK MOUNTAIN

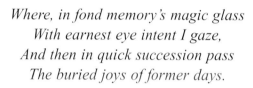

Where, in fond memory's magic glass
With earnest eye intent I gaze,
And then in quick succession pass
The buried joys of former days.

"The Death of the Buck"
Spirit of the Times
August 15, 1840

O n a clear and crisp November day in 1838, Wilburn "Burnie" Waters (1812-1875), Virginia's Natty Bumppo, roamed the land of White Top Mountain in the Southern Mountain Region of Old Dominion near Abingdon where Virginia, Kentucky and North Carolina meet in an area formerly known as Iron Mountain but known today as Pine Mountain and commonly referred to as Buck Mountain in deer hunting yarns, folklore and legend.

The 26-year old deerslayer sported a "Golden Age" 1830-vintage Kentucky flint-lock rifle with relief rococo carvings he called "Killdeer" in the best Natty Bumppo tradition. He also eventually carried a Winchester Model 1866 Carbine. The white-tailed deer, *Odocoileus virginianus,* scientifically named

Wegner's Stereoscopic Deer & Deer Hunting Collection.

ome Supper, Bob?"

When not at his permanent deer shack on Buck Mountain, Waters and his deerhound "Bob" slept wherever they found themselves including hollow logs.

by Boddaert in 1874 from a specimen collected near Jamestown, remained the ultimate object of his delight.

While pursuing venison tenderloins and white-tailed deerskins that day by still hunting, he thought about an article he had just read in the September, 1838, issue of *The American Turf Register and Sporting Magazine:* John James Audubon's classic essay "Deer Hunting." In that essay Audubon, James Fenimore Cooper's model for Natty Bumppo, characterized the still hunter as the true hunter and provided us with the first detailed definition of still hunting.

Passages from Audubon's pen lingered in Waters's mind as the muscular, blue-eyed, buckskin-clad deerslayer stalked white-tailed deer through the interior of tangled woods, ravines and morasses of Grayson County. As he approached a famous deer lick later in the day, he climbed up into a large black oak tree to study the surrounding area and watch for deer. His mind wandered but continually returned to what Audubon had written about the still hunter:

"His dress consists of a leather hunting-shirt and a pair of trousers of the same material. His feet are well moccasined; he wears a belt round his waist; his heavy rifle is resting on his brawny shoulder; on one side hangs his ball pouch, surmounted by the horn of an ancient Buffalo, once the terror of the herd, but now containing a pound of the best gunpowder; his butcher knife is scabbarded in the same strap; and behind is a tomahawk, the handle of which has been thrust through his girdle. He walks with so rapid a step that probably few men could follow him . . . He stops, looks to the flint of his gun, its priming, and the leather cover of the lock . . .

"As he proceeds he looks to the dead foliage under his feet, in search of the well-known traces of a buck's hoof. Now he bends towards the ground, on which something has attracted his attention . . . Now he moves with caution, stops at almost every tree, and peeps forward as if already within shooting distance of the game. He advances again, but how very slowly! He has reached the declivity, upon which the sun shines in its entire growing splendor; but mark him! He takes the gun from his shoulder, has already thrown aside the leathern cover of the lock, and is wiping the edge of the flint with his tongue. Now he stands like a monumental figure, perhaps measuring the distance that lies between him and the buck, which he has in view. His rifle is slowly raised, the report follows, and he runs.

"He arrives at the spot where the animal laid itself down among the grass in a thicket of grape-vines, sumac and spruce bushes . . . the place is covered with blood . . . there lies the buck, its tongue out, its eyes dim, its breath exhausted; it is dead."

Audubon's passages abruptly evaporated from his mind as two magnificent eight-point bucks suddenly appeared in front of him. They stopped and sniffed the air repeatedly. They then stomped their hooves, and – muscles stiffened – stood silhouetted against the setting sun. Silence prevailed.

Wilburn entertained the idea of trying to get both of them with one shot! In her novel about Waters, *My Head's High From Proudness* (1963), Octavia Perry imagines the thought in Appalachian dialect:

"I n'ver afore, in all o' my life, wanted airy thing like I wanted that ol' buck. Then the thought come t' me that, ifen I'd figger hit out, I mought git both o' them with jest one shot."

But that overly ambitious idea soon vanished as he brought "Killdeer" to bear on the larger of the two bucks. The giant Virginia buck snorted as his Kentucky rifle belched fire and smoke. In looking at the vanishing magnificent head of "horns," Waters could tell from its erratic stride that he had mortally wounded the animal.

He quickly climbed down the tree and followed the trail. Within a few yards he encountered the buck, apparently lifeless.

But a vicious buck/hunter skirmish was about to begin. In his biography of Waters, *The Life and Adventures of Wilburn Waters* (1878), Charles B. Coale, a friend and deer hunting partner of Waters and editor and proprietor of the *Abingdon Virginian*, a weekly newspaper where the "Burnie" Waters' hunting yarns and exploits of the old sportsman were first published, describes the scene:

"As he approached it, it sprang to its feet in a moment and came at him with the ferocity of a tiger. There was no escape from a terrible struggle for life, and he knew that his only chance was in his extraordinary strength and activity, as well as coolness and presence of mind. He scarcely had time to think even this much, when the buck rushed upon and attempted to impale him. He grabbed him by the horns and threw him several times, but the active animal was on his feet again in an instant, and so the struggle continued several minutes – to Wilburn it seemed hours – some times one on top and then the other, but

Wilburn's great strength enabled him to keep his hold, although his clothes were badly torn and his person considerably lacerated by the sharp hoofs of the animal, which cut with the keenness of a knife.

"Whilst thus struggling, he at length found time to get his knife out of his pocket and open it with his teeth. He made a desperate lunge and supposed he had entirely severed its windpipe but it made another effort for freedom, kicked him loose and plunged into the undergrowth. He followed it a short distance and found it dead with its head nearly severed from its body."

Although Waters had many hand-to-hand fights with bears and wolves, he had never been in as much danger of losing his life as he was in that encounter with a maddened buck.

The secret of his buck hunting success lay in his acute eyesight. He shot his Kentucky flintlock rifle and French double barrel shotgun with both eyes open. Many attributed his innate instinct for tracking white-tailed

Burnie and his Buck Mountain Boys head to the art studio with their white-tailed buck, all their outdoor finery and cherished weapons, 1865.

Minnesota Historical Society.

bucks to his Chowan-Catawba Indian ancestry. Coale characterized him this way:

"Whenever he finds the sign of a bear, wolf or deer, he never loses the trail, although he may have to follow it from mountain to mountain for days together and to great distances, and is almost as sure of his game as if he had it."

In his book *The Roving Artist* (1895), D. L. Clark, who painted the only portrait we have of Waters, noted, "There was in his veins just enough of Indian blood to make him a perfect hunter."

During his early manhood, the wild and rugged Waters loved to roam the deer forest with rifle, knife and tomahawk in hand, often shooting deer in the mountains for months at a time. As Paul Schullery, a prominent historian of sporting literature notes, when he returned to civilization "he was frequently in trouble; for he had a gift for fist fighting that seemed to attract others with similar gifts."

Back in White Top Mountain somewhere, according to Goodridge Wilson's Smyth *County History and Traditions* (1932), Waters used to get native lead, chopping it out of the ground with his ax. He would then mould it into bullets for his flintlock and double barrel. This was apparently the only vein of native lead ever found in southwest Virginia, all the other being a blend of ores.

He killed hundreds of white-tailed deer during his lifetime – maybe even in excess of a thousand. He was seldom seen in his deer hunting bailiwick without his faithful deerhounds Bob and Jack. Like his contemporaries Phillip Tome in Pennsylvania and Meshach Browning in Maryland, he could imitate almost to perfection buck snorts, grunts and deer bleats and the note and cry of any victim of his unerring flintlock rifle.

He pursued whitetails with the relentless religiosity of a Methodist preacher and die-

Artist unknown.

"SHOOT THE BUCK." Page 171.

While floating for deer in his canoe on Green Cove Creek and White Top Creek, Burnie frequently encountered some very trying times with escaping bucks – a familiar theme in the sporting art and literature of Waters' time. "Shoot the Buck." Frequently reprinted in various editions of S. H. Hammond's *Wild Northern Scenes; Sporting Adventures with the Rifle and the Rod,* circa 1857.

"Saved: A Hard Chase." A. F. Tait, 1874. Oil on canvas.

Private Collection.

colorful, interesting and larger-than-life characters of southwestern Virginia. Like Camuto he experienced many dreamlike moments in the deer woods. As an avid backwoods balladeer and minstrel, "Burnie" sang about these dreamy moments and played his banjo as he tramped the mountains and forests of southwest Virginia in pursuit of white-tailed deer.

> *Up in the sky-y,*
> *Sky-y so high,*
> *Thur hun-ter's moo-oon*
> *Sailed quiet-ly by.*
> *Sailed qui-et-ly by, then*
> *Sailed qui-et-ly by,*
> *Thur hun-ter's moo-oon*
> *Sailed qui-etly by.*

He also sang the ballads written by the popular song writers of the time especially A. B. Street's "Floating for Deer." According to deer hunting legend and lore, if you canoe Green Cove Creek and White Top Creek at midnight under a full moon during the peak of the whitetail rut you can still hear Old "Burnie" singing the first stanza of that famous, white-tailed deer hunting ballad:

> *The woods are all sleeping,*
> *the midnight is dark;*
> *We launch on the still wave*
> *our bubble-like bark;*
> *The rifle all ready,*
> *the jack burning clear,*
> *And we brush through the lily-pads,*
> *floating for deer,*
> *Floating for deer,*
> *And we glide over the shallows, boys,*
> *floating for deer.*

Waters loved to float for deer under the moonlight and to listen to the sounds of the big staghound music and the singing and storytelling at the fire pit where deer camp memories translate themselves into reality by the firelight and libation.

hard Sunday school teacher. Inasmuch as he was born into the romantic tradition of French Huguenot culture, Christianity strengthened his enthusiasm for the deer hunt. He read the Bible in deer camp and saw Buck Mountain as a favorable place to find religion as well as deer. He actually became superintendent of a Methodist Sunday school eight miles from his resident deer camp in the mountains. He seldom missed Sunday morning church services. When not shooting bucks and cleaning up on wolves and bears in a heroic way, he attended camp meetings and various other religious activities.

In looking at Waters' deer hunting religiosity today, we also think of another Virginian deer hunter, Christopher Camuto, and his white-tailed deer hunts on his Shenandoah Valley farm in the Blue Ridge Mountains of Virginia. In his *Hunting from Home* (2003), he admits "deer hunting has weighted my time outdoors and clarified a great deal for me, taught me innumerable practical lessons and taken me in certain dreamlike moments through the sacred pulse of being, my own and that of the game I pursue."

Waters was indeed one of the great nineteenth-century pioneer deer hunters in the central Appalachian region and one of the most

Burnie Waters' deer camp on White Top Mountain – built in 1836 and seen here in the late 1920s – still retains the Waters' name above the door.

A century and a half later in Virginia, these memories by firelight still continue in the woodlands and swamps of Ellsworth County, Virginia, as told by old "Captain Charlie" LaRue in Mr. Chips' novel *A Hound Bays in Ellsworth* (1992). Here at the Hollerin' Hound Hunt Club, where the LaRue Clan chased the old, mythic, gray-muzzled buck known as "Ole Crooked Rack," the locals still enjoyed "memorable, fun times – a nip in the fall night air, plus a little nip from a jug. There was always a crackling fire just off the old Walls Road. Around the fire several men gathered with a red-haired, freckled boy. A couple of tin lanterns gave off a dim light in the background. Under the moon would be parked the pickups with their dog boxes. This was a social event for these men. They'd come to listen to the hound music, to pass the jug and to tell the stories of the past."

Waters arrived on White Top Mountain in 1832. At first he lived in a tent. His first deer shack consisted of a three-sided structure with an open front. He lived in this traditional, primitive lean-to for four years, before moving higher on the mountain. He would lay at night with his feet outside near the fire to keep warm. The fire also served to frighten away the wolves that howled and prowled around the lone deerstalker as he dreamed of shooting monster bucks in the morning.

In 1836, he claimed 640 acres of land and erected a log cabin near a beautiful spring that gushed from the rocky mountainside. At this primitive log cabin, his sacred space in deer country, his biographer Coale once found him on a log, eating his morning meal, which consisted of corn cake, deer meat, wild honey and water from the spring. His two deerhounds stood sentinel, waiting for the deer hunting action to begin.

In his mature years, Waters roamed the land of Buck Mountain, Bearpen Ridge and Hurricane Creek in southwestern Virginia. Like Philip Tome and Meschach Browning this rugged man loved and lived on deer meat, corn-dodgers, wild honey and the rarefied air of the southern Appalachians.

He clearly believed deer hunting was a profession for which he was well adapted and one at which he could make a substantial profit. At this log cabin deer camp, he spent the rest of his life hunting deer, wolves, bears and trapping. In the evenings he sat in front of his fireplace under a dim lantern and read the classy sporting literature of the day in his primitive abode.

During the early 1870s, American deer hunters, Waters included, experienced the origins of wildlife conservation and the formation in 1873 of scores of new Sportsmen's Clubs and Deer Hunting Associations all across the nation. Rustic deer camps, like the antique Waters shack, began to dot the landscape of whitetail country. But more importantly, deer hunters now acquired a means of communicating with each other with the launching of three major national sportsmen's journals: *The American Sportsman* (1871), *Forest and Stream* (1873), and *The American Field* (1874). These popular journals began to appear in deer camps nationwide and the Waters' deer shack was no exception.

In an editorial in the October 11, 1873 issue of *The American Sportsman,* Wilbur F. Parker, the editor and proprietor and member of the famous Parker family, makers of America's finest guns, noted that while Walton commended angling as the contemplative man's recreation, contemplation for Parker meant white-tailed deer hunting. He recommended deer hunting as "a game for princes and noble persons." He called it meditative work – romance of the forests. "The exercise," he wrote, "is strictly of an intellectual sort."

Burnie Waters gave it that interpretation as well, which may surprise the modern-day deer hunter, for deer hunting today is generally considered a pursuit of the common man. But historically the origins of American deer hunting lie within an upper-class development of the 1870s that sought to define deer hunting in terms of a "religion," to create a sporting ethic and to give deer hunting legitimacy and credibility in the eyes of the general public—something it solely lacks today in American society. Indeed, editors such as Parker of the

The John Bush buck, one of the oldest mounted whitetails in the Boone & Crockett Club – mounted by taxidermist John Bush himself – dominated the "smoke talk" of Waters' time. This typical 14-pointer shot on November 9, 1870, along the Elk River in Benton County, Minnesota, scored 181-1/8.

sporting journals of the 1870s turned to the writings of Henry David Thoreau to enhance the image of the deer hunter.

Parker read Thoreau's "Higher Laws" chapter in *Walden* (1854), where Thoreau extols the virtues of hunting and views the hunter as a more perceptive observer of nature than either the philosopher or the poet. Like Thoreau, Parker and Waters ultimately viewed deer hunting as a necessary introduction to nature and believed that deer hunting must be fixed to a spiritual awareness of the wilderness and the animals being hunted, if it is to survive with any kind of credibility.

The very essence of sport and sportsmanship revealed itself in another major development in 1873: the commencement of *Forest and Stream* (1873-1911), on August 14, at 103 Fulton Street, New York, New York. Destined to enhance and reinforce the American deer hunters' ideology and image for more than four decades, this great sportsmen's journal sold for ten cents a copy.

The editor, founder and publisher Charles Hallock (1834-1917) used this weekly publication as a vehicle to promote outdoor ethics and sportsmanship and to enhance the image of the deer hunter. In an editorial entitled "Metaphysics of Deer Hunting" published on October 2 that year, Hallock summed up the spiritual meaning of the deer hunt:

"Ah! There is some soothing influence in this going apart to commune with nature in her solitudes that makes us forget the struggles of life and our worldly troubles. It banishes all inordinate desires, simplifies our tastes, and makes us contented with mere food, raiment and shelter, which, after all, constitute the sole necessaries of life."

In studying our white-tailed deer hunting heritage, I have reached one basic conclusion: the cultural value of deer hunting lies in re-enacting our historic past, in reliving our deer hunting heritage, in listening to our heroes – their stories, songs and poems – in appreciating their great works of art, in highlighting their deer hunting artifacts and memorabilia. Without doing so, we have no future.

Waters considered white-tailed venison and bear meat "the very life of man." As his big game hunting exploits grew into legend he became a folk hero in southwestern Virginia. Stories soon circulated of how he followed a 400-pound black bear, killing it in deep snow on Pond Mountain and fighting with it on the brink of an icy precipice.

The incident, which entailed riding the bear to the very brink of the precipice, occurred on January 1, 1873. On that day the 60-year-old Waters joined his hunting partner Clark Porterfield of Grayson County for a little sport with bears. Both hunters agreed to still- hunt on their own. In his book *The Bear Hunter's Century* (1988), Paul Schullery describes the hair-splitting adventure:

"The footing was wretched, snow over ice,

The Wilburn Waters (1812) portrait by artist David Lowry Clark.

so that travel in the mountains was adventure enough without trying to find a bear to shoot. . . But soon enough, the dogs were off on the trail of a bear, and the old hunter felt the thrill of it to the point that he soon . . . scrambled recklessly up the slopes – falling, rising, slipping, crawling, but always climbing – until he broke into a little clearing and saw that the dogs had treed not one but three bears. Picking the largest one, Waters took a shot with his shotgun, trying first the barrel loaded with a ball, which had no effect, then the barrel loaded with buckshot, which brought the bear down the trunk of the tree and into the midst of the dogs.

"In seconds, one dog was crippled and the bear had another one by its head. As the bear and dog slipped away from the tree and rolled down a steep gorge, Waters was after them, armed only with a tomahawk. . .

"When Waters arrived in a cloud of snow at the bottom of the ravine, the bear let go of the terribly wounded dog and turned on him. There followed a frantic dance of swipes and parries as the bear tried to get him and as he gave it what punishment he could with his tomahawk, which, judging from the effect it was having, must have been a steel-bladed ax. The bear turned from this fight and rushed for a cliff, apparently, in the hope of jumping from the cliff to nearby trees and then to safety. But Waters grabbed a handful of black fur and found himself mounted, loosely, on the back of the retreating bear. He took this opportunity to give the bear a really authoritative smack on the skull with his tomahawk, which brought it down just as its front end slid to a halt hanging over the cliff."

According to one account the 400-pound bear provided Waters with eighteen gallons of oil.

Waters became so closely identified with his deer and bear hunting ground that to the present day his name is mentioned to the tourists who travel on the Blue Ridge Parkway. In fact, the name "Wilburn Ridge" graces the fifth edition of the *Virginia Atlas & Gazetteer* (2003).

The name Wilburn Waters evokes awe among deer hunters in Southwestern Virginia. As one of his biographer's points out, "Waters was perhaps the last of his kind in Virginia — a man, like Daniel Boone and Davy Crockett, whose storied exploits in the wilderness grew into legend. On White Top Mountain the only evidence of his life are retold stories and the name of Wilburn Ridge near the summit, but his spirit still seems to hover over the mountain, the scene of many of the adventures of Wilburn Waters."

On top of a windswept, lonely knoll in a remote area of Ashe County, North Carolina, a monument honors the famed pioneer hunter and trapper Wilburn Waters. Built in 1957, this life-sized replica of a black bear stands guard over Burnie's grave, with the name Waters shown in huge letters on the very imposing pedestal. A historical marker existed at the foot of the knoll in the creek bed between the road and the old railroad track provided by the Norfolk & Eastern Railroad Company of Radford, Virginia.

You will find more information about his deer camp and deer hunting adventurers and yarns in Charles B. Coale's *The Life and Adventures of Wilburn Waters,* published in 1878. The original edition of this classic piece of deer camp nostalgia and whitetail Americana in Old Dominion sells for $375-400 in the out-of-print book market. After going through six editions, this book on the legendary deer hunts of Waters and his classic deer camp has remained in print for the past 126 years. As of this writing it fortunately exists as an e-book on the internet and in an inexpensive paperback edition for $5.95, but this edition lacks several deer hunting chapters from the original hardbound edition.

If one listens carefully on a moonlight night along Wilburn Ridge during the peak of the whitetail rut, one can still almost hear old Burnie Waters singing one of his popular ballads that demanded freedom from his dreary working apprenticeship with Sheriff Nelson Alloway:

> *Life with the Al-loways,*
> *Al-loways so dear,*
> *Chained hyar to wo-ork,*
> *Frum year to year.*
> *Frum year to year, yes,*
> *Frum year to year,*
> *Chained hyar to wo-ork,*
> *Frum year to year.*
>
> *I can-not stand hit,*
> *Stand hit I can't,*
> *Free-dom I must have,*
> *To trap and hunt.*
> *To trap and hunt, yes,*
> *To trap and hunt,*
> *Free-dom I must have,*
> *To trap and hunt.*

WOO

DEER HUNTERS' CAMP

OCOCK'S DEER CAMP

"There is no animal more intimately mingled with hunting romance or hunting traditions – none which serves more to set a hunter's blood a tingle . . . there is more excitement about deer hunting than any other kind of big-game hunting. The zest for hunting the deer is century's old and is still as keen as ever."

– *Emerson Hough,*
"Hunting the Deer," 1916

In the spring of 1903, publisher A. R. Harding of 174 E. Long Street, Columbus, Ohio, began to publish and edit numerous articles by a die-hard Pennsylvania buck hunter/mountaineer named E. N. Woodcock (1844-1917) in his magazine *Hunter-Trader-Trapper.* Harding referred to Eldred Nathaniel Woodcock as "the truest and best sportsman that ever shouldered a gun, strung a snare or set a trap."

Woodcock's articles on deer hunting, trout fishing and trapping so greatly delighted and entertained thousands of Harding's readers for a ten-year period, from 1903 to 1913, that in September of 1913, Harding published Woodcock's material in book format under the title *Fifty Years a Hunter and Trapper.* The book would remain in print for the next 100 years thanks to the continued efforts of the A.

"Deer Hunter's Camp," Hy S. Watson. Lithograph, circa 1909.

R. Harding Publishing Company; it remains in print as of this writing with the most recent edition being published in 2001.

Woodcock's book is filled with sage advice gathered from his half-century of deer hunting experiences and deer-camp adventures. With regard to guns he writes: "I am still of the opinion that a gun is similar to a man's wife, you must love them in order to get the best results." And as an enthusiastic early proponent of wildlife conservation he became an advocate of more stringent deer hunting laws and believed conservation was the answer to the declining population of all game animals.

Yes, E. N. Woodcock, the bearded bard of Potter County, was never shy or short on giving advice on a whole host of subjects and situations. With regard to the dilettantes and city slickers of the East Coast he noted: "A man that cannot mount a donkey and ride over a trail where the river is hundreds of feet

E. N. Woodcock (1844-1917), the famous Black Forest deer hunter who hunted whitetails in the mountains of Pennsylvania for more than fifty years.

When not still-hunting whitetails in Potter's County, Pennsylvania, E. N. hunted deer along the waterways all across the country – including Maine, Michigan and Canada. As a result of these trips he gained great fame as a trapper and deer hunter all the way to the West Coast.

Deer Hunting with a Canoe.

Wegner's Deer & Deer Hunting Postcard Collection.

Wegner's Deer & Deer Hunting Postcard Collection.

below or as it looks to be nearly under him, and the trail not more than twelve inches wide, hewn out of the solid rock, he had best remain in the East."

Born in Potter County, a legendary deer-hunting area to this very day, Woodcock traveled the entire country to hunt deer in such states as California, Oregon, Washington, Michigan, Canada, Indiana, Oklahoma, Missouri and New York. But he always returned to his favorite deer hunting terrain, the Black Forest, located in the extreme southeastern part of Potter County, Pennsylvania. He was born on August 30, 1844, in Lymansville, a small town named after his grandfather, Isaac Lyman, a major in the Revolutionary War and founding father of Potter County. From his grandfather, Woodcock tells us, he inherited "that uncontrollable desire for the trap, gun and the wild." From early childhood his natural inclinations led him to the streams and forests, instead of the little red brick schoolhouse on the banks

of Mill Creek. He shot his first buck near Lymansville at the age of nine.

"It was here," Woodcock recalls in his autobiography, "that I made my first bed in a foot or more of snow with a fire against a fallen tree and a few boughs thrown on the ground for a bed. At other times perhaps a bear skin just removed from the bear for covering, or I might have no covering other than to remove my coat and spread it over me. This I have often done when belated on the trail so that I was unable to reach the cabin and was happy and contented."

While on the deer trail Woodcock slept in hollow logs, hemlock-brush shanties, crude and primitive lean-tos, and tents. He was a mastermind when it came to improvising some kind of primitive deer-camp shelter when he was unable to return to his permanent deer camp located at the very head of the Allegheny River, 1700 feet above sea level. Woodcock

always maintained an open invitation to his fellow deer hunters to come to his deer camp and enjoy the wilderness at large:

"Brothers, I will tell you where my camp is and you will always find the latchstring out. My camp stands at the very head of the Allegheny River. From the cabin door you can throw a stone over the divide to where the water flows into the west branch of the Susquehanna. In a half hour a person can from my camp catch trout from the waters of the Allegheny and the Susquehanna. . . ."

His nature led him to deer trails and trap lines from early childhood; he trapped bear and hunted whitetails in the mountains of Pennsylvania for more than a half century. Like Philip Tome, the legendary Pine Creek deerslayer, Woodcock shot whitetails and bears at the age of nine and frequently tramped back to deer camp in the black wilderness with a tallow candle in an old tin lantern, which gave him about as much light as a lightning bug. Back then, he would beg or steal his father's old double-barrel flintlock shotgun called "Sudden Death" and escape to the nearest salt lick to watch for deer. He describes his early experiences in this regard:

"I would beg father to let me take the gun and watch the lick. As I was only nine years old, they would not allow me to have the gun, so I was obliged to steal it out when no one was in sight, carry it to the barn and then watch my opportunity and skipper from the barn to the lick. All worked smoothly and I got to the lick all right. It was toward sundown and I had scarcely poked the gun through the hole in the blind and looked out when I saw two or three deer coming toward the lick. I cocked the old gun and made ready but about this time I was taken with the worst chill that any boy ever had and I shook so that

E. N. Woodcock frequently dined on venison liver and onions at the hollow log where he lived snug as a bug as he traveled through Northern Wisconsin, 1893. The classic Winchester Model 1887 lever-action shotgun stands ready for action.

On Woodcock's deer hunting trip to the West Coast in 1902, E. N. slept in primitive hemlock brush shanties as well as in snazzy, romantic log cabins in Northern Wisconsin with bending meat poles.

I could scarcely hold the gun to the peep-hole. It was only a moment when two of the deer stepped into the lick, and I took the best aim I could under the condition and pulled the trigger. Well of all the bawling a deer ever made, I think this one did the worst, but I did not stop to see what I had done but took across the field to the house at a lively gait, leaving the gun in the blind.

"The folks heard the shot and saw me running for the house at break-neck speed (this of course was the first they knew I was out with the gun). My older brother came to meet me and see what the trouble was. When I told him what I had done, he went with me to the lick and there we found a fair sized buck wallowing in the lick with his back broken, one buckshot (or rather one slug, for the gun was loaded with pieces cut from a bar of lead); one slug had struck and broken the spine and this was the cause of the deer bawling so loud as this was the only one that hit.

"The old shotgun was now taken from its usual corner in the kitchen and hung up over the mantelpiece above the big fir place and well out of my reach. This did not stop my hunting."

This turn of events only encouraged the boy to hang around gun shops like that of Seth Nelson, who shot more than 3500 whitetails and instilled the love of buck hunting and arms in several generations of mountain boys, including E. N. Woodcock. At Nelson's gun shop the lad heard infamous tales of deer and deer shooting while constantly looking at and dreaming about guns. At this gun shop he heard about the notorious stags that held a veritable army of Pennsylvanian "red coats" at bay for days on end. Here he learned about the wild adventures of "Black Jack" Schwartz, who presided over deer drives that encompassed a radius of 30 miles or more and once downed 138 deer on a single drive.

By the age of twelve, he convinced his father to have the local gunsmith, Mr. Goodsil, make him a double-barrel shotgun. He now began gunning for deer in earnest; he received fifteen cents for the saddles and ten cents for the whole deer. Like every backwoods deer hunter and trapper, Nimrod Woodcock longed for taller timber and tried to get farther and farther from the "ting-tong of the cow bells." In saying farewell to the plow, his trail and trapline excursions became longer and longer. Jerking venison and feasting on trout high-lighted his deer hunting campaigns, which by the age of 17, lasted for three months at a time. He usually returned home for Christmas.

Like most deerslayers of his time, he used the railroad, a team of horses, the ever-present buckboard and a bobsled to travel farther and farther into the heart of the deer forest, where the business of deer hunting became serious. He traveled for months at a time with his buckboard loaded with whitetails and bear which he deposited at railroad stations as shipments to the next city. He traveled through several counties on these prolonged deer hunts.

On a deer hunting campaign in the fall of 1868, with his partner, William Earl, a deer hunter from Vermont, Woodcock recalled that "we were seldom in camp until after dark, and we were up early and had breakfast over and our lunch packed in our knapsacks. The lunch usually consisted of a good hunk of boiled venison and a couple of doughnuts and a few crackers, occasionally the breast of a partridge, fried in coon or bear oil. Sometimes the lunch would freeze in the knapsacks and it would be necessary to gather a little paper bark from a yellow birch and a little rosin from a hemlock, black birch or hard maple tree and build a little fire to thaw the lunch. This, however, was quickly done, and was a pleasure rather than a hardship. I have delighted in eating the lunch in this manner for many a winter on the trap line or trail, as have many other hunters and trappers."

Woodcock's hemlock shanties contained a number of essential ingredients: back issues of *Forest and Stream, The American Field and Hunter-Trapper-Trader* as well as current issues; as he traveled through deer country he always had his mail forwarded to local post offices. Standard equipment at the Woodcock deer camp generally included Winchester rifles, especially the Model 1866 Carbine, Woodcock's *Method of Trapping the Fur-Bearing Animals* (1907), Stevens Pocket Shotguns with 15-inch barrels and, of course, the ever-present Woodcock Bean Hole.

Indeed, the famous Woodcock Bean Hole became a standard fixture at his deer camp, whether it was a hemlock shanty, a tent, a lean-to or his permanent deer camp in Potter County at the head of the Allegheny River. Near the fireplace he dug a two and a half foot hole measuring about 18 inches in diameter. In the hole he placed an iron pot with a close fitting flange lid to keep out all dust and ashes. With the beans already in the iron pot, he would then rake a lot of live coals from the fireplace into the bean hole. He then covered the hole over with plenty of ashes. The beans cooked for three to four days. He detailed his method as follows:

"We prepared the beans in this fashion: After washing we soaked them for about twelve hours. The water was drained off and the beans were then put into a the kettle with the necessary trimmings, which consisted of a good chunk of pork put in the center of the beans, and two or three smaller pieces laid on top, a pinch of salt providing that the pork was not sufficiently salty. A spoonful of brown sugar or rather a little baking molasses and a little pepper. Now this kettle was allowed to remain three or four days in the hole without disturbing farther than to cover over occasionally with hot embers. You ask if beans are good baked this way – we guess yes. We have heard a great deal about the famous Boston baked beans, but we wish to say that they are not in it compared to beans baked in a bean hole."

During the late 1880s and early 1890s, Woodcock hunted whitetails in Michigan along the banks of the Manistee, Boardman and Rapid Rivers as well as in Upper Michigan near Lake Superior. During this time entire Michigan families frequently searched out his deer camps for visits with the famous deer-hunting bard from the Black Forest of Potter County. Some of these visitors customarily stayed at his deer camps for several days at a time; others remained in camp for weeks. They would target practice, play cards, pitch "quoits," conduct jumping contests and other activities including fishing, eating trout and venison along with potatoes roasted in ashes, toasted bread and always beans, beans, beans – from the famous Woodcock Bean Hole. As E. N. fondly put it, "I wish to say to the man going to deer camp for a long hunting campaign, don't forget the beans as they are bread and meat!"

Unlike legendary deerslayer Philip Tome, Woodcock preferred to still-hunt whitetails rather than to drive them. "I wish to say right here," he wrote in his autobiography, "that I do not like driving deer any better than I do the hounding and running of deer with dogs. The dog is all right but I want no dogging of deer for me." During the latter half of Woodcock's life Pennsylvania, like many other states, banned using dogs for running deer in 1873, as well as shooting deer at salt licks in 1897.

On one occasion, however, a dog greatly assisted the old Nimrod while doing battle with a white-tailed buck. After following a deer trail along a creek, Woodcock suddenly stopped and prepared to climb over a fallen tree across the trail. In his *Fifty Years a Hunter and Trapper,* he details the battle:

"I was just in the act of climbing this log when a good-sized buck went to jump the log also and we met, head on. I had no gun and if I had would have had no time to use it. I seized the deer by the horns and forced him back from the log with a startled cry at the same time. The deer, instead of trying to get away, seemed bound to come over the log to where I was, so I held to the deer's horns, not daring to let loose.

"I could keep him from raising over the log and after he tried several times to jump the log, he then tried to break loose from me, but I had the advantage of the deer owing

Superior View.

While hunting whitetails in Michigan entire families searched his deer camps out for visits with the famous deer-hunting bard from the Black Forest of Potter County.

As Woodcock hunted whitetails in Wisconsin during the 1880s, he encountered classic racks of venison like this one at a deer camp near Phillips, Wisconsin, circa 1880.

to the log being so high that the deer could not pull me over, neither could the deer get in shape to strike me with his feet under the log. I think that I was so badly frightened at the sudden meeting with the deer, that I did not know what to do so I hung tight to the buck's horns and called as loud as I could for help, thinking that someone might possibly be passing along the road, which was not so far away, hear my call and come to my assistance, but no one came.

"A man by the name of Nelson lived about a fourth of a mile away, who had a large bulldog. The dog's name was Turk. This dog would follow me at every chance that he could get. As no assistance came, I had about made up my mind to release my hold on the deer as my strength was fast leaving me, when I thought to call for Turk. I began calling as loud as I could and it seemed that the dog had heard my calling before I began, for almost before I was aware of his presence the dog sprang over the log and seized the deer by the hind leg, but the dog had barely grabbed the deer when the deer kicked him away from the path into the laurel.

"In an instant the dog, with an angry yelp, jumped and seized the deer by the throat and in a moment the deer ceased to struggle and began to settle to the ground. As soon as I dared to release my hold on the deer horns I got my pocketknife out and sprang over the log and ran the knife blade into the deer's throat. The deer did not seem to notice the knife. I think that the dog had choked the life out of him. The battle was over and it was only a few minutes but it was the hardest battle that I ever had and the dog came to my assistance none too soon for I could not have held on much longer."

These man-deer skirmishes frequently occurred during Woodcock's day and stories about them appeared in the sporting literature of the time. The sporting literature during this period also contained descriptive accounts of deer hunters pursuing phantom, mythic bucks. Each district had its phantom buck. And there was always a legendary deerslayer in hot pursuit.

For many years, Woodcock pursued a mythic buck called "Old Teddy" because, like Theodore Roosevelt, he could not be downed. This giant buck had top-heavy antlers: a 14-pointer with 5 inch basal circumferences and brow tines reaching one foot apiece. Its main beam measured 25 inches each in length. He led the raids on corn and wheat fields, fought dogs and even attacked a bull. One of Woodcock's hunting companions claimed "he had a rack of horns as big as any elk!" Woodcock's brother Roscoe Woodcock finally downed the old boy in 1914.

Woodcock followed with great interest the stories and photos of Pennsylvania's legendary white-tailed bucks. He considered the majestic Strohecker head with 26 ebony-stained points shot in 1898 in the High Valley section of the Seven Mountains and the bizarre 28-pointer shot on December 8, 1910, by William Pearl "Bunker" Rhines to be the two most spectacular bucks of his day. At his legendary deer camp in the heart of the Black Forest, Woodcock read newspaper accounts of these giant bucks and studied their rack configurations in the photographs. He also read the classic sporting literature of his day and kept the memories of these tales alive at his fire pit.

Sometime during the fall of 1880, Woodcock met a tall, lean, black-haired deerslayer named John Q. Dyce (1830-1904), who tramped through the endless mountains, broad river valleys and steep gorges of the Black Forest country of Clinton County, just south of Woodcock's deer hunting bailiwick. On a long narrow ridge known as Spring Run Ridge, the two Pennsylvanian mountaineers shared a campfire and exchanged buck hunting tales, adventures and ballads.

According to Pennsylvania's deer and deer hunting historian Col. Henry W. Shoemaker, Dyce carried an old percussion Kentucky rifle with considerable brass and silver inlay, called "Kill Buck." Although the maker's name was illegible, the word "Philadelphia" could be seen on the lock. It was probably a Tryon.

According to legend, Dyce seldom went anywhere without his 13-inch Pennsylvania Mountain Hunting Knife with stag-horn handle and pewter mountings, made by John E. Smith, a famous Clearfield County deer hunter. As the 6' 5" deer stalker slowly moved along the side of the Spring Run Ridge, his deeply-inset, dark, black eyes – "black as any raven's wings," as Shoemaker would have it – suddenly focused on a buck, doe and fawn standing together.

Bang! Sounded the old Kentucky rifle. According to Shoemaker's *Stories of Great Pennsylvania Hunters* (1913), "the bullet pierced the brain of the buck, the throat of the doe and lodged into the heart of the fawn. It is said to be the only case of this kind recorded in Pennsylvania deer hunting annals." Shoemaker documented the distance of the shot at 100 yards. As a result of this episode, Shoemaker listed Dyce in the Pennsylvania "Honor Role" of legendary deerslayers. In the only portrait we have of him, his distinguished black beard makes Dyce look a little like an ancient philosopher of Greece and Rome.

In many ways Dyce, like Woodcock, was indeed more than just a famous deer hunter in the Highlands, as we learn from a brief glimpse of his life. The so-called celebrated "Poet Hunter" of the Bald Eagle Mountains was born on the banks of the West Branch of the Susquehanna near McElhattan on May 31, 1830, the year Pennsylvania deer hunter Arthur Young downed Pennsylvania's #9, 12-point typical buck in McKean County, which still reigns supreme as the oldest buck in the Boone & Crockett Record Book, scoring 175-4/8.

E. N. Woodcock considered the majestic Strohecker buck with 26 ebony-stained points shot in 1898 in the High Valley section of Pennsylvania's Seven Mountains to be one of the most spectacular bucks of his day.

Dyce was a descendant of a prominent family from the Highlands of Scotland. The Dyces distinguished themselves as soldiers, artists, surgeons and scientists in the British Isles. John Q. received his education in a log schoolhouse at McElhattan and later studied at the Dickinson Seminary at Williamsport to become a Methodist preacher. After encountering a variance with theological dogmas, the restless adolescent imbued with intense buck fever left the Seminary and for many years led the life, like Burnie Waters, of a die-hard buck hunter, poet and minstrel ballad singer in the deer camps of the Highlands. His repertoire embraced more than 100 folk songs, some of them centuries old.

He acquired a great love of nature and possessed a wide knowledge of animals, trees, plants and flowers. In doing so, he soon became a regular contributor of poems and lyrical prose for the *Clinton Democrat* published at Lock Haven and other newspapers as well. As a great lover of deer hunting dogs, he possessed first-class stock. Some of his deerhounds came from Kentucky. With his cherished deerhounds he pursued deer with great delight and as the deer population began to decline in Clinton County, he extended his deer hunting territory into the northern portions of the state including the area Woodcock hunted.

In his discussions with Shoemaker, Dyce related how in 1858, he shot what he thought was a large spike buck also on Spring Run Ridge, but when he started to field-dress the buck he found it was a doe with antlers. He also reported killing a book on Kearns's Run in Clinton County, which had antlers in the velvet in late October. He also shot many large atypical racks, which he insisted always had more points on the left side than the right.

During his lifetime, Dyce shot more than 500 white-tailed deer, many of them, especially the bigger bucks, in a sacred place called Long Hollow back of McElhattan, not too far from the infamous Deer Head Tavern where he hung out and sought sustenance—social and liquid. The better antlered racks and skulls he nailed to the side-walls of the woodshed at his deer camp along the banks of the West Branch of the Susquehanna River. Unlike many of his pioneer deer hunter colleagues, who found life too complicated to undertake the task of collecting trophy antlers, Dyce acquired an early interest in preserving unique, white-tailed deer antlers.

Like many Keystone deer hunters of his day – "Burnie" Waters and E. N. Woodcock included, Dyce traveled the waterways of the Bald Eagle Mountains and fire-hunted deer at night. Nighttime deer hunting was not banned in Pennsylvania until 1917. As one of Pennsylvania's greatest mountain minstrel singers, he sang, like Waters and Woodcock, the popular folk song of his day, "Floatin' fur Deer" by James Ballard, as he traveled the West Branch in pursuit of deer in his jacklighted canoe:

Yon nook! Spring the locks!
The deer's eyeballs of fire
Still, still as a shadow!
Hush! Nigher, yet nigher!
He falls! Draw him in!
Now away in good cheer,
Through the lily-pads blithely
from floating for deer,
Floating for deer.
Back to camp, through the shallow,
from floating for deer.

His nighttime fire-hunts often generated as many as four deer per night. His fire-hunts for whitetails ended at his deer camp along the banks of the Susquehanna with music, singing and reading in front of the blazing hunter's fire. Passages from Isaac Mclellan's classic *Poems of the Rod and Gun* were heard late into the night:

Now, from the sweet
aquatic grass
Whereon they feed,
they raise the head,
To watch with curious gaze
the flame
Athwart the inky river shed;
Then when the red
reflected light
Gleams on their glassy
eye-balls clear,
The volleying gun disturbs
the night,
And dies with gasping moan
the deer.

John W. Dyce (1830-1904), the famous Clinton County deer hunter who killed three deer with one shot and wrote the classic deer-camp ballad "All is Vanity, Saith the Preacher."

Music and singing prevailed at his deer shack for it contained a whole host of musical instruments: violins, mouth organs, accordions and even a few dulcimers and harps. Like many Native Americans, this premier ballad singer and buck hunter of the Highlands believed that deer themselves were attracted to music. In his *Pennsylvania Deer and Their Horns* (1915), the centerpiece of Pennsylvania's deer hunting tradition and mystique, Shoemaker notes "that Fiddler's Green on Potato Creek in McKean County was named for a famous greensward where deer danced to the music played by an eccentric back woodsman named Vincent Hogarth."

Dyce's primitive backwoods deer shack took on the atmosphere of Nineteen Hundred & Tobacco. Everyone present frequently listened to the old bard as he conversed about the rare sport of the day and recited Reverend C. H. Dudley's "The Huntsman's Camp" at the end of the day:

> Pale and vanishing moonlight,
> Retreating shadows
> of naked autumn trees,
> Morning breaking
> on the mountain-tops,
> A faint light below the horizon.
> A stir in the hunters' camp,
> A thrill of life electrifies sleeping forms,
> Quick crawling forth
> from piled blankets,
> Coffee, rolls, smoking bacon,
> Boundless animation, excited talk,
> burnished guns,
> Off to the woods – and the kill.
>
> Primeval man – primeval instinct –
> a primeval world,
> A wooded solitude;
> The hot and crowding emotions
> Of man going forth to slay,
> The hunting cry of the wolf pack
> In his heart and burning through his veins,
> Rare sport this day.
>
> Slowly the sun climbs above a far range,
> Darkness dissolves and fades away,
> A light snow like a bridal veil
> Makes a paradise of whiteness
> Over all God's world:
> The hunt is on.

In the deer woods Dyce wore a coonskin cap, deerskin hunting shirt, buckskin leggings and moccasins. Deerskins sold in those days for 75 to 90 cents. He coveted the deer as a grand prize. No finer dish than venison graced his table. No more beautiful trophy ever adorned the walls of his humble cabin on the West Branch than the antlers of a fallen white-tailed buck.

When the deer hunt was on, each day ended in intense storytelling by the fire. Many Dutchmen called it "Smoke Talk" – a rich blend of truth mixed with downright lies and sundry libations. One of the stories told and retold by Dyce and his boys focused on the wild adventures of Curley Pete Quick, a noted deer hunter from a family of famous hunters. The incident occurred in November of 1874 when Quick wounded a massive buck in the Big Log Tavern Pond, near Milford.

According to numerous reports in the sporting literature of the day, especially *The Field*, Curley Pete Quick encountered a ten-pointer as he ran into the pond near the Big Log Tavern. Quick jumped into his canoe and followed the buck. After getting into close range, he discharged both barrels of his old 12-bore double breech-loading shotgun made by "Wm Moore & Co." According to Curley, he "hit it bad!" But it kept on swimming in the Big Log Tavern Pond.

Re-doubling his efforts, he sped the canoe along side the wounded buck and dropped his double barrel in the bottom of the canoe. Like Natty Bumppo and in the adventurous spirit of Woodcock, he attempted to dispatch it with his Pennsylvania buck knife. He seized the "horns" and tried to hold them, but the buck plunged forward at the same time, throwing Quick backward and almost capsizing the canoe. Regaining his equilibrium, old Curley again seized the buck by the "horns" but this time he was thrown from the canoe on to the deer's back – capsizing the canoe.

The wounded buck managed to throw Quick in front of him and strike him several times with his flailing hooves, stripping Quick of his buckskin hunting shirt and forcing the dazed hunter to retreat from the scene of battle. In a painful and weakened condition he headed for shore and the Big Log Tavern on the opposite side of the pond, half-naked and benumbed with cold. Quick found the buck dead the next day a quarter of a mile away from the skirmish.

These deer-men fights frequently occurred due to the primitive nature of the weapons used and became a leitmotif of the sporting literature and art of the time. Dyce finished his tale about Curley Pete Quick's buck fight at the Milford Big Log Tavern by singing one of his favorite deer hunting songs, "The Horns:"

> *Tally Ho my Boys,*
> *the Horns forever, Hey Tally Ho,*
> *Tally Ho, Tally Ho.*
> *And in our hunting may we never*
> *miss the Buck*
> *And kill the Doe.*

The strong antagonism to shooting does – a practice that would haunt Penn's Woods for almost a century and a half until the arrival of Gary Alt – is obvious in the stanza of this popular deer hunting song.

When the colorful mountain minstrel John Q. Dyce, the legendary Clinton County deer-slayer who shot three deer with one bullet, died on December 3, 1904, he died, according to Henry W. Shoemaker, singing the song "All is Vanity, Saith the Preacher," which recalls what happened one Sunday at Welcombs. As the song has it, with snow lying deep on the ground a Presbytery clergy-man, Reverend Thompson, was reading the second lesson, when a deer hunter suddenly opened the church door and shouted in, "I've got 'un!" All the men in the congregation with the exception of the Pastor and old Billy

Whether at his tent or the one-room deer camp, Woodcock loved to tell deer-hunting stories and engage in the mystique and romance of camp fire dreams, circa 1900.

Tench arose and withdrew immediately to follow the buck in hot pursuit:

> *The singing o'er, the prayer was said,*
> *But scarcely had the text been read,*
> *When, panting with fatigue and fear,*
> *Rushed past the door a hunted deer.*
>
> *Prayer, hymn and text were all forgot,*
> *And for the sermon mattered not—*
> *Forth dashed the dogs—not one was mute—*
> *Men, women, children followed suit.*
>
> *The men prepared the deer to slaughter,*
> *None staid but lame old Billy Tench,*
> *Who sat unwilling on his bench.*
> *Not for the sake of hymn or prayer,*
> *Did Billy keep his station there,*
> *But, as he said, with rueful phiz—*
> *"For a damned spell of roomatiz!"*
>
> *The Parson groaned with inward pain,*
> *And lifting up his hands amain,*
> *Cried, dolefully, "'tis all in vain!"*
> *Up starting nimbly from his bench,*
> *"'Tis not in vain," cried Billy Tench,*
> *"When my good hound, old Never-Fail,*
> *Once gets his nose upon the trail,*
> *There's not a spike buck anywhere,*
> *Can get away from him, I'll swear."*

John Q. Dyce, like Burnie Waters and E. N. Woodcock, loved to keep deer-camp memories of the past alive by telling and re-telling past and current deer hunting stories at the campfire. At times, dinner for two at the hollow log merely consisted of Woodcock himself and his cherished hound Mage – "the best hunting hound that ever trod the earth!" At other times, however, local deerslayers of renown, balladeers, and mountaineers assembled to listen to his deer-hunting tales, which became a rich blend of personal experiences mixed together with deer hunting lore from the sporting literature of the day.

As the beans simmered in the Woodcock Bean Hole, the "Smoke Talk" at the fire pit revolved around the mythic, white-tailed bucks that roamed the Pennsylvania Mountains and the strange and bizarre deer-hunting events that occurred in the Black Forest such as the tale of Ezra H. Prichard, an old buckboard maker, and the buck that ran off with his new Winchester repeating rifle in 1866. While

Outing Magazine, circa 1910.

"Smoke Talk." Woodcock loved the camaraderie and storytelling at the fire pit. From a painting by Oliver Kemp.

still hunting the hills at the head of Joerg Run with his buddy Burt Olson, according to Woodcock, Prichard shot a magnificent ten-pointer. As he started to field dress the buck he rested his brand new Winchester against a tree – one of the first Winchester Model 1866s to be used in Potter County.

As Woodcock told the tale, at the first prick of the knife the buck suddenly strug-

gled to its feet, caught one antler in the guard of the rifle and plunged on down the hill. Pritchard, in a dazed state of mind, dropped his knife and yelled to Olson to save his precious Winchester. Both men hastened after the fleeing buck. Woodcock refined the tale repeatedly: "The buck slumped down at the first knoll. A few rods distant – dead as the proverbial door nail – but the rifle slipped

WOODCOCK'S DEER CAMP   65

from the antler and kept on its course for many yards." After a long and patient search Ezra recovered his cherished Winchester with only a small bruise on the stock.

Woodcock also fondly told the tale of Reverend Samuel Hull's wife Margaret, of the East Fork District, who nailed her buck with an axe in 1870. In hearing a disturbance in the woodshed one day she discovered a fight between her dog and a very large white-tailed buck. As the buck thrashed the dog, she seized an axe and joined the fracas. A well-directed blow saved the dog from being trampled without wasting any lead or precious gunpowder and added venison steak to the dinner table that night for Samuel, their son Joseph, and herself.

Woodcock's repertoire of bizarre deer-hunting tales remained endless. He told the tale of Fulsome Ferris of McKean County, who proudly killed three deer with a single shot as well as the incredible tale of a buck/bear/three-man deer fight that occurred on November 20, 1879, near Coudersport.

He also, of course, told the story of how he himself shot the legendary white seven-point white-tailed buck of Lymansville on a hillside between there and Coudersport on December 3, 1879.

"One day, a Mr. Hill came to my house in great haste. He had been cutting logs on a hill, and looking across onto a hill opposite where he was working, saw the white buck, and came to tell me. I took my gun (an 1873 Remington #2 Sporting rifle), went up the hill until I was sure that I was well above the deer, then cautiously worked my way down. There being no snow on the ground, and the deer being white, I soon discovered it lying in its bed. I crept up within shooting distance and fired, killing it instantly."

Historian Robert Lyman recorded what happened to what undoubtedly remains the oldest full-mounted albino deer in America: "The deer was mounted by a taxidermist and sold to Prudence Lyman Boyington, at Roulet for $100.00. After her death it went to her daughter, Dora Boyington, and then to (Topsy) Rossella Lyman Tauscher, who passed it on to Annis Coleman. After her death it was claimed by her daughter Leo Coleman, who on May 15, 1964, presented it to the Potter County Historical Society. Now, with unseeing eyes it gazes out at the hills to the east where it romped so gaily long ago."

In the past, albino whitetails were rarer than they are today. Woodcock's mounted albino played indeed an interesting part in the history of Roulet. For many years Mr. Boyington kept it in the Roulet House, where thousands of people marveled at what they referred to as a freak of nature. It remained on display and in countless parades in several towns and eventually became a symbol of Roulet.

In a recent interview with Bob Currin at the Potter County Historical Society in April of 2007, I learned that Woodcock's white buck was being refurbished and placed in a special wooden-glass diorama for all to view at the Potter County Historical Society as a special artifact of early North American white-tailed deer hunting.

Although crippled with "a damned spell of roomatiz," by the age of 69, after 50 years of deer hunting in the mountains of Pennsylvania, E. N. Woodcock continued to dream of legendary white-tailed bucks and the endless miles of deer trails he tramped while hunting them in the Black Forest of Potter County and all around the nation. In 1917, at his death at the age of 73, he had missed only two deer seasons from the time he started deer hunting at age nine.

As an avid reader of *Forest and Stream* he had read the great reporting on white-tailed deer and deer hunting in this journal by one of his contemporaries from Iowa, the wildlife conservationist/author Emerson Hough (1857-1923), best known perhaps for his novel *The Covered Wagon*. E. N. often

Like many deer hunters of the time, Woodcock proudly displayed his quarry in the art gallery. This unidentified hunter dressed for the occasion and brought his cherished Remington Model 8 Auto-Loading Rifle with him, circa 1910.

quoted Hough at great length, especially Hough's classic essay "Hunting the Deer":

"There is no animal more intimately mingled with hunting romance or hunting traditions – none which serves more to set a hunter's blood a-tingle . . . there is more excitement about deer hunting than any other kind of big-game hunting. The zest for hunting the deer is century's old, and is still as keen as ever."

E. N. Woodcock believed that, and he remains one of America's greatest deer camp tribesmen of the rough and tumble sort, showing no interest, as he readily admitted, "in the high boot, fashionable, corduroy suits and checker cap business!" This primitive, rugged, folksy, backwoods character traveled the nation via buckboard, stage, canoe, bobsled and train in pursuit of the whitetail; he will remain in our white-tailed deer hunting memories forever.

THE ECH

CHAPTER 5

ECHO LAKE DEER CAMP

With whatever proficiency in still-hunting any mortal ever reaches, with all the advantages of snow, ground, wind, and the sun in his favor, many a deer will, in the very climax of triumphant assurance, slip through his fingers like the thread of a beautiful dream.

– *T. S. Van Dyke,*
The Still-Hunter,
1904 Edition

On Tuesday, November 8, 1904, Wisconsin's legendary deer hunter H. C. ("Bert") Scofield and his Echo Lake Deer Camp boys, known later in Wisconsin deer hunting lore as "The Perkinsville Pirates," left Sturgeon Bay at 6:00 PM via boat – "The Sturm Sailor Boy" – for Marinette They arrived at 8:30 and put up for the night at the Hotel Marinette. Those present included J. C. Dana, Honorary Member; H. J. Hahn, President; J. H. Elliott, Vice President; H. B. Jennerjahr, Steward; H. C. Scofield, Secretary; and H. M. Walker, Treasurer.

Poker, schnapps and beer prevailed, as did wild story telling and recitations from T. S. Van Dyke's newly revised 1904 edition of *The Still-Hunter,* the most popular deer hunting book of the day. Late into the night they examined Van Dyke's proposition that "the

Courtesy of the Remington Art collection.

"Whitetails in Cutover Country." Oil on canvas, 1972.
Tom Beecham.

combined ingenuity of Earth, even assisted by light from on high, could not improve upon the quintessence of perfection for deer hunting known as the Winchester of '73."

The next morning at 8:12 AM they boarded the Wisconsin & Michigan Rail Road and headed for Norway, Michigan. After arriving there at 10:14, they met up with three more club members: Bert, Ned and Harry Chapman. After a rigorous and adventuresome eight-hour buckboard ride through the piney woods and cedar swamps of northeastern Wisconsin, the boys arrived at their classy backwoods retreat along the banks of Echo Lake, a short distance northeast of Pembine in Marinette County – in what my father always referred to as "The Heart of Wisconsin Deer Country."

Thursday, November 10, the boys spiffed up their picturesque and romantic 20′x30′ log cabin overlooking beautiful Echo Lake. The smell of cigars, wood smoke, baked beans and onions hinted at high hopes of venison liver and heart to come! And venison liver and heart came the next day – the opener – when "Bert" Scofield (1859-1951), the former Mayor of Sturgeon Bay, nailed a 12-pointer near Buck Mountain with his Winchester Model 1895 repeating rifle – the first successful box magazine, lever-action repeater ever placed on the market. Several days later the *Sturgeon Bay Advocate* proudly announced that H. C. Scofield killed a 275-lb. buck the first day out!

The diary entries in the official Echo Lake deer hunting journal remain sketchy for the rest of this deer hunt. But we do know the hunters spent Thanksgiving Day in the deer woods. The faded picture of the club house for 1904, pasted into their journal, highlights their meat pole with nine deer and some very fine bucks in the hangings. They arrived back in Sturgeon Bay on Saturday, November 26, at 10:30 PM.

The 20-day Wisconsin deer season that year

(November 11-30) generated 76,000 license sales with a two deer of any size or sex season; when the 1904 Wisconsin deer season ended nine whitetails with their tails properly placed up and all facing to the right hung on the Echo Lake deer camp meat pole according to tradition and deer camp bylaws.

On Thursday, November 9, 1905, the Echo Lake deer camp boys left Sturgeon Bay on the "Sturm Sailor Boy" for Marinette at 8:20 AM. After a series of railroad connections they arrived in Pembine where they dined out at the Hotel Algonquin. They reached their

Their picturesque, classy, romantic deer camp – a 20'x30' log cabin – was located along the banks of Echo Lake, a short distance northeast of Pembine, Wisconsin, in Marinette County. From left to right: Aug Rieboldt, Joe Elliott, H. Hahn, H. B. Jennerjahr, Ned Chapman, Bert Chapman and Claude Gard. November 1906.

cherished log cabin at Echo Lake at 6:30 PM. After supper, house cleaning and arranging their gear, they listened to music on their gramophone and retired at 10 PM.

On this 1905 deer hunt, 73,474 hunters participated in the 20-day/two-deer/any-size-or-sex season. The 1905 season saw the prohibition of hunting deer with dogs and the use of salt licks. After a long and involved breakfast on Friday morning the Echo Lake gang spent the day scouting, sighting in rifles

and preparing for the opening day.

On the sacred, long-awaited Opening Day, the bell rang at 4:30 AM. Breakfast was served at 5:30 and consisted of bacon, sausages, potatoes, biscuits and coffee. At 6:00 AM the boys bent their course for Cooks Camp #3 below the Beaver Dam, where they made their first drive but to no avail – no deer were spotted. They then drove the balsam thicket near "Wild Cat Hill." On this drive they started a doe, which Elliott dropped in its tracks.

After eating lunch at Dunn's Camp, they made several more deer drives including "Johnson's Clearing" where Scofield burned his barrel hot at a large buck and a doe but without making a hit. At the close of the opening day eight hunters (Hahn, Elliott, Jennerjahr, Scofield, Russell and the three Chapmans) saw 28 deer, shot 19 times and killed two deer. After hot soup, bacon, sausages, potatoes, bread and coffee for supper the boys took flash pictures of the cabin's interior.

On the second day of the hunt the weather turned warm and uncomfortable with no deer seen and no shots taken. On the third day a cold wind blew from the northeast with snow squalls. Several members stayed in camp, read Van Dyke and worked on domestic chores while Hahn, Scofield, Bert and Charlie Chapman and James Russell made a series of drives on their walk to Faithhorn, Michigan. On their way they spotted eleven deer and shot three times but scored no hits. While walking along the Zoo Line railroad tracks they crossed the Menominee River on the bridge and walked into Faithorn, where they stopped at Harters Hotel for drinks and camaraderie. Before returning to camp they purchased deer hunting postcards, which they mailed out every year, and beer for camp.

Tuesday, November 14, dawned clear, still and frosty – eight degrees above zero. The boys drove the heavy brush below Beaver Dam Swamp with no results. They then took on the heavy timber near the Soo Line Bridge but again failed to move any deer. Several more failures followed. Even drives at the legendary Cat House Swamp and Wild Cat Hill only produced one sighting and one shot taken by Charlie Chapman with his new Winchester Model 1905 self-loading rifle but with no results for the meat pole.

The next couple of days produced no starts and no shots according to their deer camp diary. There might have been some shots of brandy taken, however, to ease the frustration of sitting on stumps all day to no avail.

Booze was an item listed in their expense ledger but not discussed much in the content of the diary.

Before the '05 deer hunt ended, deer drives at Smitty's Hill and Buck Mountain produced two more deer for the meat pole. On this 20-day deer hunt, eleven hunters saw 78 deer, shot 71 times and downed nine deer. They enjoyed a splendid Thanksgiving Day Dinner at the Hotel Algonquin in Pembine before returning to Sturgeon Bay on November 30 aboard "The Sturm Sailor Boy." The Echo Lake camp expenses that year totaled $44.37.

The twenty-day deer hunt for two deer of any size or sex continued for the Echo Lake Deer Camp boys in 1906 in northeastern Wisconsin. On the second day of that hunt the boys once again burned their barrels hot with the weather being cold, blustery and snowy. With two inches of snow on the ground that day they first drove the Beaver Dam. Scofield, the club's secretary, records the events of the day in their deer camp diary:

"Ned starts a deer and gets a snap shot. Harry shoots seven times at it but no hits. Drive out Halls Chopping. Plenty of sign but no shots! Drive out the 'Brush.' Hahn gets five shots at two deer but no results. Elliott gets three shots at another deer and Scofield kills it in five shots. Eat lunch at Barkers Chopping that we later drive out but get no starts. We then drive out Madigans Chopping and get after Old Square Toes but do not see him."

Every deer camp has their legendary phantom buck. Old Square Toes haunted the minds of the Echo Lake deer hunters as he snuck around as a shadow lurching within a shadow. (He eventually died of natural causes.) In the November 12 diary entry, Scofield reported six deer sightings and 21 shots fired with one deer going to the meat pole.

After 14 days of blazing away and many deer drives at Buck Mountain, Cat House Swamp, Cooks Camp #3 and Wild Cat Hill, Scofield tallied up the final figures for the 1906 deer hunt: eleven hunters saw 54 deer,

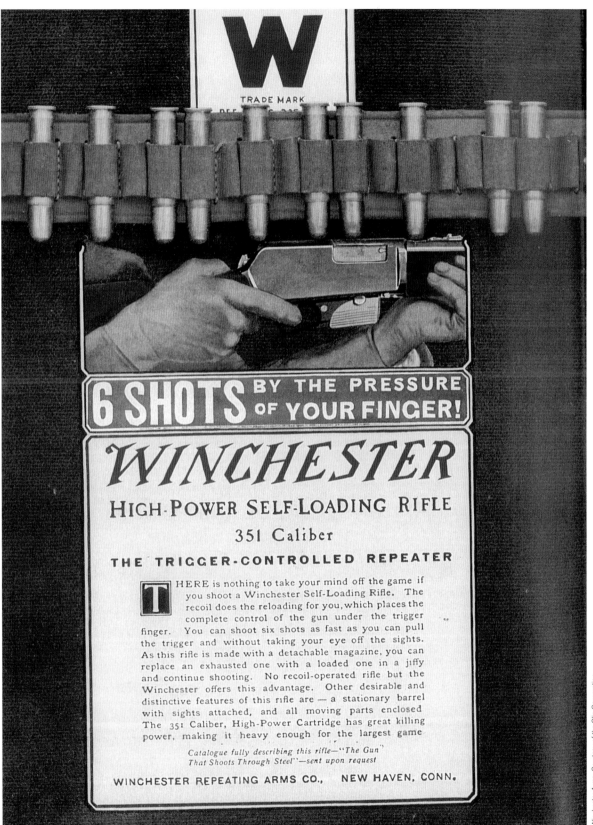

In 1910 Scofield used his new .351 Winchester Model 1907 Self-Loading Rifle, which allowed him to shoot six shots as fast as he could pull the trigger. In doing so that year he shot two bucks – one at Halls Chopping and the other at K. C. Creek.

shot 89 bullets and bagged seven deer. Wow! They fired enough lead, didn't they? The total expenses for the Echo Lake Deer Camp that year reached an even $50.

The length and type of deer season remained the same for 1907, the only change being that state law now prohibited the use of scaffolds for deer hunting. On November 9, "Aug" Rieboldt, H. M. Walker, Joe Elliott, H. B. Jennerjahr and H. C. Scofield left Sturgeon Bay on "The Sturm Sailor Boy" and arrived at Menominee at 10:50 AM. After dining at "Murrays Restaurant" they took the Milwaukee & Northern Railroad to Pembine and then Van Durn's buckboard to their Echo Lake retreat.

The opening day on November 11 dawned clear with a light northeast wind and snow on the ground. As they began to drive the Beaver Dam, Walker jumped a big buck near "Neds Mound." Bang! Bang! went the Winchesters. Rieboldt shot three times. Jennerjahr shot three more. And Walker levered out another four balls of lead into the air – all to no avail, for the buck continued to elude the meat pole and ran on into obscurity. Back at camp all agreed: "There's a lot a room around 'em! And don't forget it!"

A Perkinsville Pirate ready to board the Soo Line Train in Medford. Camaraderie aboard the train while en route to deer camp. Front cover of the September 1916 issue of *National Sportsman*.

The railroad played a prominent role in our modern-day, deer-hunting culture. The Perkinsville Pirates traveled from one railroad depot to the next en route to deer camp. Circa, 1915.

As the hunt progressed, a number of drives on Porcupine Ridge produced six deer for the meat pole. Every evening after supper the main event revolved around listening to music and playing penny ante poker. In fact the interior design of the camp architecture was originally built to accommodate a large poker table surrounded by bunks.

When the hunt ended on November 30, seven deer graced the Echo Lake meat pole after ten hunters sighted 35 deer and shot 52 times. When one looks at the sheer volume of bullets fired during these days, one can understand the devastating number of human causalities and injuries that these early deer hunts sustained.

That year Wisconsin reached for the first time 100,000 deer hunters who killed an estimated 11,000 deer in the 35 open counties. At the time Marinette County still followed the traditional 20-day season with two deer of any size or sex. During this season they drove and still-hunted their favorite deer hunting area called "Buck Rodge" with great success. During the 14 days they hunted that year the five hunters saw 17 deer, shot 33 times and killed six deer.

Jack Welch's deer camp in the heart of Taylor County between Donald and Perkinstown. November, 1915. State Historical Society of Wisconsin.

Scofield himself downed several bucks with neck shots on *"Buck Ridge."*

On Monday, November 9, 1908, Elliott, Jennerjahr, Walker and Scofield left Sturgeon Bay on "The Sturm Sailor Boy" at 8:00 PM and after a rough passage on Lake Michigan arrived in Menominee, where they dined at "Murrays Restaurant" After a hotel stay they arrived at the Echo Lake Club House on Tuesday via buckboard for the 1908 deer hunt.

On November 15, 1909, Scofield noted in the Echo Lake deer camp diary that the trip from Sturgeon Bay to Pembine for Elliot, Walker and himself cost $3.38. He also underscored the strong tradition of buying and mailing deer hunting postcards. During the 1909 deer hunt the boys hunted with great regularity on Buck Ridge and along Tin Pail Road near Deer Tail Camp. They traveled the area with a horse-drawn sleigh. The total bill for the hunt that year

reached $31.86. Four hunters saw three deer, shot seven times and killed two of them. That year 103,000 deer hunters participated in the one-deer-per-season limit now as the deer population continued to decline.

The 1910 deer hunt found only two regulars of the Echo Lake Club in camp: Joseph Elliott and "Bert" Scofield. Scofield brought for the first time his new .401 Winchester Model 1910 self-loading rifle chambered for 250-grain bullets with which Scofield shot two bucks: one at Halls Chopping and the other along the banks of K. C. Creek. That year Elliott and Scofield saw nine deer, fired 24 shots and killed four deer. The trip cost $24.28. The highlight of the year revolved around the Echo Lake Club Banquet held on Monday night December 5, at Wageners Restaurant in Sturgeon Bay. Henry C. Scofield and Henry Grasse presided over the venison supper. The following speeches and toasts were given:

Not only did the boys enjoy the spirits and venison tenderloins but the deer hunting stories and jokes as well. The hot topic of discussion that night, however, revolved around the record-book eleven-pointer taken by Robert Hunter in Vilas County in November with a maximum outside spread of 30-1/2 inches and a field-dressed weight of 256 lbs., today's #4 typical for the state of Wisconsin scoring 191-3/8.

The 1911 Wisconsin deer hunt commenced on November 11, as usual. Elliott, Walker, Bingham, Druetzer and Scofield showed up at the Echo Lake Club House at 6:00 PM carrying an Airedale pup sent along by Hahn. License sales reached 125,000 that year. With 21 inches of new snow on the ground, the boys played a lot of poker and enjoyed sundry libations. They did manage to shoot one deer in the Briar Patch near Charlie's Stump – a doe shot in its bed by Scofield on Wednesday, November 22. The final score: five deer seen, 29 shots fired, and one deer went to the meat pole for good measure. The highlight of the deer hunt appeared in the *Sturgeon Bay Advocate:*

"Dr. Norden took a bath Saturday night while trying to demonstrate as a log-walker. He and Frank Stroh and H. C. Scofield got lost in the dark near "Shivering Sands," and in crossing a narrow creek on a little log, Doc sat down on the log and tried to juggle four loaves of bread while he was immersed to the waist in the icy water."

In 1912, the Echo Lake Deer Club members did not return to their club house but hunted deer instead at Ellison Bay. The log book indicates no explicit reasons; declining deer numbers probably caused their absence. They did return to Echo Lake for the 1913 deer season, however, but that would be there last pilgrimage. Deer numbers were in decline and the Echo Lake deer camp boys began to search for another deer hunting hotspot.

They would eventually settle their deer hunting operations for the club near Perkinstown, Wisconsin, in 1915, at the Jack Welsh Deer Camp in Taylor County. There they would become known as the Perkinsville Pirates. Their last hunt at Echo Lake in 1913 cost $57.45 for six hunters and produced three deer sightings, eight shots fired and no deer taken back to Sturgeon Bay. The *Sturgeon Bay Advocate* describes the end of an era:

"H. C. Scofield, Bert Keith and Joe Elliott returned Tuesday from a week's hunt in Northern Wisconsin. The gentlemen did not see any deer just to their liking so did not bring any venison home with them. The other members of the party, Uncle August Rieboldt, Dr. F. C. Huff and Frank Stroh went to Three Lakes where it had been reported that the deer were more plentiful and tame. It is possible that Uncle August will not be seen in Sturgeon Bay again, it being reported that he had taken a solemn vow that he will not return until he has killed a deer."

On Wednesday, November 10, 1915 – the year Wisconsin installed the famous or infamous Buck Law, depending upon your point of view – Wisconsin's legendary deerslayer H. C. "Bert" Scofield and his six "Perkinsville Pirates" left Sturgeon Bay on the 2:00 PM Milwaukee & Northern Railroad for Jack Welch's deer camp in the heart of Taylor County near Perkinstown. The tickets for Stevens Point cost the Echo Lake Deer Club boys $3.41.

The Perkinsville Pirates traveled between Medford and Sturgeon Bay in snazzy black Model T Touring cars en route to Jack Welch's Deer camp in Taylor County, November 19, 1915.

Wegner's Deer & Deer Hunting Postcard Collection.

After having lunch in Green Bay they reached Stevens Point at 9:30 PM. They got off at a railroad crossing and walked to the Soo Depot where they bought tickets for Medford for $1.36. They then jumped on the Soo Line train at 1:20 AM and arrived at Medford at 4:30 AM, where they got breakfast at the Hotel Fayette for 50 cents. They then arranged their trip to Welch's deer camp with Pope's Livery and left in great haste. Heading in a northwest-erly direction from Medford they now traveled in two snazzy black Model T Ford touring cars with 20 horsepower each.

Arriving at Welch's camp at 9:30 AM and with no time to waste, they jumped into their deer hunting togs and made a deer drive in the hardwoods along the School House Road. But according to Scofield's *Echo Lake Club Deer Hunting Log, 1904-1926,* it produced no results. After dinner at camp they spent the rest

A typical Taylor County deer camp near Medford. November, 1915.

Wegner's Deer & Deer Hunting Photo Collection.

of the day still hunting and driving deer. "No starts. No shots." And so ended day one of the 1915 deer hunt for the Perkinsville Pirates, who found themselves in the deer woods that year with an estimated 134,000 deer hunters who would kill 7000 deer with half of them being taken by market hunters, according to Otis S. Bersing's *A Century of Wisconsin Deer.*

Each night after the hunt Scofield meticulously recorded deer sightings, shots, kills and hits for each hunter in the deer camp diary, as well as weather conditions and poker scores. On Friday, November 12, the club secretary reported that Will Wagener saw one deer and fired 11 shots in the process with his Winchester repeater. Apparently, that Winchester barrel was so hot that Attorney Wagener had to put the gun down before trying to construct in his mind some sort of illogical, legalese explanation for the flawed shooting that the kangaroo court back at camp would never tolerate. The next day proved to be a little better in this regard while hunting the area of Mud Lake and Polack Lake. Lloyd Scofield saw two deer and shot eight times to no avail, while old Frank Rose, however, saw two deer and killed two deer with two bullets. OK, Frank!

Despite their somewhat indiscriminate blazing away, the Perkinsville Pirates got good news coverage back in Sturgeon Bay in the local *Advocate:* "The Scofield party that left here last Wednesday afternoon for Taylor County, near Medford, has proved its ability as deer hunters. Reports come in from the camp that even at this writing the party has shot five or six deer, which speaks for itself as regards the marksmanship of these sportsmen." Apparently club member H. M. ("Cap") Walker worked for the *Advocate.*

Welch's deer camp was located within walking distance of Perkinstown, for one entry in the camp log noted the boys frequently walked to town after supper for tobacco and 12-quart pails of beer.

Heavy snow and a blowing gale from the northwest forced the camp on Friday, November 19, to call Pope's Livery for the Model Ts. Pope sent out two Ford touring cars. One stalled out in heavy snow at Richter's Lake and the other Ford that got to camp also got mired down on its way out before reaching Medford Road. A team of horses and a sleigh finally reached Welch's deer camp and got the boys to Medford at 11:05 PM just in time for the Soo Line train at 11:16. After changing trains at Spencer, they reached Stevens Point about 2:30 AM and stayed at the Majestic Hotel for the night. The last item in the deer hunting log for 1915 indicated that seven hunters saw 27 deer, fired 59 shots and in the process killed seven deer.

For unknown reasons Bert recorded only one entry for the 1916 deer hunt at Welch's deer camp in Taylor County. They hunted for nine days with ten gunners, who shot two

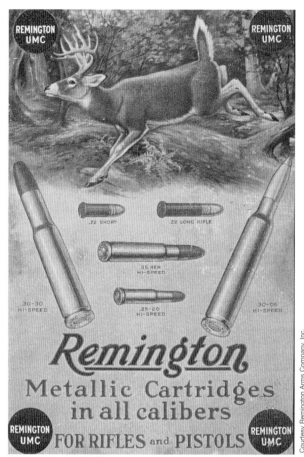

Scofield used Remington metallic cartridges in his favorite Remington Model 8 rifle.

spike bucks and a doe. Once again they completed the journey between Medford's Hotel Fayette and Welsh's camp via two Ford Model T touring cars. Automobiles were becoming quite popular in the deer woods; Wisconsin licensed 115,645 autos in 1916.

In 1917, the Wisconsin Department of Conservation shortened the deer season to ten days (November 21-30) due to declining deer numbers for the 30 open counties. They also reversed themselves on the Buck Law and now reverted to the any-deer season. Although the Department insisted that "a one-buck law is the only law that will protect the deer and provide an annual open season," the Legislature rejected the idea. License sales fell dramatically from an all time high of 155,000 in 1914 to 53,593 in 1917. The Department also required paper deer tags for

2 mile carry

"A Three Mile Carry." Two of the regular Perkinsville Pirates: Hunt Master Bert Scofield bringing the deer meat back to camp, ably assisted by Joe Elliott who carries the smoking hot Winchesters. Circa 1915.

the first time, each of which cost ten cents. The year 1917 remains historic for two other reasons: 1) the Department subjected Indian deer hunting off the reservations to all game laws, and 2) it prohibited the use of any kind of light while hunting deer.

On Saturday November 17, the Perkinsville Pirates including Joe Schauer, Will Wagener, Bert Carmody, Louis Werkheiser and H. C. Scofield left Sturgeon Bay at 1:45 PM and reached Green Bay too late for the Green Bay, Winona & St. Paul to Stevens Point, so they took the Interurban Electric Car to Neenah – arriving there just in time for a 7:00 PM supper at Valley Inn Hotel. They then took in a show "Stop, Look, Listen" and left on the Soo Line Rail at 10:15 PM.

After arriving at Medford at 5:15 AM Sunday, they had breakfast at the Hotel

Fayette and left for Welch's deer camp in a classy Maxwell driven by a friend named "Warsaw." En route they spotted three deer between Wigger and Richter Lake. "Great hustling to get our guns out but failed to get any shots." Interestingly enough the season didn't open until November 21, but traditional deer camp meat was frequently taken any way it could be taken in those days. The results of their 10-day hunt that year: two bucks and one doe. *The Sturgeon Bay Advocate* chronicled the hunt:

"DEER SLAYERS RETURN. Attorney W. E. Wagener, H. C. Scofield and Register of Deeds Bert Carmody, returned home Thursday morning from their hunting expedition bringing with them a deer apiece. Mr. Wagener bagged the biggest one of the party, being a buck that tipped the beam at 175 pounds.

The Perkinsville Pirates loved to travel at high speeds to and from Billy Wolff's camp near Tipler, Wisconsin, in their black, convertible Model T Roadsters loaded with plenty of white-tailed venison, Shell Motor Oil, an occasional wolf and even a Lady Diana dressed in black for good measure. November, 1922. *(An interesting note on the back of this postcard indicates that it appeared in the 1923 Menomonee Falls Periscope School Annual on page 36.)*

Wegner's Deer & Deer Hunting Postcard Collection.

Joseph Schauer and Louis Werkheiser, who were members of the same party, did not return home until the end of the season – not having been able to get their deer until the day after their comrades left for home.

"Attorney Wagener secured the largest, a buck weighing 175 pounds. As Billy has been chasing deer in Taylor County for the past three seasons, without meeting with success, no one envied him his good luck. Bert Scofield, the crack shot of the party, secured the smallest, his deer weighing but 67 pounds. He explains this fact, however, by stating that any one that can shoot a gun should be able to hit a big 175 pound deer, but that it takes some skill to hit a little 67 pounder jumping along like a rabbit."

Statewide, 53,593 deer hunters shot an estimated 18,000 deer in 1917.

The *Advocate* documented the 1918 deer hunt of the "Perkinsville Pirates" as a huge success with most of the deer shot on "Hardwood Hill:" "The hunting party consisting of H. C. Scofield, Captain August Rieboldt, W. E. Wagener, Joe Schauer, Joe Elliott, Louis Werkheiser, Bert Carmody, D. E. Bingham and Leo Schauer bagged nine deer and a red fox. They left here on November 19 and returned home Saturday morning, November 30. They had the finest kind of weather for the sport and not a day passed but that they secured a deer. Three days were consumed in going and coming home, so that they had only a week's actual hunting. The fox was shot by W. E. Wagener and is a beautiful specimen. He will have the hide tanned. Every one of the party feels that this was one of the most enjoyable hunting trips that it had ever been their pleasure to participate in, not only because of the success they had, but from a social standpoint as well." Heavy snow forced the boys to leave that year via two teams of horse-drawn sleighs.

More than 70,000 deer hunters shot more than 25,000 deer in 1919. Even though more deer hunters were taking more deer, the most frequently bandied-about statement at the train depots and backwoods taverns went something like this: "The close of the hunting season in 1921 will see Wisconsin deer practically wiped out!"

In search of a better deer hunting bailiwick the Echo Lake Deer Club again changed their base of operation to William (Billy) Wolff's deer camp near Lake of Dreams and Chipmunk Rapids at Tipler, Wisconsin, in northwestern Florence County for the 1920 deer hunt. Resorts in that area at the time still served venison on the menu. The Department of Conservation reverted back to the Buck Law in 1920 – one buck with "horns" not less than three inches. That deer season also saw for the first time the use of metal deer tags that needed to be fastened around the hock joint. Scofield and his boys arrived in camp on November 18, after walking the last eight miles over a right of way behind horse-drawn wagons in one of the most rugged sections of the state. The ten-day hunt for the eight gunners from Sturgeon Bay resulted in very few sightings or shots with only one buck – weighing 169 pounds – taken by H. C. Scofield.

In reporting on the hunt the *Sturgeon Bay Advocate* told a tale of woe: "The hunters ran into hard luck this season, otherwise they would have returned with four or five deer. They encountered 14 inches of snow on their second day, which drove the deer out of the slashings. The gentlemen state that between deep snows, scarcity of game, the Buck Law, and poor shooting, all combined to make the trip a failure from the amount of game brought home."

On November 12, 1921, the year the state started the deer season one week earlier (November 13-22), the Echo Lake Deer Club regulars returned to Wolff's deer camp in Florence County for another deer shoot-out. In reading their deer camp diary it seems that the boys once again reverted to indiscriminant blazing away and poor shooting with their Winchester repeaters and automatics. With a great deal of specificity secretary Scofield reported the following results: seven gunners saw 73 deer, fired 112 bullets and killed seven deer. Oh! Where is Old Frank Rose when you need him? To save great embarrassment for all concerned, the *Sturgeon Bay Advocate* remained silent, probably on "Cap" Walker's insistence. The Echo Lake Club members used a staggering amount of lead. Indeed, one can understand

Courtesy Wegner's Deer & Deer Hunting Photo Collection.

Nov. 1919 **NATIONAL SPORTSMAN** **15 Cents**

85,000 Copies, the Largest Net Paid Circulation in the Field

The Perkinsville Pirates were avid readers of the deer and deer hunting stories published in the highly popular *National Sportman* magazine.

why the *Advocate* ran such headlines as "The Deer Shooting Season Starts Tomorrow" when documenting the adventures of this legendary deer camp.

But things took a turn for the betterment of all concerned when the legendary Perkinsville Pirates again returned to Billie Wolff's deer camp on November 11, 1922, the year in which the Department of Conservation narrowed the deer hunt down to only 23 open counties. Some of the boys now traveled all the way from Sturgeon Bay to Tipler in their Ford Model T touring cars (193 miles) while others still traveled via the railway system. Buckboards, sleighs and horse-drawn wagons were still being used,

THE ECHO LAKE DEER CAMP 83

Wegner's Deer & Deer Hunting Postcard Collection.

Oh! How romantic – traveling in snazzy black Ford Model T touring cars and horse-drawn buckboards.

depending on the weather. Some new names also appeared on the roster: A. E. Doolittle and Joe Welniak.

The action started on Monday, November 13, when Scofield killed two bucks before 8:00 AM on Hardwood Hill: three shots and three hits each. Shortly thereafter Carmody shot another buck with one shot at the west end of the hill. Everyone got shooting, with

a total number of 63 deer being seen before noon. Due to bad snowstorms, the hunt ended earlier than anticipated with the hunters seeing 163 deer and getting four bucks.

During their 1923 deer hunt, the year the deer tag increased to 50 cents, Scofield, Wagener, Elliott, Walker and Doolittle returned to Billie Wolff's deer camp and experienced the best week of weather ever for chasing white-tailed bucks. During the 10-day deer hunt the five hunters saw 71 deer, shot 34 times and killed three bucks.

On Thursday, November 13, 1924, Scofield and his boys were again at Wolff's deer camp for the opening day. Secretary Scofield describes the beginning scene of the opener: "Cloudy and cool with a light west wind. Wagener goes to his place on Camp 4 Road. Martin and Carmody to Prince Albert's Stump on the east end of Hardwood Hill. Scofield to his runway near the right of way. Martin and Carmody get eight shots at three deer before they are located on their stumps. Wagener and Scofield see flashes from their guns as it is still dark. No damage. Light fall of snow nearly all day." On November 24, the last day of the hunt Scofield sums up the results for himself, Wagener, Martin and Carmody: four hunters see 43 deer, shoot 61 bullets and kill three bucks. The number of cartridges used during these early hunts must have delighted the folks at the Winchester Arms Company.

In 1925, the State Legislature closed the deer season; thus began the alternating annual closed-and-open deer seasons during the Twenties. The 1926 deer season (December 1-10) may have opened past the rutting season but possibly ran into the period when deer yard together. In any event, that year 47, 330 Wisconsin deer hunters downed an estimated 12,000 white-tailed bucks, but Scofield and his boys did not contribute to that estimate.

On Tuesday, November 30, Schofield, Carmody, Martin, Wagener and two new faces, W. J. Bourgeois and Albert Conjurski, left Sturgeon Bay on the 7:00 Interurban Electric Car for Tipler, Wisconsin, with high hopes of successful buck shooting with their Winchester repeaters and automatics. They arrived at the Tipler Depot at 4:30 PM and were greeted by Willie Wolff's team and sleigh. The weather was bitterly cold, blowing and snowing with 14 inches of crushed snow on the ground and subzero temperatures.

The 1926 deer hunt, the last official hunt recorded in the Echo Lake Deer Club Hunting Journal, resulted in a colossal failure. Deer drives on Big Hill and to Prince Albert's Stump usually successful now failed repeatedly. Still hunting and runway watching on the shores of Balsam Lake also produced no sightings and no shots from the Winchesters. Driving the ridges around Deer Lake also proved futile. More time than usual revolved around playing poker and talking about how Gene Tunney defeated Jack Dempsey for the heavyweight boxing title on September 23 of that year.

When the 1926 deer hunt ended, the *Sturgeon Bay Advocate* offered its condolences with the following headline: "LATE SEASON IS FAVORABLE TO DEER." The article documented the trip:

"Some deer hunters are not as fortunate as others. The party consisting of H. C. Scofield, W. E. Wagener, Bert Carmody, Joe Elliott, Wm. Bourgeois and Albert Conjurske returned home Sunday from Florence County, where they spent ten days chasing the elusive bucks. In fact they were so elusive that they failed to bag a single one.

"The snow was so deep and traveling through the woods so difficult that it was a most strenuous job for the hunters and a boon to the deer.

"Notwithstanding the disappointment of failing to bag a beauty of the forest they had a good time. This was the first time that Messrs. Wagener, Scofield, Elliott and Carmody were ever skunked."

According to an unpublished letter to Walter E. Scott of the Wisconsin Department of Conservation (now the DNR) from Attorney W. E. Wagener dated February 14, 1955, we learn that H. C. ("Bert") Scofield continued to hunt deer with Wagener at Lattermann's Deer Camp on the Pine River in Florence County for a number of years and then for four or five years more at Madeline Island before his death in 1952. Scofield planned and participated in 78 consecutive deer-

A Taylor County Deer Hunt*

By H. C. "Bert" Scofield

Liver & onions for supper. Early regular members of the Echo Lake Deer Camp / Perkinsville Pirates, November 18, 1897. (Left to right). Jule Collard, Joe Elliott, Dr. H. C. Sibree, H. C. Scofield, Ross Wright, Rob Brooks, Capt. Joe Brooks, Lester Cheeseman, H. E. Tanner.

Door County Historical Museum.

Slowly the November sun was dropping behind the bleak hills of Taylor County. The day had been one of desperate and unfruitful toil.

Since early morn the desperate pirates of Jack Welch's far famed gang had tramped the hills in a vain search for venison.

And now as evening was falling Bert's favorite song was still and ever strong, the hardy little Spitz, no longer emitted his plaintive bark, which in days gone by never failed to start Mr. Buck from his lair.

The last drive was slowly drawing to a close, when the sudden roar of Harry's .45-70 infused new life into the entire gang. As the echoes died away each man eagerly waited for the celebrated death call of the pirates but it came not, so they silently gathered to talk it over. A short search revealed blood and soon the "Spitz" was ferociously barking on a blood trail.

Quickly and silently the gang ran out and around the woods to find where the trail led. It was my luck to get the extreme outside stand and I chose for my position a stump in the center of an old logging road. Scarcely had I reached my goal when the roar of a gun close by announced that the game was on its way.

Soon my straining ears heard the rustle of the leaves and the occasional cracking of brush as the deer approached. A small doe suddenly burst from cover and my old .35 roared a welcome. She took the first shot thru the front quarters and kept coming. My second shot got her too high through the back and she jumped sideways into the brush and stood.

As I drew on her for the final shot it flashed thru my mind that this shot must be the last for right upon us and within 5 rods was another camp whose eager hunters were already rushing forward to be in on the finish. Quickly the gold bead came to rest on her left shoulder just at the rise of the Winchester I touched the trigger and was amused by a tiny little click which sounded as impotent as a Republican Campaign Platform.

I looked at the old .35 in dismay. Never before in her long history of faithful service had she failed me in an emergency. I hastily ejected the unfired shell and inserted another and the next pull on the trigger might be finis for Mrs. Deer. As she fell she fell into the outstretched arms of the greedy gang who arrived just too late to finish her and claim her. The fact that I did finish her is all that saved the "Boss," alias Bert Scofield, – Scofield Hahn Company, – and the H. M. C. Company from an untimely end.

As my old friend Willie Shakespeare says: a poor shell, rains hell.

Edited from a hand-written, unpublished manuscript from the Wisconsin State Historical Society by Robert Wegner.

hunting treks to the North Woods in quest of white-tailed bucks. When the Legislature closed the deer seasons he traveled northward to Canada to hunt deer. Only on rare occasions did he return from the deer woods without a deer. In 1951 at the age of 91, he shot his deer seven minutes after the opening of the season. He was indeed a legendary Wisconsin deerslayer. Shortly after his death writer Jim Robertson paid him the final tribute in a newspaper article titled "Claim to Oldest Hunter Dies with Bert":

"With the passing of H. C. (Bert) Scofield Surgeon Bay and Door County lost claim to having the State's and quite possibly the nation's oldest deer hunter. Unlike many men, who choose to forget about active participation in sports at half or less of his 92 years and then see even a spectator interest gradually diminish, Bert was a true-blue sportsman up to the end of his colorful life. In fact, there are those who believe that Bert's participation in his favorite sport of hunting was conducive to his longevity. They will tell you that hunting was Bert's life; that he no sooner was over one deer hunting trip than he was planning for another."

Oh! How romantic and nostalgic: traveling to Jack Welch's deer camp in the heart of Taylor County via the Interurban Electric Car, the Chicago, Burlington & Northern Railroad and the classy Maxwell driven by "Warsaw" and then the snazzy black Model T Ford touring cars; retrieving dead bucks on horse-drawn sleighs under the moonlight; drinking beer out of 12-quart tin pails; the fine meals at the Hotel Fayette in Medford; burning Winchester barrels hot on Hardwood Hill, Krause's Clearing and Prince Albert's Stump; and driving deer at Deer Lake, Balsam Lake and Mud Lake more than a century ago. I wish I could have hunted bucks with Bert Scofield and his boys during those golden days of the Wisconsin white-tailed deer hunt.

M

MINNISINK DEER CAMP

Rod Crossman.

"The Cabin."

Autumn has come again to our Mountain.
Through the dim outline of white birch,
on the farther shore, a light gleams
to welcome you.
In a moment, you are penitent.
A word, unspoken, has weaned your spirit
from the wild:

"The Cabin."

– Oliver Howard Wolfe,
Back Log and Pine Knot: A Chronicle of the Minnisink
Hunting and Fishing Club, 1916

When one thinks of the cultural history of Pennsylvania's great white-tailed deer hunting traditions, we think of the Keystone State's legendary bucks: the Arthur Young buck shot in McKean County in 1830, with a score of 175-4/8, the oldest buck in the Boone and Crockett record book; the majestic Strohecker head with 26 ebony-stained points shot in 1898, in the High Valley section of the Seven Mountains of central Pennsylvania, a legendary buck that the great deer taxidermist, Charles H. Eldon, made remarkably lifelike; and, of course, the bizarre, 28-pointer shot on December 8, 1910, by William Pearl "Bunker" Rhines, the famous pitcher for the Cincinnati Reds, whose awesome burr points almost touch one another and measure 16-7/8 and 17-3/8 inches.

The famous Cameron County deer head shot in Pennsylvania by William Pearl ("Bunker") Rhines on December 8, 1910.

David Rhines.

The origins of the Minnisink deer camp consisted in deer tenting near Hemlock Swamp and Big Spring in 12'x12' canvas wall tents, 1900.

J. T. Rothrock, Pennsylvania Historical and Museum Commission – Division of Archives and Manuscripts, Harrisburg PA.

We also think about Pennsylvania's legendary deerslayers: the hair-splitting adventures of Philip Tome (1782-1855), the Pine Creek deerslayer, who relentlessly tracked deer to their deaths in the east-central part of Potter County; E. N. Woodcock (1844-1917), who tracked endless miles of deer trails in pursuit of his quarry in the Black Forest and once shot seven deer in one day and 3,000 deer during his lifetime deer hunts in the northwestern counties.

When we recall Pennsylvania's grand, deer-hunting traditions, deer-hunting historian Henry W. Shoemaker's blue-chip deer book, *Pennsylvania Deer and Their Horns* (1915), comes to mind with all of its glorious tales of Pennsylvania deer and deer hunting. More recently, when we think about Pennsylvania deer and deer hunting, we remember the classic, deer-hunting illustrations and deer prints of Ned Smith (1919-1985) that vividly entertained countless American deer hunters.

But we also recall the hundreds of thousands of legendary deer camps that dotted the landscape of Pennsylvania deer country. We remember, for example, the legendary Minnisink Hunting and Fishing Club in the Pocono Mountains, thoroughly documented for us in Oliver Howard Wolfe's *Back Log and Pine Knot: A Chronicle of the Minnisink Hunting and Fishing Club* (1916), one of the most cherished books in my deer and deer hunting library of more than 2,000 titles. This privately printed deer camp diary is exceedingly rare and very expensive.

The Minnisink Hunting and Fishing Club deer camp, located southwest of Milford in Pike County near High Knob, one of the highest landmarks (2062 ft.) in the Pocono Mountains, near Dingman's Falls in northeastern Pennsylvania, was a special place, a sacred space, for ten deer hunters: William L. "Bill" Fox, O. Howard "O. H." Wolfe, Horace W. "Hoddy" Shelmire, David R. "Dave" Shelmire, Walter "Wawa" Peirson, Jr., Dr. George R. "George" Fleming, S. Judson "Pop" Parrott, Dr. George E. "Doc" Levis, and two Honorary Members, David Shelmire and J. M. Wolfe. O. H. Wolfe describes the special-ness of their Mountain:

"A Tolerable Hold Up." The greenhorn dilettantes toil homeward from Hemlock Swamp with "Old Teddy" aboard the riding meat pole, 1908.

"High Knob inspires you as the bubbling spring does the thirsty woodsman, or the smell of bacon crisping over a wood fire inspires the heavy footed deer hunter on a bleak November night."

The Minnisink Hunting and Fishing Club came into existence in May of 1900, when O. H. Wolfe and Bill Fox camped out with blankets near Perkiomen Creek. O. H. fondly recalls the first campsite: "That first night was spent on Mother Earth under a very crude shelter of green boughs that oozed and dripped dew and red ants till morning brought a blessed relief to aching joints."

During the early years of the twentieth century, members of the club hunted deer from 12'x12' canvas tents near Big Spring above Dingman's Ferry. The terrain in this area possessed a natural charm and beauty beyond that of any other portion of the Delaware River. This blessed land up to the Lackawaxen River was known as THE MINISINK, the cherished domain of the Minsi Indians. The word "Minisink" from the Indian means "the water is gone." Wolfe for some reason unknown to this author chose to spell the word with two n's instead of one.

The deer camp suppers in these tents were elaborate affairs with the best stocked larder that could be bought and hauled 20-odd miles back into the mountain. Their deer camp suppers consisted of pheasants, rabbits, wild duck and deer liver. "Deer liver, as only Bill can cook it, is a treat unknown to the city dwelling epicure," O. H. wrote in the deer camp diary.

One famous deer camp supper in the old tenting days inspired O. H. to trochaic quatrameter. Two neighbors, encamped by Big Spring shot a buck near Hemlock Swamp and being tenderfeet, staggered seven miles back under their burden, fifty pounds heavier because they failed to field dress the animal on the spot. That incident prompted O. H. to write the following meter on eating venison liver in deer camp somewhat suggestive of Longfellow:

. . . . And the Hunters toiling homeward,
Brought the deer with all his blood in;
Lights and liver, heart and kidneys;
Came they from the Swamp of Hemlock,
Seven weary miles of labor,
Knowing not that they were bone-heads.
Then up rose Old Bill, the Boy Scout,
He the butcher, cook and baker,
Said, "I'll snatch that gory liver;
We will feed our guests upon it,
End the days of fast and watching
For Pot-meat-a, the white swamp hare.
For cant-hit-em, the hen pheasant.
So he took his trusty snicker,
Ripped the red buck through the mid-rif
Till he found a three pound liver
That had urged the red deer onward
Where the gentle doe had lingered
In the swamp to wait his coming.
In the pot, Bill placed the trophy,
Till the blood and evil passions
All had left the crimson slices.
In the pan with hissing bacon,
On My-ril-la's heated bosom
Fell the tender slabs of fresh meat,
Filling all the woods with perfume.
Came the guests unto the feasting,
Came with joy into the tepee
On each face the look of hunger,
Fell they then upon the muffins,
Drank the broth of tails of oxen,
Ate the green herbs from Turn Villa.
But the best of all that banquet
Was the liver of the ten prong
That had roamed the swales and thickets
Through the red brush and the laurel.
Then they smoked the pipe of plenty,
Smoked the peace-pipe, smoked Tux-e-do:
Though their own game tree was barren,
Said the Hunters, "We should worry!"

The best of that festive banquet was indeed the liver of the 10-pointer in the grand Pennsylvania deer camp tradition of masculine rites and rituals. At that ceremonial dinner the young deer hunters came of age. Historically, it was cooked ritually the day of the kill; it testified to the success of the hunt during the first days of the season. The hunters became totally immersed in the deer hunting life, and in the Native American tradition, they became the deer when they ate its organs.

The Minnisink deer camp boys discussed the deer hunting tales of Marcus N. B. Killam (1815-1902), the greatest deerslayer of Pike County to ever roam the deer woods, who killed 900 deer, including a superb buck weighing 306 pounds dressed. During the first decade of the twentieth century these fire pit stories revolved around a vast variety of subjects such as the great conservation work of Dr. J. H. Kalbfus, the Secretary of the Game Commission, who worked hard to preserve the heritage of white-tailed deer hunting; who banned buckshot in 1905; who introduced deer restocking in 1906; and who solved the buckshot murder of Game Protector Seely Houk on March 2, 1906, by Rocco Racca, who was convicted and hanged in 1907. And, of course, the famous Buck Law of 1907 also got rehashed to death over many pipes of tobacco and glasses of high-octane whiskey.

In 1914, the club received permission to lease an acre of land and erect a deer shack with a rough stone fireplace and a massive chestnut log for the mantel. It was soon agreed upon they would build the deer shack with their own hands and it would stand on the "Point" at Peck's Pond, the little open piece of ground made famous by the original bivouac where O. H. and Bill lay in a drenching rainstorm while fighting mosquitoes for two long nights.

In his chronicle of the Minnisink deer-hunting club, O. H. describes the location of the deer shack, which eventually became known with great reverence as The Cabin:

Many Pike County deer camps brought their own certified cook to camp who dressed in formal attire. And they reached their camp at Peck's Pond on Hawley Road (familiarly known among Peck's Pond fraternity as the "Pike"] via the buckboard, 1916.

A typical Pennsylvania State deer camp in Pike County on leased land, 1916.

W. H. Schwenk, Clinton County deer hunter with a typical buck taken at Green's Gap, 1914.

Pennsylvania Deer and Their Horns (1915), that choice piece of whitetail deer camp nostalgia containing one of the finest photo collections of Pennsylvania's greatest deerslayers and their camps ever assembled.

Rumbles and bumps occurred on the Hawley Road as the season approached. In his chronicle of the camp, O. H. captures the scene as Peck's Pond mobilized its little army of corduroy and khaki-clad, red-capped riflemen for the annual foray:

"There is no time for visiting yet. All is bustle as wagons are unpacked, wood fetched in, and fires started. Since the law has permitted cabins in these woods, the familiar sound of tent peg driving, with its accompanying profanity, is no longer heard in the land. Trying to drive a white birch peg through a half ton rock, neatly covered with four inches of top soil, is a diversion calculated to ruin anyone's disposition.

"As the sun begins to sink behind Southwest Ridge, only the Knob shows up clear in the waning light. Soon it, too, grows purple as the sun goes down back of the notch, and the short day draws to a close. Columns of bluish white smoke drift straight up through the taller oaks as the camp cooks prepare the evening meal. The sound of a good axe rings clear as the blade bites into the red oak log.

"What music is sweeter than that of steel as it strikes into hard timber on a clear crisp November evening? It suggests the fireside circle of whole-hearted, strong muscled friends; the roaring logs and the crisping bacon. It is heard at its best as you come within hearing distance of your cabin after a trying day in the woods, especially if you have been lost just previously in the 'red bresh.'

"You are tired as you finish your chores the first night in. Your back and arms have grown soft, you find. You are glad to wash up at last and take your place at the table while George carries in stacks of boiled potatoes, fired ham and stewed onions, to be raided as soon as you

"The traveler who has the courage to walk, drive or motor up the Hawley Road (familiarly known among Peck's Pond fraternity as the 'Pike'), will see a small sign-board nailed to a pine tree at the entrance of our land which modestly informs him that the M. H. and F. C. is located hereabouts. We boast no high wire fence in which to enclose trained deer for target practice but we are a bit jealous of our patch of oak, chestnut, pine and white birch. The latter beautiful tree is very bountifully distributed all about us and there are no lovelier or more graceful specimens than those, which grow at the edge of the lake beside The Cabin."

As the 1915 Pennsylvania deer season approached – the year in which the Pennsylvania Game Commission authorized the appointment of 60 Game Protectors – the Minnisink deer camp boys read with great delight Col. Henry W. Shoemaker's

have finished your steaming bowl of ox-tail soup. You drink your tea finally, draw around the fireplace and lay plans for tomorrow."

As O. H.'s narrative unfolds, the whole group decides to go to their favorite deer stands. "Pop" decides to go to the Hogback; Doc and Dave prefer Hickory Crossing. Bill announces that he will climb his pet tree at

Trophies o

Deer camp, 1915 – a special place in sacred space where man hunts whitetails and communes with nature.

shack fo
modate
Fred an
Young,

On t
six buc
Road L
clear a
to the c
Mount
back lo
pine kr

The
bottle
all to t
In this
old tir
older
age. A
fired

Fred
ma
191

gu
the
the
nic
fir
Cu
W
at
So
hi
Ja

w
b
th
c
o
a

9

BENT'S CAMP

"When Dad goes the deer hunt will go with him and when it comes time for those who are left to join the others in the Bent's Camp of the Happy Hunting Ground, we will see Dad there, waiting on the dock, flashlight in hand, counting in his last boy as he comes in over the long trail."

– *"Franny" Manierre,*
"The Story of the Clow Deer Hunt," 1938.

O n the Wisconsin 1928 deer hunt, William Ellsworth Clow, Sr. – "Dad" Clow as he was affectionately known – counted every one of his deer camp boys from the dock on Mamie Lake as they came off the deer trails surrounding the legendary Bent's Camp on the Wisconsin/ Michigan border in the Land O'Lakes area on the Vilas/Gogebic County borderline. That year 14 members of the Clow deer hunting clan shot ten quality bucks at Bent's Camp as seen on their meat-pole postcard. The season ran from December 1 to December 10. That year the agency required deer hunters to wear an official Conservation Button while deer hunting.

"Starting the Hunt." Warren Baumgartner, 1938. Two plaid shirts leaving with their guide for the start of the deer hunt with two classic Remington standbys: the Remington Model 8 Auto-loading Rifle and the Model 14 Slide-Action.

Courtesy: Remington Art Collection.

Many parts of the State at the time had no deer at all, as seen on Leopold's 1928-29 deer population map. Statewide, 69,049 deer hunters killed 17,000 bucks; the Clow boys got ten of them with some remarkable shooting during the buck-only season. The year 1928 also stands as a landmark year, for that was the year the Wisconsin Conservation Department created the Game Division.

For 14 deer hunters from one camp to get ten bucks in 1928 with a very low buck density in the area was a remarkable event indeed. And "Dad" Clow, President of James B. Clow & Sons – one of the largest jobbers of plumbing and heating supplies and manufacturers of cast iron pipe located in Chicago – quickly sent a letter to his friend Henry W. MacKenzie, Director of the Conservation Department, informing him of their fine shooting success. One of "Dad" Clow's sons set a record for shooting four bucks in four consecutive seasons with four shots.

In 1928, the deer hunters at Bent's Camp read William Monypenny Newsom's blue-chip deer book *White-Tailed Deer* (1926), as did Aldo Leopold, and discussed Leopold's prophetic ideas as well as quality deer hunting, land leases and deer hunting clubs and cooperatives – ideas way ahead of their time. When it came to Vilas County's trophy bucks, they talked about Robert Hunter's 11-pointer shot in 1910 which eventually scored 191-3/8 typical Boone & Crockett points and C. Callup's 14-pointer shot in 1913, which scored 193-3/8 typical points – two bucks that reigned supreme for many years as Vilas County's best record book bucks.

The Clow clan consisted of buck hunters of the first order from Lake Forest, Illinois – not only shooting lots of bucks, but big bucks with large racks as they traveled through the largest inland chain of lakes that surrounded Bent's Camp. It was a sight to behold: The Tar Baby (a large wooden, steam-driven, wood-fed, tar-

William Ellsworth Clow, Sr. – "Dad" Clow as he was affectionately known – counted every one of his deer camp boys from the dock on Mamie Lake as they came off the deer trails surrounding the legendary Bent's Camp.

The "Tar Baby" – a large wooden, steam-driven, wood-fed, tar-covered boat – hauled the Clow Clan to and from their cherished deer stands.

Courtesy Bent's Camp/Lisa Stemen.

Wegner's Deer & Deer Hunting Postcard Collections.

The Clow Clan traveled to Bent's Camp via the Chicago-North Western Railroad and Charlie Bent's two-runner logging sleighs.

covered boat), an entire flotilla of canoes small and large, row boats and scows in tow for heavy loads, all arriving at Bent's dock under the watchful supervision of "Dad" Clow.

Here amidst the historical grace and beauty of the Cisco Chain of Lakes they pursued legendary white-tailed bucks, many of which eventually graced the birch bark walls and ceilings of the rustic dinning room and barroom and fireplace mantelpiece. Great deer camp tales and lore revolved around many of them. The legendary taxidermist Carl Akeley of the Chicago Museum of Natural History even mounted some of them for display in the country estates of Lake Forest, Illinois.

The camp's log dining room with its large stone fireplace served as the social centerpiece of the entire deer-hunting experience. The walls

Group portrait of the 1928 Clow deer hunt. Ten hunters with their chef downed ten bucks. Like hundreds of thousands of deer hunters making postcards at the time, they turned their meat pole scene at Mamie Lake into a postcard and labeled Bent's Camp the deer "Hunters' Paradise" of Northern Wisconsin.

lined with white birch bark held in place with cedar bark strips gave the camp a quaint and rustic aura. White-tailed racks looked over the entire proceedings as deer-hunting storytelling continued late into the night. The spectacular dining room joined the kitchen, which stood on the lakeshore with screened porches above the water and offered magnificent views.

The Clow deer hunting party started to deer hunt from Bent's Camp in 1898, the year of disastrous forest fires in northern Wisconsin and Michigan. They traveled for several days on the Chicago & North Western Railway from Chicago to Appleton Junction and then to the Wisconsin–Michigan Line to what is today the city of Land O' Lakes. "Franny" Manierre, the camp historian, described the terrible ordeal of waiting in railway stations:

"The benches were merciless to the youthful in denying them the privilege of lying down in the presence of prohibitive arm rests. We traveled all the next day, as I recall it, in a stuffy day coach packed with lumberjacks, deer hunters and whatnot, all smelling equally bad or anyway the car did."

They then traveled west for more than

When traveling through Europe, "Dad" Clow drank Hubertus Pils and read the great hunting journal of its day, *Deutsche Jagd*. At Bent's Camp in Northern Wisconsin he drank Ashland White Label Beer – the brew "Dad" Clow knew – and read the leading wildlife conservationist journal of the time, *Forest and Stream*.

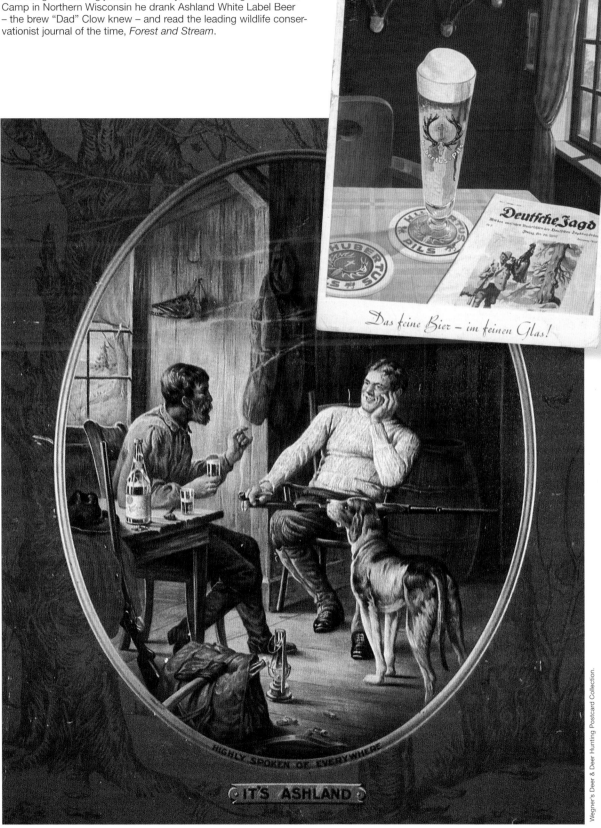

Das feine Bier – im feinen Glas!

HIGHLY SPOKEN OF EVERYWHERE

IT'S ASHLAND

four miles in Charlie Bent's buckboards and two-runner logging sleighs on very rough tote roads to Mamie Lake. The 20-day deer season ran from November 1-20, with a limit of two deer of any size or sex.

For the next 40 years, the Clow deer hunting party went to one place for one purpose: to hunt whitetails at Bent's Camp – a special place in sacred space – and they did so for more than forty continuous years. During that period of time workers from the James B. Clow & Sons' plants from Coshocton, Birmingham, Newcomerstown, Chicago and Marble Mill eventually traveled via train, buckboard and bobsleds of hay to Bent's Camp for the annual Wisconsin deer hunt with the Clow clan huntmaster "Dad" Clow. Sometimes as many as twenty huntsmen joined the gang.

From the high society of Lake Forest, Illinois, with its classic country estates and mansions and the wheeling and dealing of the corporate headquarters at 212-214 West Lake Street, Chicago, the Clow clan, specialists in plumbing fixtures and cast iron pipe, traveled to the primitive, white birchbark rusticity of Bent's Camp to escape, recreate and hunt deer while enjoying great white-tailed deer cuisine prepared by Lizzie and Charlie Bent. They eventually rented the entire camp, brought most of the food and even their own cook, "Ole Black Joe," the wonderful African-American gentleman who as Waube Kanish reports, "helped bring up the Bent children and grandchildren. While the Clows were there the Bents were guests, a yearly vacation."

In a unique postcard of the period we see a Green Bay & Western Railroad car converted into a portable deer camp itself with five deer hunters posing with their guns and five whitetails hanging from the railroad car. Deer hunters often rented railway cars for traveling deer camps at the time. A cook stove and hanging lantern appeared in the center of the car. Railway cars and depots stood as the main social centerpiece of the entire deer hunting experience in the early years of the twentieth century. And so did backwoods taverns such as the one shown in the Ashland White Label Beer ad. In looking at this delightful beer/deer ad we can almost hear these two deer hunters talking about "Bent's Camp of the Happy Hunting Ground" as they take a shot and a beer for the road.

In his history of this legendary Wisconsin deer camp, *The Story of the Clow Deer Hunt* (1938), author and fellow campmate "Franny" Manierre notes that "the Clow party became a cultural institution. The State of Michigan regarded it as such, for the Conservation Commission always issues #1 license to 'Dad' Clow and the consecutive numbers following to the rest of the party." Since they hunted both sides of the border, they purchased licenses from both states. The Wisconsin Conservation Department also issued "Dad" Clow their #1 non-resident deer- hunting license for many years.

"Dad" Clow, with his incredible enthusiasm and energy, unfailingly kept the crowd together for more than 40 years, promoting it to the enjoyment of lifelong friendships. In December of 1938, the Wisconsin Conservation Bulletin proudly announced in an article entitled "Clow's Deer College" that "this past November was the 58th time he has come this way on deer hunts. It is doubtful if any native or anyone else can match that record."

In 1937, "Dad" Clow wrote an article entitled "Half Century of Deer Hunting" for the *Wisconsin Conservation Bulletin*. In it he wrote: "It is now over 55 years since I first hunted deer in Wisconsin. At that time I had to go up on the Leopold and Austrian Line and have Indians from the Odanah Reservation meet me with a wagon at Bayfield. From there we would trail in on the old tote roads and such other rough roads as we made ourselves, to the hunting ground." In 1937, "Dad" Clow was 77 and reportedly more active than the majority of deer hunters who were 30 years his junior.

Some members of the clan came to Bent's Camp from Chicago, while others came from Wisconsin and Michigan; "Dad" Clow came from his classic country estate in Lake Forest, Illinois – an extraordinary two-story mansion. During the early years they all arrived on the Northwestern Railroad 12 miles east of Bent's Camp at the railroad station now known as Land O' Lakes. It then took about four hours to drive to Bent's Camp with a team of horses on a very rough tote road. According to Manierre, it was easier to walk it than to ride on the spring-less wagon. "Charlie Bent and his son Austin met us at the station with a two horse team harnessed to a two runner logging sleigh with a sort of a hayrack body and, fortunately, plenty of hay. Al Awalt drove the team while Charlie rode the famous little Indian pony Nixie, the mother of Nigger, the black colt known to all Bent's campers as the black horse that turned pure white in his old age. Austin trudged alongside in the woods,

popping off a partridge now and then in a spruce tree, with a twenty-two Stevens pistol, before it got too dark.

In his younger days Charlie Bent had worked as a game hunter for the logging companies but after establishing Bent's Camp in 1896, he gradually became what his nephew "Dunny" Bent, the regional historian, called "a mild conservationist" who took a dim view of market hunting. In his early days Bent dressed in buckskins and used a Winchester .45-90.

From a panoramic photo of Bent's Camp taken in 1903, we see ten different log cabins plus four boathouses. Some members of the Clow party stayed in the "Tenderfoot Cabin," and others resided in the "Robbers' Roost." Manierre reports that "such ribald and boisterous characters as Harry Clow, Bill Clow, Freddy McNally and Andy McNally always occupied the Robbers' Roost. There the liquor was free and candy, pop-corn and sweet tid-bits sent up by loving but unknowing

Two Bucks and a Doe.

Clow's boys dressed appropriately for the occasion, following in the tradition of ultimate respect for their downed quarry: large white-tailed bucks, c. 1907.

Charlie Bent (1867-1955), a wildlife conservationist who loved the North Woods and worked
to protect and improve it for others, circa 1928.

According to deer hunting lore, even the legendary "Spike
Horn" Meyer hunted whitetails at Bent's Camp during the late
1890s.

wives were displayed at all times in most tempting fashion. But, otherwise, the place was a pig-pen. Empty toddy glasses, sticky spoons, deflated lemon halves, wet and smelly clothes, and other miscellany, were in all directions, mostly on the floor. The room was filled with men and smoke, both tobacco and wood, and the language was terrible. No wonder it was called the Robbers' Roost."

An interesting array of characters hung out at Bent's Camp, a well-known Mecca for deer hunters, owned by Charlie Bent (1867-1955). As a wildlife conservationist, Bent loved the North Woods and worked to protect and improve it for others during his lifetime. One also thinks of old Bill Bent, Charlie's father. He took on the appearance of James Fenimore Cooper's "Natty Bumppo" himself. Manierre describes old Bill Bent:

"Tall, powerful, with tobacco-stained white beard, corncob pipe in his mouth and dressed in buckskins, he presented a picturesque figure with his old hound, Hobart, always at his side. Old Bill Bent was a great deer hunter and trapper and carried a Winchester lever-action repeating buckshot gun, the likes of which I had never seen before or since."

According to deer hunting lore, the legendary "Spike Horn" Meyer even hunted white-tails at Bent's Camp during the late 1890s. He used a muzzleloader of monumental proportions and unknown vintage the likes of which none of the Clow party or even old Bill Bent had ever seen before or since.

During the early years of the twentieth century, Bent's Camp became a public resort charging $8 a week for board. During the deer season, however, the camp was dominated primarily by the Clow deer-hunting clan. Mrs. Bent prepared all the meals and reportedly served venison three times daily on many occasions. In those deer-hunting days of yesteryear, as Ernie Swift recalls in his *A History of Wisconsin Deer* (1946), "game belonged to no one in particular, except the man who took it. The natural practice was, therefore, to feed the 'sports' on venison. Eating venison was a part of the romance and mystique of their wilderness trip. A resort which accommodated any substantial number of guests together with a guide crew fed many pounds of deer meat during a season."

Wisconsin deer hunters at the time killed many of these deer by spotlights from boats and salt licks. Some resort owners paid the guides as much as five dollars a head. Serving venison in resorts remained common into the late 1920s; it only gradually ceased to be a common practice with the advent of better law enforcement.

During the Prohibition years the commercialization of illegal venison became part and parcel of the whiskey running business. Cheap alcohol was shipped from Chicago to northern Wisconsin and traded for cheap venison. Lumberjacks and hunters consumed the whiskey while white-tailed venison graced the tables of expensive hotels in Chicago.

Charlie Bent, a conservationist at heart, did not participate in these affairs. According to "Dunny" Bent, Charlie's nephew and prominent historian of the area, Charlie believed the whitetail should be properly

The young Charlie Bent coming into camp with his favorite Remington Model 8 Auto-loading Rifle, circa 1908.

Polly and Lizzy Bent joined the Thanksgiving Day deer hunt with great gusto.

managed by sportsmen. The Clow clan also did not participate in these affairs – believing instead in legitimate stand hunting, still hunting and driving – but "Dad" Clow and his boys experienced these events first hand, as well as the major developments in early Wisconsin deer hunting shown in the accompanying sidebar.

During each deer season Mrs. Bent staged the Thanksgiving Dinner Party as a gala affair. "Dad" Clow would invite a large

number of men, women and children from the surrounding countryside. The dining table groaned under the weight of roast turkey, cranberries, fresh vegetables, venison tenderloins and marvelous pies and pastry. Hot stoves and hot toddies did their wonders, as did the extra whiskey pump priming at the Robbers' Roost. They lead to singing, dancing and wild and exaggerated speeches on such topics as buck snorts, deer beans, farts and jammed deer rifles. Wild talk on Winchester and Remington rifles went deep into the nighttime hours. But every hunter was in position the next morning well before sunrise – "Dad" Clow saw to that!

In their method of deer hunting they

During the 1920s and 1930s the white-tailed deer hunting paintings of Frank Stick – "Whitetail Hunter" (1927) – and the numerous illustrations of white-tailed bucks in flight by Lynn Bogue Hunt hung in the dining room and barroom at Bent's Camp.

Courtesy Winchester Arms/Olin Corporation/Winfield Galleries LLC.

Courtesy Field & Stream / Wrights Reprints

and some who merely came along for the camaraderie and fun of the chase. "Dad" Clow dearly loved the white-tailed deer hunt; his avid enthusiasm became infectious. His oldest son Bill, second son Kent and Franny Manierre planned each day's hunt to the last detail at the early morning council with "Dad" Clow in attendance. Bill placed the men on their stands, Frannie led the drivers, and Kent did whatever he wanted. Such dignitaries as Fred McNally of Rand McNally Publishers, a company owned by the Clow family, and Bob Thorne of Montgomery Ward also participated in the chase. Bill shot most of the deer because he got the best stands while Manierre emerged as the best hunter seldom if ever failing to get a magnificent rack.

In the early years they used deerhounds as drivers but later the guides did the driving. "Dutch" Dickman and Ray Bingenheimer served as guides for many years at Bent's Camp; both loved pipes and Winchesters. According to Manierre, "the guides were the more important members of the "dog pack," for on their younger legs and stronger backs fell the most walking and deer hauling." John Knobel, a very picturesque character of the North Woods also guided the hunters. He was allegedly long on stories and cussing, but short on wind and strength but amusing and a fine marksman nonetheless.

At the fireside the boys at Bent's Camp talked about the big bucks of 1937: the 16-pointer weighing 237 pounds dressed that was shot at Orr, Minnesota, by R. J. Herrington;

usually employed large scale drives in and around the lakes connected with Mamie Lake. "Dad" Clow insisted that every shot be accounted for and after the drive would give the time, exactly, of every shot fired and ask for the results.

The Clow party usually consisted of twenty guns: some great hunters, some good hunters

Charlie relaxing at one of the cabins, c. 1938.

John Mattews' 14-pointer with 5-3/4 inch basal circumferences shot in Nova Scotia; Bruce W. Campell's 12-pointer with 7 inch basal circumferences; and Joe Violetti's 32-pointer shot at Eagle Lake, ME with 8-1/2 and 7-3/4 inch basal circumferences. They also saw pictures of a giant New Brunswick's head shot by an unidentified French Canadian farmer. This magnificent whitetail rack that looked like a mule deer was not scored until 1952, when the mystery buck with 14 points scored 180-6/8 T and appeared as No. 1 in the 1952 Boone & Crockett third edition of *Records of North American Big Game.* One of the main beams measured 31-6/8, inches making it a world-class buck. But the classy Homer Pearson buck, a 43-pointer shot just east of Sand Creek in the Township of Roosevelt, Burnett County, Wisconson, received the most attention.

As fall approached, hunters read the deer hunting stories of Jack O'Connor and Archibald Rutledge in *Outdoor Life* and scoured the pages of *Hunting and Fishing,* America's most widely read sporting magazine of the day with a circulation of 457,647, for the latest information on hunting white-tailed bucks. As they dreamed of trophy bucks, little did they know that they as a husband/wife team would bring home an instant Wisconsin legend on November 28, 1937, that would score 233-7/8 non-typical Boone & Crockett points and weigh 309 pounds on the hoof.

Nineteen-thirty-seven was indeed a very significant year in the history of Wisconsin deer hunting. Aldo Leopold, the Chairman of the newly-founded Department of Wildlife Management at the University of Wisconsin at Madison, issued a very serious warning of an impending white-tailed deer irruption. Leopold's friend, Gordon MacQuarrie, who just became the outdoor editor of the *Milwaukee Journal,* also echoed his concern of an exploding deer herd as well.

In 1937, the year the deer license cost one dollar, the Wisconsin Conservation Department conducted deer drives throughout the state and estimated the deer population at 28.6 animals per section. A buck-only season each even-numbered year prevailed from 1924 to 1937. In 1937, the Conservation Commission recommended the beginning of a more liberal deer harvest. By the end of the 1930s, historian Otis Bersing reports in his A Century of Wisconsin Deer, "more than two times as many bucks were bagged than during the buck and any deer seasons of the 1920s."

The 1937 Wisconsin deer hunt was the first consecutive deer-hunting season since 1923 and 1924. That season witnessed the first emergence of the "Save the Deer" clubs and stringent public criticism of deer management policies. The season lasted for three days, November 26-28, with a bag limit of one forked-horn buck. It opened the day after Thanksgiving. Researchers estimated that 90,906 deer hunters participated in the hunt, resulting in a total kill of 14,835 white-tailed deer which represented a 16 percent success rate.

As the Clow deer hunt became more popular and complicated, the plans for their massive deer drives became more intricate and the gadgets more fascinating and marvelous. Snowshoes, bob sleds, boats with steel runners, and mysterious-looking implements of all kinds suddenly appeared at Bent's Camp. A massive wooden raft, known as "the good ship Pere Marquette" and drawn by horses, moved the Clow boys alone the shoreline of Mamie Lake. The Tar Baby also provided a similar service.

The Clow deer hunting clan that year consisted of only 11 hunters, but they managed to take eight bucks to the meat pole after three days of very intensive deer drives. The entourage arrived at Bent's Camp with a '37 black Ford pickup truck, an old Ford woody wagon, and several spiffy black '37 Deluxe club coupes.

Another major event at Bent's Camp that year revolved around one of the longest-standing members of the Clow deer hunting clan, who not only shot one of the biggest bucks at Bent's Camp that year but entered baseball's Hall of Fame in 1937: Denton True Young (1890-1955) – the man who pitched baseballs so fast his Boston Red Sox teammates called him "Cyclone" Young, later shortened to "Cy." His 511 wins set the baseball record in major league games. The

Cy Young Award has been given each year since 1967 to the best pitchers in each major league. His friend Babe Ruth sent Cy a picture to Bent's Camp that year with the caption: "I would have shot more bucks Cy but I ran out of bumpers and fenders on my Nash Ambassador Sedan!" One of those bucks the "Bambino" shot that year on his Nova Scotia deer hunt received honorable mention from the Boone & Crockett Club in 1940.

In Manierre's description of a typical Clow deer hunt we learn that deer hunting was only incidental to having a good time in the North Woods with laughter, camaraderie, spirits, storytelling, superb venison cuisine [sometime three times a day] and beautiful wilderness-scenery:

"We get started in the good ship Pere Marquette," Manierre says. "We arrive at the first stop, to count noses and give and take instructions. The standers are segregated and put in charge of Bill Bent. The "dogs" (the drivers), are told their part, from where to start, what direction to take, and where and

Courtesy Bent's Camp/Lisa Sternen.

Cy Young, the famous pitcher for the Boston Red Sox's remained one of the longest standing members of the Clow Clan and shot some of the biggest bucks at Bent's Camp.

Major Milestones in Wisconsin Deer Hunting

1880 – The Lund Homestead, a legendary deer camp near Iron River

1896 – Bent's Camp, Lake Mamie, Vilas County

1898 - Disastrous forest fires

1899 - Height of lumbering production

1900 - Federal Lacey Act prohibits interstate commerce of deer

1901 - Hunting with dogs during open season prohibited

1902 – Sale of venison prohibited

1903 – First deer tag required

1905 – Use of salt blocks prohibited

1905 – John Pettinggill downs heaviest buck (live weight of 477 pounds) in Iron River on November 13

1907 – Use of elevated scaffolds prohibited

1908 – Hundreds of thousands of acres burned in the north

1908 – Age limit of deer hunting licensee increased from age 12 to 15

1910 – Charles Berg's 23-point, Bayfield County buck scores 228-2/8 N-T

1910-1935 - The Legendary Deerfoot Lodge, Vilas County, Star Lake

1910 – Robert Hunter's 11-pointer taken in Vilas County scores 191-3/8 T

1913 – First deer farm started at Trout Lake, Vilas County

1913 – C. Callup's 14-pointer scoring 193-3/8 typical B&C points

1914 – World-class record buck shot by Jim Jordan (206-1/8 T) in Burnett County

1915 – First "one-buck" law passed by legislature

1916-1928 – The Famous Bucks Camp, Ladysmith, Northern Rusk County

1920 – First use of metal deer tags costing ten cents

1925 – First closed deer season/open seasons every even-numbered year

1928 – Deer Hunters required to wear official conservation button

1928 – 1972 Buckshot Inc., a legendary deer camp near Cable, WI

1929 – First licensing of deer farms

1930 – Roy Case shoots first buck with bow and arrow under special permit on December 6

1934 – Wisconsin Conservation Congress organized

1934 – Artificial feeding begins in the northern deer yards

1934 – Earl Holt's 33-point, non-typical from Bayfield County scores 227-4/8

1935 – CCC deer census drives begin

1937 – First "Save the Deer Clubs" established

1937 – Homer Pearson's 43-point Polk County buck scores 233-7/8 N-T

1938 – Publication of Manierre's *The Story of the Clow Deer Hunt* (1898-1938), detailing the events of the legendary Bent's Camp

when to meet for the lunch fire. The timing element is calculated so that the deer will not be put through before the standers arrive.

"Our drive invariably takes us through a beautiful piece of country of alternate hardwood and hemlock and spruce swamps. The trees are heavily laden with snow and all is a Christmas scene, especially the little Christmas spruce trees which, if you giggle them too much, will precipitate a cold shower down the back of your neck. The woods are still and quiet except for the occasional whistle of a Canadian Jay, the croak of a raven or perhaps the knock-knock of a woodpecker or the scolding of a squirrel. A partridge may scare the living daylights out of you when it jumps up from under your feet. The drivers walk cautiously along through the woods out of sight of each other, keeping their line as nearly as possible.

"Suddenly you see legs below the boughs of an evergreen. In a second a massive set of horns appears and there is a big buck right in front of you. Your heart thumps and in the excitement the instinct to kill has done the deed without remorse. Someone later helps you drag the buck to the shoreline and from thereon everyone takes a turn.

"Dad hears more shots than any of us and always accuses someone of having missed and holding out. And how he loves to ride anyone who has missed. We meet at the lunch ground, - hot coffee, sausages, and maybe scrambled eggs and sandwiches glace (for unless you toast one the butter is as brittle as ice) are devoured. The story and experience of the morning's hunt is told by all, and the afternoon hunt is planned. A smoke and then we are off for the hunt again, - then back to camp and dry clothes, hot stoves, hot toddies, a good dinner, hunters' conversation or maybe a game of bridge, a smoke again and then to bed early.

Courtesy Bent's Camp/Lisa Sternen.

Lizzy Bent, dressed in traditional buckskin with her classic Winchester rifle in hand, plays with her favorite dog.

"And so the Clow deer hunt has gone on for forty years."

Bent's Camp remains a classic example of how man converted the antique, quaint lumber camps of the old lumbering era into romantic deer camps and recreational resorts of the early twentieth century; how these old time lumber camps became great enclaves of manliness and refined sportsmanship with a pronounced wildlife conservation ethic. Yet women also emerged into this rustic atmosphere as well, as we see in those two great deer hunting photos of Lizzy Bent with her classic Winchester rifle in hand and Henry and Ruth Voss posing with their trophy whitetail at Manitowish Waters – two photos shown in the Wisconsin Public Television Documentary "A State of Escape." Bent's Camp still exists today in all its magnificent splendor; in the interior of the camp with its beautiful, sapling wainscoting deer hunters still converse, tell stories, and in the North Woods around the camp reconnect with the ancient rhythms of nature.

Before the 1906 deer hunt ended, close to two thousand pounds of venison decorated the massive Camp Comfort meat pole – the meat pole to end all meat poles.

Camp Comfort member Frank Onderdonk from Grand Rapids dressed in buckskin poses in front of their classy abode.

CAMP COMFORT

The venison chops are on the table, just dripping in their fat;
And I wish someone would tell me, what is sweeter than that.
Close beside are the partridge, with the dumplings lying near;
You bet your life we're living high, now the hunting time is here.

The old buck follows the trail, 'round the big hemlock tree,
And the deer run just as sassy like, whenever they see me.
In old Camp Comfort with the boys, there's an interest most sincere.
For it makes the heart beat faster, when the hunting time is here.

– A. B. Richmond

When I think of Michigan deer and deer hunting, Ilo Bartlett, Fred Bear, Ted Nugent, The Yoopers, *Escanaba in da Moonlight* and Camp Comfort come to mind. Indeed, in 1900, another legendary deer camp like Bent's Camp, Michigan's Camp Comfort, founded in 1894, was well under way on the south shores of Cusino Lake in Schoolcraft County in the Upper Peninsula less than 60 miles west of Shaffmaster's Silver Creek Camp and Osborn's Deerfoot Lodge.

Like Shaffmaster and Osborn, its hunt-master, Alva "Buckskin" Richmond (1854-1918), the Secretary-Treasurer of the Consolidated Sportsmen's Association, one of Michigan's early prominent conservation organizations, directed the deer hunting affairs afield and afloat, while leaving a fine literary record including poems and exquisite Kodak photographs of the camp's activities which frequently appeared in *Outdoor Life*. He also served as First Lieutenant in the 32nd Michigan Volunteer Infantry in 1898 during the Spanish-American War and, like Shaffmaster, he too read the tales of the legendary Song of Hiawatha.

Not much is known about the deer herd in 1900 in the Upper Peninsula. In his standard pamphlet "Michigan Deer" (1950), Ilo Bartlett, Michigan's legendary deer researcher of the period, merely indicates that intensive market hunting between 1880 and 1890 so depleted the herds that whitetails were at very low ebb by around 1900. In 1900, 13,366 residents purchased a deer hunting license for $.75; 77 non-residents purchased a license for $25.00 that year. Open season

The Grondin Hotel in Seney, Mich., served as the loading place for supplies which the Camp Comfort boys transported to Cusino Lake by foot and horse drawn wagon.

ran from November 8 to November 30 with a bag limit of five deer of either sex. In 1900, more than 13,000 deer hunters bagged about 12,000 deer with most of them taken in the Upper Peninsula.

Like the boys from Silver Creek, Buckskin Richmond and his Camp Comfort clan – including Doc (Dr. Hudson, the great lover of the Winchester .25-35 from Grand Rapids), Frank Onderdonk (also from Grand Rapids), and Niel Richmond and A. B. Richmond, Jr. – often walked more than 25 miles from the Grondin Hotel in Seney leading a horse-drawn buckboard heavily laden with a month's supplies for life at Camp Comfort.

The wild, raucous, hellish behavior in the saloon at the Grondin Hotel where whiskey-drinking, fist-fighting loggers went to Boot Hill as a result of gunfire makes Jeff Daniels' hunter behavior in *Escanaba in da Moonlight* look like commonplace mediocrity. One cultural historian referred to Seney as the "Hell Town in the Pine" where a vast array of wild,

bizarre desperadoes of the bush hung out waiting for the next macho rumpus in the bush – which seemed to be an ongoing affair at any time of the day. What a place: the whole shebang burned down to the ground on at least two occasions. Hemingway called this raw, violent place with a legendary history of violence "a good place to camp!"

The Camp Comfort clan traveled to the Michigan North Woods (which Hemingway immortalized in his Nick Adams stories) via the Duluth, South Shore & Atlantic Railroad, arriving in Seney, where they then went on horse-drawn wagons to the southern shores of Cusino Lake, near Shotgun Creek. The Cusino town site was named after an early French trapper in the area, Cusineau, but later shortened to its present, more phonetic spelling. As they walked along behind the wagon the clan neatly clipped off the heads of grouse with their Winchester rifles for the first meals at camp.

The legendary teamster, Tommy, an original son of the "Ould Sod" arrives at Camp Comfort

They too had their legendary teamster, Tommy, an original son of the "Ould Sod," who maintained a cheery disposition through every crisis imaginable and provided a proverbial ready wit when necessary. He became a standard fixture, sitting up high on stacks of baled straw. All members of the camp had nicknames: Buckskin, Deerslayer, Trail Maker and Buckshot.

On their deer hunt in 1900, they arrived in Seney on October 29 on the Duluth, South Shore & Atlantic Railroad. After a thirty-mile tramp they reached Camp Comfort. In an article in *Outdoor Life* titled "A Deer Hunt in the Snow," Buckskin acknowledged, "I doubt very much if a more congenial or happy lot of brother Nimrods could be gotten together for any hunting expedition than the five whom we will dub Doc, Frank, Alva, Niel and A. B., who annually make a trip into the wilds of the Upper Peninsula of Michigan in quest of the wary deer."

Camp Comfort's hunt master Alva "Buckskin" Richmond in a reflective pose while on his favorite deer stand, circa 1907.

Despite the fact that it snowed for days on end they consistently killed deer with their Remingtons, Winchesters and Marlins. By the end of the third day five deer graced the

Alva Richmond Jr., and his father's deer hunting partners - Harry, Byron and Doc - relax in front of Camp Comfort during one of their month-long deer hunts in Upper Michigan's Schoolcraft County, circa1900.

Camp Comfort meat pole. They feasted on venison steak, partridge, duck and all the fancy dishes Buckskin could muster. In commenting on the beautiful snowy landscapes Buckskin reported, "In the early morning the whole landscape would glint and sparkle in the bright sunlight, making it appear like a great fairyland, covered by the deep blue canopy of heaven, broken in the north by a great bank of pure white clouds."

During the three-week hunt they shot 25 deer and consumed two in camp. "The three weeks we were in camp was a continual round of pure enjoyment and pleasure. We were all materially benefited by the rest obtained and our health bettered by the outing and exercise." In the grand tradition of the Back to Nature movement in America, they lived out the Arcadian myth at their secluded deer camp which they viewed as the "Church in the Wildwood."

In 1903, the boys again arrived at their "dear old shack," Old Camp Comfort, where they ate venison steak for breakfast and venison roasts for supper. After supper they smoked their pipes and toasted their shins before the blazing wood fire and reminisced over old deer hunting adventures. On this particular deer hunt, Doc Hudson, a die-hard still-hunter, was reading William J. Long's book *Following the Deer* (1901). Every so often he would punctuate the deer shack dialogue in the dim light of the lantern with one-liners from Long's briar-patch philosophizing on the art of still-hunting whitetails:

"October, the superb month, found me again in the same woods, this time not to watch and learn, but to follow the big buck to his death. . . So the days went by, one after another; and still the big buck held his own against my craft and patience. He grew more wild and alert with every hunt, and kept so far ahead of me that

Arriving back at Camp Comfort with a massive 10-pointer afloat in the hold of a primitive wheel barrel.

only once before snow blew did I have even the chance of stalking him, and then the cunning old fellow foiled me again masterfully."

Ah, yes. Being eternally foiled by the "ghost" buck in the North Woods! But not all ghost bucks escaped. Rumors were surfacing at the Grondin Hotel in Seney, the loading place for supplies, that a deer hunter named Dan Kothman had just recently got the upper hand and shot an 80-pointer in Mason County, Texas on October 24, 1903. In studying the photo of this legendary white-tailed buck as it eventually appeared in *Outdoor Life,* I realized it was the so-called Brady Buck – the world's number five non-typical from Texas (284-3/8 B&C).

In the article under the header "Classed as a World's Record," *Outdoor Life* noted that this wonderful head was owned by Alexander Schlelyer, a well-known Texas sportsman, who valued it as a trophy above anything in his personal possession. "As to beauty, symmetry and number of points, we doubt if it can be beaten." The deer hunters at Camp Comfort read about this legendary buck – which eventually graced the walls of Albert Friedrich's famous Buckhorn Saloon at the Corner of Houston and Soledad Streets in San Antonio, Texas – with great delight. It is interesting to note that the fourth edition of the Boone and Crockett *Records of North American Whitetail Deer* (2003) lists this head as being shot in McCulloch County with the hunter being unknown and the date uncertain.

Historically, even though deer were scarce at the time, as many as 17 Boone & Crockett bucks came from the first decade of the twentieth century. Texas deer hunter Basil Dailey, in almost a Ripley's Believe It or Not manner, shot one of them in Frio County, Texas in 1903. The story of that buck reached deep into the deer country of the North Woods and became talk of the saloon at the Grondin Hotel, the social centerpiece of early U. P. deer hunting. In his history of Texas trophy whitetails, Big Rack IV, John Stein recorded this most bizarre event in deer hunting lore:

"There was a bitter, north wind blowing across the Blackaller Ranch that morning in

At the old table the boys consumed many venison tenderloins fried in bacon and onions.

Courtesy Mert Cowley.

mid-December as Mr. Blackaller and Basil had decided to split up and hunt in different directions. They agreed to meet at a central location, at a large stock tank, that afternoon; and walk back into camp together. Both hunters then started out across the ranch, spirits high, in search of their quarry.

"But it was a tired and disappointed Basil Dailey that made it to the stock tank first that afternoon. After a long and tiring hunt, he saw nothing all day and guessed the wind had kept the deer bedded down. The sun was beginning to set as he leaned against a small mesquite tree, starring across the water.

"Then out of the brush came a bounding buck, and to Basil's amazement, jumped into the water. Nearly freezing, and this buck wanted to take a bath. The big deer dunked head and antlers under the frigid water, raised them up again and shook his head furiously. Who was going to believe this story?

"Mr. Blackaller would, because he had quietly slipped up behind Basil Dailey and witnessed the whole affair. Then lowly said, 'Take your time Basil, that's the biggest buck I've ever seen.' Basil did just that, squeezing down on the old .303 Savage and firing. On impact, the buck whirled, sending water flying in all directions. The buck fell dead, not seventy five yards from the amazed hunters."

The buck dressed out at 230 pounds and later scored 192-2/8 typical Boone and Crockett points. For many years this impressive buck dominated the décor of Basil Dailey's bedroom. The character, dimensions and score remain almost unsurpassed in the history of Texas white-tailed deer hunting. It still stands as the Texas #3 typical white-tailed buck with an all-time rank of 51. In lore and legend this buck stirred the imagination of the Camp Comfort buck hunters.

Courtesy A. B. Wells & Lynn W. Wells.

Seated at the poker table, several of the boys demonstrate there are other ways to take a buck at the old "Church in the Wildwood."

Despite the low deer densities nationwide at the turn of the century, nowhere on earth did hope bloom so eternally than in the deer shack of H. S. Canfield, who summed up his great optimism in an article, "Following Deer Trails in Northwestern Woods," published in the November 1904 issue of *The Outing Magazine,* one of the most popular sporting journals of its day, published in New York City and read with great delight by the boys at Camp Comfort:

"The deer are there, swift, beautiful, cunning and timorous, the miles of massive woodland, the balsam airs, the keen and friendly emulation, the strenuous endeavor, the tired muscles, the gnawing appetite, the dreamless sleep – sleep so deep that it is no longer sleep but slumber . . . Around the inner walls of the deer shack the firelight leaps rudely and falls on contented faces."

In November of 1904, the Camp Comfort still-hunters returned to the shores of Cusino Lake filled with similar gusto and extensive information on the techniques of still-hunting whitetails. The 1904 edition of Van Dyke's classic book on the subject had just been reprinted and many deer hunters including Frank, Barney, Buckskin and A. B. were reading it with great interest. Van Dyke was widely considered at the time to be the final authority on deer and deer hunting. Since they lacked snow on the ground that year and found the woods extremely noisy, what William T. Hornaday and Paulina Brandreth were saying about this mode of hunting in the sporting literature at the time also gathered their attention as well.

They agreed with Hornaday's assessment of still-hunting in his standard essay on "The Deer Family," published in his book *The American Natural History* (1904):

Courtesy A. B. Wells & Lynn W. Wells.

"He jumped from his bed . . . and Doc put him down . . . and then the long haul back to Camp Comfort."

Courtesy A. B. Wells & Lynn W. Wells.

"Still-hunting is the true sportsman's method of outwitting white-tailed deer which for genuine keenness of eye, ear and nose, have, I believe, no superior in the whole Deer Family. One fine old white-tailed buck killed by fair and square trailing and stalking is equal to two mule deer or three elk."

Despite the lack of snow cover for proper still hunting, the Camp Comfort boys secured five nice large bucks in 1904. Perhaps the most interesting event of that year occurred January 16, when a full-page ad in *Forest and Stream* announced that Schlitz Beer, "The Beer That Made Milwaukee Famous," had arrived at deer camps throughout the land. The ad argued that beer keeps one well! "It is a noticeable fact that those who brew beer, and who drink what they want of it, are usually healthy men. You find no dyspeptics among them, no nervous wrecks, no wasted, fatless men." I am sure the Camp Comfort boys wholeheartedly agreed. The modern day Yoopers certainly do!

While the backwoods tavern had always served as the social centerpiece for the American deer hunting experience in the Upper Peninsula and elsewhere, the deer/beer connection was greatly enhanced with the

The Camp Comfort clan loved to still-hunt whitetails on the snowy lane that led from the camp to Cusino Lake.

"What a flood of memories envelops by the sight of the old cabin ..." Camp Comfort, 1904.

The Camp Comfort clan utilized every form of transportation available, train cars as well as man-drawn buckboards.

publication in the sporting literature of the day of lithographs such as the John Gund Brewing Company's portrait of a Wisconsin deer hunt entitled "The Return – Two Bucks." In the lithograph the advertisers proudly announced Gund's Peerless Beer won the 1904 Louisiana Chase Exposition's Gold Metal.

Buckskin's descriptions in 1904 of the dear old shack – old Camp Comfort – took on a heightened degree of religiosity:

"What a flood of memories envelops by the sight of the old cabin and those old familiar places, and, involuntarily stopping, the mind of the hunter turns back in retrospect to the many times he had approached this dear old spot under similar conditions, full of anticipated pleasures in the days to come, recalling this adventure and that disappointment, until he is awakened from his reverie by the distant mournful howl of a wolf, to a realization that it is time to move on.

"Drawing in a deep breath of the crisp evening air, and with unexpressed feelings of thanks to the Creator for the opportunity

Before the deer season ended they took pictures before heading back to Seney, Michigan.

Courtesy Mert Cowley.

to again enjoy this contact with nature, he hastens forward. A few steps bring him to the door of the dear old shack. Raising the latch, which is never locked, the door creaks naturally as he pushes it open and steps into the dim interior."

In 1905, Buckskin Richmond and his comrades returned to Camp Comfort, but since he did not write an article for *Outdoor Life* about this annual deer hunt, specific details remain sketchy. We know Buckskin and his partners read the sporting literature in an in-depth manner, and it seems likely he read Theodore Roosevelt's *Outdoor Pastimes of an American Hunter* (1905), in which the President – like Audubon, William Elliott, and Judge Caton – chased deer with horses and hounds and glorified the tradition despite the intense controversy between hounding and still-hunting nationwide:

"To be able to ride through woods and over rough country at full speed, rifle or shotgun in hand, and then to leap off and shoot at a running object is to show that one has the

qualities which made the cavalry of Forrest so formidable in the Civil War."

In November of 1906, Buckskin Richmond and his partners returned for another four-week stay in the grand old woods of the Upper Peninsula of Michigan to chase those "steel-gray shadows." They arrived in Seney on November 3 and were soon settled in at cozy Camp Comfort on the southern shores of Cusino Lake. As a lover of nature with poetry in his soul, Richmond viewed these escapes from the world of business as a "refuge from the frivolity of society." Richmond set down his thoughts in verse:

When the air is getting cool and sharp,
and you feel a frosty bite,
Creeping up your back when you
go to bed at night;
When you wake up in the morning,
and the snow squeaks sharp and clear;
It is then that you remember,
hunting time is here.

Old Comfort's walls are all chinked up,
your last year's undershirt is there;
Stuffed in the window sash to keep out
old winter's frosty air.
The wood is cut and in the shed,
the provender stored near;
Oh, won't we have a glorious time,
now that hunting time is here.

The venison chops are on the table,
just dripping in their fat;
And I wish someone would tell me,
what is sweeter than that.
Close beside are the partridge,
with the dumplings lying near;
You bet your life we're living high,
now the hunting time is here.

The old buck follows the trail,
'round the big hemlock tree,
And the deer run just as sassy like,
whenever they see me.
In old Camp Comfort with the boys,
there's an interest most sincere.
For it makes the heart beat faster,
when the hunting time is here.

"On the venison steak,
Jovial feasting they make,
While the flask going round
Helps with the cheer:
And the log burning bright,
Keeps them warm all the night
As they rest after slaying the deer."

One of the customs of Camp Comfort was to begin to eat venison the first day of the season. With the hunting time at hand on November 10, the boys took to the field in their quest for camp meat. Rich headed for the hills. Frank chose to still-hunt around Round Lake. And Buckskin left for the Wolf Lake district. Rich soon jumped a buck but failed to get a shot.

A. B. "Buckskin" Richmond designed his own white camouflage clothing for still-hunting whitetails in the snowy woods of the Upper Peninsula of Michigan. Circa 1906.

Frank saw a fleeting glimpse of a white flag blowing in the breeze, which generated nothing but symptoms of heart failure. Buckskin, in his deerskin moccasins, stalked a doe and two fawns and managed to take a fawn for the pot. By dust that night the Camp Comfort boys dined on prime venison tenderloins and onions fried in bacon. Deer camp for Richmond and his clan and for the "Yoopers," as the U. P. residents call themselves today, is really less about deer hunting than it is about being boys in the wilderness of deer country.

On November 16, A. B. arrived in camp as did their first good tracking snow, so their still-hunting campaign began in earnest as a foursome. "It is a good time to begin our real hunt," Buckskin announced, and all agreed. Frank took to the hills while Rich and Buckskin headed south of the camp into the Moulder territory. A. B. started for Round Lake. They all left camp with great gusto, for after all, the latest U. M. C. cartridge ads in the sporting journals just announced, "It is deer hunting

Camp Comfort is now long gone; nothing remains but black and white pictures and a few mounds of debris to preserve the grandiose memories of that great, legendary deer camp of yesteryear. Note the ever-present deer camp cook dressed in proper white attire.

time and reports from the Big Woods up North indicate better sport than ever!"

Frank soon discovered a buck browsing near the base of a hill. Bang! Went his new Remington Model 8 semi-automatic rifle and down went the buck. But immediately he was on his feet again. Then the fun began. Bang! Bang! Bang! At every open spot between the trees the Remington semi-automatic cracked but to no avail. Finally on the fifth shot the old buck pitched forward and did not rise again. It seems likely that Frank was using U. M. C. ammunition, for the Union Metallic Cartridge Company of Bridgeport, Conn., was running a current ad in the sporting literature of the day, especially *The American Field,* announcing that "your fusillade will not be stopped by a misfire or a jammed cartridge if you shoot U. M. C. cartridges. They make the deer drop his flag!"

After going around an old fallen treetop a buck suddenly jumped out in front of A.B. He stood right in the open. One shot and another buck went to the meat pole. After crossing Wolf Creek, Rich and Buckskin separated. Buckskin took the swamp on the south side and followed it for some distance. He soon jumped a buck, which he missed, but minutes later he spotted a doe in a group of hemlocks and dropped her in her tracks with a well-placed ball at the base of the neck.

The luck of the day continued for the Camp Comfort boys as Rich followed a hemlock ridge running parallel to Wolf Creek. Innumerable buck signs gave Rich eternal hope. But no deer! Then out of nowhere a buck appeared and broke through the underbrush and headed towards the creek bottom. When it hit an opening Rich fired his Winchester. The buck struck the ground immediately but was up and away again.

"Then the bullets began to sing through the tag alders," Richmond writes, "like hail on the roof of an old barn." With the last Bang! Bang! The old fellow – weighing in over 200 pounds – hit the forest floor dead as a doornail. Rich hastily dressed the buck out and hung it in a tree. As he started to return to camp he accidentally ran into another huge buck moving along a well-used deer trail. The buck stopped, snorted and took off straight up the trail. When he saw hair in the Lyman sight, Rich pulled the trigger and

Leaving for the Grondin Hotel in Seney with a sleigh full of venison, circa 1909.

one more report from the Winchester echoed through the tag alders. A second buck also weighing more than 200 pounds lay dead in the deer woods. Two bucks over 200 pounds each in one day for A. B.!

Well before the 1906 Michigan deer hunt ended, Camp Comfort had all the deer allowed by law. With the larder full they spent the rest of the season whiling away time in perfect enjoyment of deer camp life. More than a thousand pounds of venison bent the meat pole to the limits. In an unpublished poem Buckskin reflected on the real and lasting pleasures of the deer hunt:

Though every season is gladsome,
And never a month that is drear;
There's not one thing
that quickens the pulse,
Like the sight of a Camp Comfort Deer.

Though the mountains are
a wonderful beauty,
And the slopes of exquisite hue;
One glimpse of our old camp in the woods,
Would make a happy dream come true.

Though the birds sing in the trees,
Through every month in the year;
My heart would welcome the change,
To the white deep snow
and the wily old deer.

I would forgo sunshine and beauty,
And the sky of cerulean blue,
Could I again see old Camp Comfort,
The deer, the woods, Frank and you.

It seems likely that the Richmond clan continued to hunt deer at Cusino Lake throughout the first decade of the twentieth century, but the historic record remains very sketchy. The last personal recollections for the Camp Comfort hunters we find in an article titled "A Michigan Deer Hunt" published in *Outdoor Life* in November of 1914, which describes their 1913 deer hunt at a shack located on the headwaters of Driggs Lake in Schoolcraft County near Buck Lake, just west of Cusino Lake. This quaint, warm and roomy log building supplied with a good cook stove was owned by a trapper known simply as "Old Pete." That year the agency cut the limit to two deer. While the counties in the U. P. remained open, eight counties in southern Michigan were closed due to dramatic declines in deer numbers. In 1913, the deer license sold for $1.50; 22,656 residents bought one –an all-time record for license sales.

With a fresh tracking snow lying on the ground that Opening Day of November 10, Buckskin began a long involved still hunt – following the faint outlines of old deer trails. Suddenly he jumped a large 10-pointer. When the Lyman showed plainly on the buck's fore shoulder Buckskin pressed the trigger of his rifle. Bang went the .38-72 Winchester Model 1895 and the buck disappeared over the top of a ridge. Minutes later he again jumped it beneath a hemlock tree and emptied his rifle with four fast shots. – Bang! Bang! Bang! Bang! The war was on, thought his comrades in the field.

"The fusillade of shots rattled down through that tall timber, resembling the long roll of a snare drum, and just as I emptied my magazine, down went the old monarch to raise no more. . . My first deer was down, and inside of thirty minutes from the cabin. There he lay in all his 190 pounds of fallen majesty." Before eight o'clock that opening morning Buckskin's first big buck hung in all his majesty in front of their cabin door for all to admire. But Richmond knew the real benefit of the hunt was not the downing of the buck but rather the more lasting and greater benefit that came from the freedom offered by escaping the shackles of modern civilization and returning to Nature, to commune with the Gods of good cheer.

BOB KUHN

STILL HOUSE INN

From here I come, and here I must return,
A rightful habitant to claim his own.
As any sharp – eyed creature's in the fern,
This mountain is my property alone.

– Lionel Wiggam

When one thinks of Pennsyl-vania's legendary deer camps, one thinks of the Orrstown Hunting Club's Still House Inn. In 1948, the Orrstown Hunting Club published a history of their deer camp, *Meat on the Pole,* limited to 100 numbered and signed copies. Of the more than 2000 books on deer and deer hunting in my library, I consider this privately-printed limited edition to be one of my favorite deer camp books. *Meat on the Pole,* by Charles D. Minehart, Club Historian, as told to Louis Lester, documents the story of one of the nation's oldest and longest running deer camps, located in Still House Hollow in the South Mountains of Franklin County, where the legendary Fred Bear started to hunt deer.

Although the Club owned only 20 acres, nestled high within the slopes of these mountains, its members roamed far and wide as

a club for more than half a century. They knew every trail, hill and hollow for miles around intimately. They thought of the South Mountains as "our" mountains and frequently quoted the poet Lionel Wiggam in this regard while emphasizing their special attachment to this sacred place in the woods:

This mountain is my property alone:
A hard expanse of cocklebur and pines,
A lace of grass subsiding into stone,
And overhead a purple fret of vines.

These are my woods,
and this my personal scene:
Where fallen underfoot the balsam boughs
And partridge-feathers pattern each ravine,
And where the hornet plots his paper house.

For no man knows this place so well as I;
Not one has seen this roof of branches torn
By sun, or watched the overhanging sky
Scraped by a wing as sharply as a thorn.

Illustration by Bob Kuhn, circa 1948. Courtesy Bob Kuhn/ICasey Kuhn.

Fred Bear, Pennsylvania's native son, with his second whitetail taken in 1916 at the Cameron Road deer camp at South Mountain.

This place is mine,
where evening breeds alarm:
A thin disquiet sharpened with despair,
Where dusk approaches like a locust – warm
Spreading its copper rumor down the air.

From here I come, and here I must return,
A rightful habitant to claim his own.
As any sharp – eyed creature's in the fern,
This mountain is my property alone.

As the crow flies, the Club was located about five miles south of Shippensburg, or eight miles east and a little north of Chambersburg. Minehart gives us this precise description: "If you drew a line on a map from Gettysburg to Shippensburg and another from Fayetteville to Carlisle, where

the two lines cross will be just about hollerin' distance from the cabin. At least, it will be so close that if a deer were killed on the spot, the cook would slip outside to see what the shootin' was all about."

In his historic account of this deer camp, Minehart noted that this section of Pennsylvania deer country is rich in history, romance and tradition. But he suspected that if the old trees could talk, they would reveal some mighty strange tales that would clearly shake the family trees of some of his good and respected neighbors to the very foundations. He gave two examples.

"According to the stories told by the Rev. George Perry and old 'Banty' Fry, who lived in this section for many years, back in the old charcoaling days, Still House Hollow not only got its name but a rather questionable reputation at the same time. It seems the natives in this section did not look too kindly upon the Revenue Tax, and since the Mason and Dixon Line and Maryland are not too far away, the boys just moved into the mountains and set up stills of their own. Apparently they did a rather thriving business, because some of the old foundations for the stills may be seen today along the creek. From time to time Revenue Agents were sent into the mountains, but many never made their reappearance back into civilization. What happened to them, we can only guess."

The Orrstown Hunting Club came into existence on May 1, 1897, the year the Game Commission outlawed salt and deer hounds for hunting deer, when William "Pappy" Kane and some of his friends gathered in his blacksmith shop in Mongul to draw up and adopt the Constitution and By-Laws of the Orrstown Hunting Club.

Deer were scarce at this time, so these hunters didn't shoot deer very frequently. They more often talked about deer tracks at the fire pit in their "smoke talk." In 1904, they developed shooting matches with the expressed objective to improve their shooting skills and better their chances of getting a deer, if one ever presented itself. These shooting matches became extremely popular and a major highlight of deer camp life.

It wasn't until 1906, when the Game Commission began to transplant and stock deer, that the Club started to shoot deer. Pennsylvania's deer restocking plan consisted of two phases: the first involved purchasing deer for release from such states as Michigan, Maine, North Carolina, New Hampshire and Kentucky, and the second involved trapping and relocation.

As intense deer hunting got underway in 1906, the atmosphere in the field became extremely dangerous to say the least. In April of that year the killing of Game Protector Seely Houk, who had set out to vigorously enforce state game laws, dominated the game law news

and deer camp dialogue of the day. (His murderer, deer woods rogue Rocco Racco – no, I did not make that name up – was eventually hanged for the murder.) In addition, fourteen Game Protectors were shot at in 1906 alone and three of them died. Three more were seriously wounded, one slightly injured and one citizen killed while assisting a Game Protector. At the time the Commission declared bucks legal "with horns visible above the hair."

In the 1910 deer season, the boys at Still House Inn established a "new high" in bagging deer when they secured four bucks. That was the first year since the club's inception that they killed more than one deer during a season. Philip Cover picked off a seven-pointer on Devil Alex; the distinguished Reverend George Perry finished off a four-pointer on the Sand Bank, and later at the same spot, an eight-pointer received a one-way ticket to the meat pole from the rifle shouldered by Benjamin Hostetter. As Minehart noted, "our spirits were high and a real Still House Inn celebration followed!"

At that glorious December deer camp feast, Minehart cooked the Deer Hunter's Dish of fresh venison liver with onions and bacon in celebration of the successful hunt. He served it up with several cans of Heinz 57 Varieties that had just appeared in the grocery stores nationwide. Whiskey that year sold for $3.50 a gallon and the boys consumed a judicious amount as they told and re-told deer hunting stories until the ambers dimmed.

The long and endearing tale that night revolved around a newspaper account brought to camp by a late-comer about a massive 28-pointer downed by William Pearl "Bunker" Rhines, the famous pitcher for the Cincinnati Reds, known for his unorthodox underhanded pitching style. According to the early newspaper account, "Bunker" downed the legendary monarch in the wilds of Cameron County with a .30 caliber U. S. Army Winchester rifle issued to him by the Pennsylvania National Guard. The buck would eventually

During the early years of deer camp tenting, Minehart's Boys drilled several nice bucks for the bending meat pole, 1910.
Credit: Michigan Technological University Archives.

become known as "the celebrated Cameron County Big Head" and score 206 Boone and Crockett non-typical points.

When the members of Still House Inn left for home that year their Model T roadsters were loaded with quality deer meat and their minds filled with priceless memories and tales of a great Keystone deer hunt.

During the next 13 years they wandered around like gypsies but stayed primarily in the Still House Hollow area while living out of large canvas tents. In 1911, the year the Game Commission appointed 30 more Game Protectors, they bought 20 acres of land from Levi F. Weest for $60. They now dreamed of erecting a bona fide deer shack.

But ten more years of deer tenting would pass before that event would occur. Meanwhile, they continued to improve the property and the logging road that ran through it. As the years passed, they saw and bagged more deer as the deer herd continued to grow.

Minehart notes that in tenting in those days, the old sheet-iron stove kept them very comfortable despite zero-degree temperatures. During the 1915 deer hunt, the tent became so completely encrusted with snow and ice they had to leave it in place until the following spring. Around 1915, the cut-over forest began to re-grow into the seedling/sapling stage and the white-tailed deer population in Still House Hollow began to erupt.

When the members of Still House Inn left for home their Model T. Roadsters were loaded with quality deer meat for the pole, 1910. After arriving back in Orrstown they paid homage to the fallen bucks with dignity and respect; dressed in black chic attire for their triumphant return to civilization they looked like distinguished "Dutch Pallbearers."

Wegner's Deer & Deer Hunting Postcard Collection.

As a political activist, Minehart kept the readers of his Still House Inn chronicle informed not only on Pennsylvania state politics but on the affairs of the country as well. In my copy of his *Meat on the Pole,* I found a folded political commentary taken from the July 1915 issue of *Forest and Stream* written by a member of the Old Guard named "Old Camper." In it "Old Camper" makes his views clear about World War I, views Minehart shared:

The' ain't no sense in talkin' war,
it's foolishness at best
We all agree, that's had part in that game,
But if Uncle Sam'l calls us
or puts us to the test,
There won't be ary hyphen in our aim!

During the 1915 deer season (December 1-15), the club members were reading Captain Henry W. Shoemaker's popular *Pennsylvania Deer and Their Horns* (1915), a compendium of deer hunting stories and tales about legendary bucks and famous deerslayers such as Phil Wright of Franklin County, who killed more than a 1000 deer and hung out at the famous Deer Head Tavern.

During this time, the deer population rose in a dramatic way. In 1913, 300,000 licensed deer hunters took 800 bucks out of Pennsylvania's deer hunting grounds. In 1915, when only 250,000 licenses were sold, hunters killed more than 1,200 bucks. By 1919, when total license sales increased 30 percent over the 1913 figures to 400,000 deer hunters, the total buck kill increased more than 250 percent to 2,939. Pennsylvania's remarkable

By the 1920s when the logging road to Still House Inn improved, some of the deer camp members drove their "Apotheosis of Tin-Can Comfort" right into Still House Hollow.

buck kill during the regular season at this time received nation-wide notoriety.

As the war came to a close, the Orrstown Hunting Club again hunted deer in earnest. The 1921 deer season became a banner year. Not only did the club members adopt a resolution to build a new club house on their 20 acres, but by the end of the 1921 deer season, the year the Game Commission declared bucks with antlers four inches long legal, they shot six bucks reaching the limit for the camp. Sixteen die-hard buck hunters hunted that year at the newly built Still House Inn.

In the fall of 1922, the Still House Inn boys read the November issue of *Forest and Stream.* In it Archibald Rutledge described white-tailed deer hunting as "the master wildwood sport," and highlighted his article with that title with a photo of a massive Pennsylvania buck with 24 points and a spread of 27 inches that apparently escaped the record books. But Minehart and his boys nonetheless took notice and dreamed about downing such a giant.

The 1922 deer season proved highly successful for the club. They again bagged the limit for the camp. "We maintained the record by bouncing off six deer again this year when meat was brought in by Roland Smith, John Mowery, Wilmont Mowrey, Harry Miller, W. Chester Wise, and my son, John Minehart. The figure 6 seems to be the lucky number for the club, as John killed the sixth deer on the sixth day of the season. The preceding year the sixth deer was also killed on the sixth day the club hunted."

In 1922, the State of Pennsylvania elected Minehart to the Pennsylvania State Legislature. In 1923, the Game Commission gave landowners the right to kill deer to prevent damage to crops. That year also saw the creation of the first antlerless deer season. With an increased deer herd density that year, the boys at Still House Hollow once again got several fine deer, including one ten-pointer over on the Little Polk, shot by member Frank Beam. This 1923 antlerless deer hunt, however, brewed controversy with deer hunters all across the nation.

Wildlife conservationists sold the Buck Law so well that many deer hunters still viewed the doe as a "sacred cow" and preferred to shoot bucks only. The constant hype of big bucks in the sporting literature of the day did not change the hunter's mind, Minehart's included.

Indeed, large antlered bucks continued to grace the pages of *Forest and Stream.* Their August issue of 1924 featured Captain Elwin S. Lackey of Alexandria Bay, New York, with

As time passed, the deer camps in the Pennsylvania Mountains acquired a very dignified look indeed – such as the Deysher family's deer camp where women joined in the celebration as well with their official cook in attendance dressed in formal attire, circa 1938. A good number of the legendary Remington Model 14 Slide-Action Rifles stand at attention.

Deer camp camaraderie and smoke-talk at the fire pit about the phantom white-tailed bucks that get away. During the 1930s artists painted deer hunters as heroic, action-type figures.

his massive, heavily-palmated 21-pointer with a 34-3/4 inch spread that he shot in the Adirondacks – another world-class whitetail that apparently escaped the record book.

The following year also proved to be successful with John Walters, C. E. Foust and Bill Beam each tying their tag to a nice buck; with three deer hanging outside on the meat pole, joy reigned supreme at Still House Inn. The boys sent a message to the Game Commission back in Harrisburg telling officials that pretty good rifle shots prevailed at Still House Inn and mighty fine venison hung from the meat pole. Twenty-six guns participated in the 1924 season.

In 1925, 30 members of Pennsylvania's "Pumpkin Army" assembled at the Inn to chase deer and escape the rigors of an over-civilized society. Orin Clippinger, Harry Miller and John Minehart sent three bucks to the meat pole. And again, they sent a good news message back to Harrisburg officials. Statewide that year, hunters bagged 7,287 bucks.

After attempting many methods to improve the deer herd situation, the Game Commission declared, for the first time since 1907, a general season on antlerless deer (with the exception of 16 counties) and a closed season on bucks. Hunters shot 25,097 antlerless deer. The Game Commission's classic Bulletin #12, "The Pennsylvania Deer Problem," reported that this event "aroused so much antagonism that the controversy echoed in the nation's press from ocean to ocean."

Despite the 1929 stock market crash, 25 club members made the annual pilgrimage to the Inn in the Mountains and some of them had a small portion of venison for Christmas dinner as a result of roaming through the hills. The state deer kill that year reached 22,822 antlered bucks.

As a member of the State Legislature, Minehart kept the club members well informed of new and pending deer hunting legislation. When he arrived in camp in December of 1930, he brought with him copies of the Game

Commission's famous Bulletin #12. In reading this historic bulletin, the members of the club soon learned that in 1927, due mainly to the fact that the deer hunters did not properly cooperate in the doe season, special sharp-shooters of the Board, known for their superior marksmanship and knowledge of deer hunting, were dispatched to kill off a number of does throughout the state. This action engendered protest. Many felt that the Game Commission was depriving them of sport and venison that should rightfully belong to the hunters, who had annually paid their license fees. That action sparked disagreement statewide.

The highlight of the fireside stories that year, however, centered on Ira Kane's Winchester Model 1887 lever-action, repeating, 12-gauge shotgun:

"If you haven't seen that lever-action Winchester shotgun of Ira Kane's you better take a good look at it! I imagine Ira and his boys have thrown more pumpkin balls out of that antique into the sides of more deer than any other gun that has been carried over these mountains. The Winchester folks only made a very few lever-action 12-gauge guns, and dozens of collectors have tried to get that gun from Ira, but it's no sale as far as he is concerned. The Winchester Company is very anxious to have it for their collection, and have offered Ira the pick of their catalog in exchange, but Ira wants his gun and he is keeping it. I guess a man's gun is sorta' like his right arm, or his dog, and can't be parted with too easily."

Members of the club prided themselves on the vast variety of shooting irons at the Inn on the Mountain. "Just listen to this Camp Roster we have here now: 32 Remington; 25-20 Stevens; 30-30 Winchester; 35 Remington; 12 Gauge Winchester; 30-06 Winchester; 303 Savage; 32 Winchester Special; 32-40 Winchester; 30-06 Remington; 300 Savage; 16 gauge Pump Winchester; 30 Remington; just to mention a few!"

In 1934, the club leased the Still House Inn

One of Pennsylvania's phantom bucks that did not get away: Edward Dodge's 238-6/8 non-typical 30-pointer shot on November 30, 1942 in Erie County. It was Pennsylvania's non-typical state record at the time.

to the Civilian Conservation Corps to be used by them during the off-season. During the mid-1930s, the club members often hunted with the boys from the C. C. C., and it was not unusual to have sixty to seventy young lads driving the entire mountainside. By1936, the membership of the club had peaked at 30 gunners.

Criticism was immediate and direct to the first statewide season for antlerless deer only in 1938, when hunters shot 171,662 antlerless deer. Legislator Minehart summed up the feelings for many members of the club:

"Every time I think of that year, I shudder all the way down to my shoes. It was awful! Believe me, it was worth a man's life almost, to move in the woods. And if he didn't move, some fool with lots of shells and no brains would bang away just to hear the noise! Why half the population was not stretched out with the deer that were slaughtered, I'll never be able to explain. I'm not exaggerating when I say the woods was literally filled with hunters and anything with four legs was shot. Lots of them with two legs were shot, also.

Roy Wagner, Charles Shunk, J. Goodhart and Harry Stroble pose with two of the three bucks they shot in Lycoming County, 1937. (Below.) In 1938, the sex of the deer changed riding the fenders as Pennsylvania experienced its first antlerless deer only season.

"The boys up in Harrisburg who figure such things as the number of deer in relation to food availability, will prove to you that a doe season at intervals is healthy, and actually means more game each year. They have census figures, number deer killed, number alive, number for each year, and lots of other statistics. They may be right, but . . . . . I'm a little hard to convince!"

In 1940, the club added an electric light plant to the Inn. And with another liberalized season, the Inn's meat pole hung heavy with deer.

That year Pennsylvania reached an all-time deer harvest of 186,575 animals: a dramatic increase from the 150 deer shot in 1898.

During the 1940s, the buck harvests remained fairly stable at around the 30,000 mark. The Pennsylvania Woolrich-clad also downed some real quality bucks during this time: one thinks of Lewis Hajos' buck (162-4/8, typical) shot in Lackawanna County in 1941, Edward Dodge's 238-6/8 non-typical shot in 1942 in Erie County and the Paul

"White-Tail Wilderness." Water color painting by Francis Lee Jaques, circa 1947. Courtesy: *Outdoor Life* / Wrights Reprints.

Corley buck (186-7/8, non-typical) shot in Bedford County in 1944.

Despite the uproar with the first antlerless-only deer season in 1938, hunting "female and immature deer under state control seemed widely considered an occasional, if distasteful, necessity," as historian Louis Warren notes in his provocative book, *The Hunter's Game* (1997). Yet, the hunting of does still weighed heavily on the minds of the older hunters in Still House Hollow. As the club reached its fiftieth anniversary in 1947, Minehart addressed the question of the aging process:

"Well, some of us are getting along in years now, and probably do our best hunting in an easy chair along side this old chunk stove.

We have the experience and desire, but there comes a time when the old legs and heart just won't take the hard punishment any longer. We can help out occasionally, or perhaps do a little pot hunting, but for the real stuff, we're depending on these younger fellows to carry on with the spirit and tradition of the club. "Fifty years is a long time . . . . !"

As the aging buck hunter penned those melancholy, bitter sweet lines Minehart starred at Francis Lee Jaques' great deer print in the November 1947 issue of *Outdoor Life* and longed to get back on the deer trail of those phantom, mythic, white-tailed monarchs of the deer woods as he so joyously did in his early manhood.

SILVE
DEER CA

R CREEK
MP 1897-1903

Carl Rungius.

"White-Tailed Deer in the Adirondacks." Oil on canvas, 1904.

"Go, my son, into the forest,
Where the red deer herd together,
Kill for us a famous roebuck,
Kill for us a deer with antlers!'
All alone walked Hiawatha
Proudly, with his bow and arrow.

– Longfellow,
The Song of Hiawatha, 1855

In 1904, a die-hard buck hunter and magazine editor named Allen Dyer Shaffmaster from Bronson, Michigan, wrote a delightful diary of his deer camp's adventures. The book, *Hunting in the Land of Hiawatha*, an out-of-print, blue-chip deer book, captures the mystique of deer camp life as few books do. Reading this deer-hunting diary allows one to relive the savory and pungent odors and manly camaraderie of Michigan deer camps of yesteryear. The book's superb collection of old Kodak exposures on all aspects of deer camp brings to life the very essence of this sacred place in the alder bushes and birches where the mythic Hiawatha, the deer hunter and hero of nature worship, shot the "red" deer (as the white-tailed deer was commonly called at the time), in Henry W. Longfellow's grand epic poem published in 1855.

Hiawatha became the apotheosis of the deer hunter – his deification and glorification – at the beginning of the twentieth century.

Shaffmaster's diary narrates seven individual white-tailed deer hunts at the Silver Creek Deer Camp, 1897-1903, at the precise location where Shaffmaster believed Longfellow placed the scene for his legendary epic poem, *The Song of Hiawatha:* thirteen miles northwest of Eckerman where Silver Creek flows towards Tahquamenon Bay near the shores of Lake Superior in what is known today as the Hiawatha National Forest – East Side.

Each of these seven deer hunts became a mystic pilgrimage to reenact, recreate and preserve the legendary event of Hiawatha killing the white-tailed buck. The cultural and historic significance of this literary deer-hunting event is in decline because anti-hunting editors and publishers have consciously taken this scene out of the children's editions of the poem as well as the anthologies of Longfellow's writings for adults. Purging this scene from American literature spells trouble for the future of American deer hunting.

In 2003, however, an accurate rendering of Hiawatha's deer hunting scene and beautifully illustrated for children appeared by Maragret Early (Hand Print Books) with stunning images for children. And in 2004, the paperback edition by publisher David R. Godine featured Frederic Remington's illustration of Hiawatha shooting the buck on the cover as well as deer hunting illustrations and paintings on deerskin throughout the highly illustrated text.

When first published on November 10, 1855, *The Song of Hiawatha,* one of the finest poems we have in the Romantic tradition of the deer hunt, attained instant popularity and great acclaim. Five thousand copies sold in the first five weeks, ten thousand in the next six months and 45,000 by 1859. Today in America, Longfellow is unfortunately out of fashion and *The Song of Hiawatha* languishes in the dustbins of popular culture. Fortunately for the deer hunter, an English publishing house named

Allen Dyer Shaffmaster, author of the great deer-camp memoir, *Hunting in the Land of Hiawatha, or the Hunting Trips of an Editor* (1904).

Wegner's Deer & Deer Hunting Photo Collection.

J. M. Dent in London, founded in 1906 as The Everyman Library, still keeps the book in print in America with annual reprints in paperback for $6.50 as of this writing.

In his "Introduction" to The Everyman Edition, Professor Daniel Aaron of Harvard University notes that when the book first appeared "Performers in Indian costume chanted its incantatory lines; portions of it were set to music. Hiawatha pencils appeared

Michigan's legendary Deerfoot Lodge, owned and operated by that well-known sportsman/editor/author/traveler, Hon. Chase S. Osborn. From left to right: Barney, the deer camp cook; Governor Osborn; Roys J. Cram; and Judge Joseph H. Steere.

on the market along with Hiawatha sleighs decorated with scenes from the poem. A New York saloon served a Hiawatha drink, contents unspecified but guaranteed it was said, 'to make the imbiber fancy himself in the happy hunting grounds.'"

Shaffmaster sought to preserve this historic event and so should we. Indeed by 1904, the American cult of the whitetail was well anchored in the legend of Hiawatha thanks to A. D. Shaffmaster. He studied Longfellow's papers in consultation with his friend, Michigan Governor Chase S. Osborn, at Osborn' legendary deer camp, Deerfoot Lodge, located on Deerfoot Lake, south of Eckerman. At Deerfoot Lodge, Shaffmaster and Osborn not only hunted whitetails together but studied topographical maps and geographical evidence in their pursuit of the sacred place where Hiawatha, the legendary deer hunter, downed his buck.

Hiawatha became the apotheosis of the deer hunter – its deification and glorification – at the beginning of the twentieth century.

By the end of the century, however, the deer hunter, like Hiawatha, seemed doomed to vanish into the vapors of history. For by the dawn of the twenty-first century the deer hunter constitutes only about seven percent of American society and his numbers decline at about 75,000 hunters annually. As deer hunter densities continue to decline and deer numbers increase, chronic deer mismanagement produces Lyme disease, crop damage, deer-vehicle collisions and chronic wasting disease. The scene of Hiawatha's Departure, when read today, 150 years after its publication, seems to prophesize the demise of the American deer hunter and sounds like the funeral oration:

On the shore stood Hiawatha,
Turned and waved his hand at parting;
On the clear and luminous water
Launched his birch canoe for sailing,
From the pebbles of the margin
Shoved it forth into the water;
Whispered to it: 'Westward! Westward!'

*And the evening sun descending
Set the clouds on fire with redness,
Burned the broad sky, like a prairie,
Left upon the level water
One long track and trail of splendor,
Down whose stream, as down a river,
Westward, westward Hiawatha
Sailed into the fiery sunset,
Sailed into the purple vapors,
Sailed into the dusk of evening.*

*And the people from the margin
Watched him floating, rising, sinking,
Till the birch canoe seemed lifted
High into the sea of splendor,
Till it sank into the vapors
Like the new moon slowly, slowly
Sinking in the purple distance.*

*Thus departed Hiawatha,
Hiawatha the Beloved,
In the glory of the sunset,
In the purple mists of evening,
To the regions of the home-wind
To the land of the Hereafter!*

Every American deer hunter should have and read a copy of The Everyman Library edition of this classic book if we are to preserve our white-tailed deer hunting heritage. Shaffmaster and his boys read and re-read this "beautiful pen picture of the mystic Hiawatha and the killing of the roebuck," as Shaffmaster described it.

The real meaning of this legendary epic poem not only reflects the traditional Native American way of story-telling, but it places the deer hunt in our uniquely American cultural context, while emphasizing the utilitarian principle of venison consumption and deerskin utilization and preserving the national essence of the American white-tailed deer hunt. Like Hiawatha, Shaffmaster tramped the deer woods of the Upper Peninsula of

Michigan in deerskin moccasins. In reading the poem one can almost see and smell Hiawatha's yellow shirt and moccasins of deerskin.

*From his lodge went Hiawatha,
Dressed for travel, armed for hunting,
Dressed in deerskin shirt and leggings,
Richly wrought with quills and wampum;
On his head his eagle feathers,
Round his waist his belt of wampum,
In his hand his bow of ash-wood,
Strung with sinews of the reindeer;
In his quiver oaken arrows,
Tipped with jasper, winged with feathers;
With his mittens, Minjekahwun,
With his moccasins enchanted.*

From his lodge went Hiawatha, Dressed for travel, armed for hunting, Dressed in deerskin shirt and leggings. H. W. Longfellow, 1855. In the tradition of Hiawatha this Silver Creek deerslayer dressed in deerskin. His well-filled cartridge belt, hatchet and favorite lever-action repeater indicated he was ready for action.

"Go my son into the forest And kill for us a deer with antlers."
The Song of Hiawatha, 1855. The Winchester Model 1895 lever-action repeating rifle with the non-detachable box magazine was highly cherished by Zane Grey and Theodore Roosevelt, among others.

Wegner's Deer & Deer Hunting Photo Collection.
Bob Kuhn Illustration courtesy Remington Art Collection.

The poem ultimately represents a celebration and glorification of the environment of the deer woods. In it we follow Hiawatha, the deer hunter and teacher, from his first deer kill to his rites of passage into manhood.

According to the first entry in Shaffmaster's diary, we learn that the 1897 Michigan deer season opened on November 8, with the deer population at an all-time low due to heavy market hunting, logging operations and fire, but still at higher levels than anywhere else in the country. After traveling more than 650 miles on trains and many hours on a horse-drawn wagon with the legendary teamster, the reliable Sam McMullen – who drove the Stage from Eckerman to White Fish Point delivered the mail and hauled more whitetails carcasses than any other man in America – Shaffmaster and his hunting partner Dick Addicks reached the land of Hiawatha and were soon settled down in a freshly-built, handmade, 8'x12' spruce shanty near the Tahquamenon River.

Travel to and from deer camp at this time consisted primarily in railroad cars and walking along with horse-drawn wagons and buckboards. Many days passed without a deer sighting, but then on November 21, Shaffmaster reports, "I caught a faint glimpse of a phantom-like, brownish-gray, streak vanishing with the rapidity of a streak of lightning through the vista of scattered timber in the distance."

Bang! Bang! Bang! cracked his Winchester .38-55 and venison soon hung on the Silver Creek meat pole. That night they dined on venison tenderloins and read passages from the newly reprinted 1891 edition of *The Song of Hiawatha* with the newly commissioned fanciful and romantic pen and ink drawings by Frederic Remington which reeked with the wood smoke of Indian culture and the romance of deer and deer hunting.

"Go, my son, into the forest,
Where the red deer herd together,
Kill for us a famous roebuck,
Kill for us a deer with antlers!"
All alone walked Hiawatha
Proudly, with his bow and arrow.

To the ford across the river,
And as one in slumber walked he.
Hidden in the alder bushes,
There he waited till the deer came.

One year later, on November 10, 1898, the editor and George H. Brown, an old deer hunter with the vigor of youth stamped on his face, left Bronson on the Duluth, South Shore & Atlantic Railroad and arrived in Eckerman on the next day. Shaffmaster believed this famous railway system reached more of the best deer hunting grounds than any other railway in the midwest. On this hunt, they camped in a canvas wall tent and by the end of the day "a brisk fire soon cast a glow of warmth and comfort around us, and a big appetizing supper, consisting of boiled potatoes, fried onions, grouse, fried in butter and big flaky flapjacks, Silver Creek spring water and rich coffee, put us in good humor."

After several failed days of intensive still-hunting in the cherished land of Hiawatha and lively discussions on T. S. Van Dyke's principles of still-hunting, George finally downed a magnificent ten-pointer with Shaffmaster's Marlin .30-30. The dragging of the buck back to camp took the boys through about a mile and a half of dense timber. The buck soon hung from a pole propped up against two big pines.

As the hungry Silver Creek still-hunters ate their venison steak that night, the lantern cast a soft amber light over them from its suspended position on the center pole where it swung back and forth like a clock's pendulum. A crackling fire created grotesque shadows that danced along the walls of their canvas tent. Following in the footsteps of Hiawatha, the editor and proprietor of the *Bronson Journal* continued to read more passages from *The Song of Hiawatha*:

And his heart within him fluttered,
Trembled like the leaves above him,
Like the birch-leaf palpitated,
As the deer came down the pathway.
Then upon one knee uprising,
Hiawatha aimed an arrow:
Scarce a twig moved with his motion,
Scarce a leaf was stirred or rustled,
But the wary roebuck started,
Stamped with all his hoofs together,
Listened with one foot uplifted,
Leaped as if to meet the arrow;
Ah! The singing, fatal arrow,
Like a wasp it buzzed and stung him!
Dead he lay there in the forest,
By the ford across the river.

The following day they left for home, thus ending their second annual deer hunt at Silver Creek. As they passed through Eckerman, Trout Lake and St. Ignace on their way to Bronson, they saw wagonloads of deer at the train depots; piles of deer carcasses being shipped home, piled as high as man could pile them. Tens of thousands of deer carcasses passed through the Straits of Mackinac during the first decade of the twentieth century. Such scenes we will never see again:

"It was a grand sight for the sportsman to behold, and could not help but send the sporting blood tingling through one's veins as one contemplated the spectacle and ruminated on the scenes and transpiring events which must have occurred to bring each and every one of those beautiful inanimate animals from its home in the heart of the deep forest."

On November 2, 1899, Shaffmaster and Brown and another deer hunter from Bronson, M. M. Clark, the well-known hardware man, arrived in Eckerman for a 28-day deer hunt along the banks of the beautiful Tahquamenon. This year they replaced their tent by reconstructing an abandoned logging camp office. Grouse fried in butter remained the key source of food for the first couple of days. On the nearest stage coach road several miles from their camp they nailed a wooden U.S. mailbox on a tree and wrote on the lid of the box:

A. D. Shaffmaster
George Brown
M. M. Clark
Camp 2 miles west

This mailbox allowed other hunters to find them for visits and group hunts and allowed Shaffmaster and his comrades to get the current issues of *The American Field, Forest and Stream* and *The National Sportsman,* in which Shaffmaster's byline frequently appeared. As voracious readers of the sporting literature of their day, these hunters looked for the daily stagecoach delivery of the mail by the big, bronzed and smiling Sam McMullen, the local teamster who also owned the mail route.

On November 8, George shot a buck and a doe and on Thursday, November 9, Shaffmaster's boys dined on their first venison supper in 1899. "I proceeded to cut off slice after slice of the dark red and flavored venison, which is soon transferred to the hot frying pan, where it is done to a turn with butter and plenty of salt and pepper to season." The meal ended with story telling and smoking their pipes around the big blazing logs for several hours before retiring for the night to their beds of freshly-cut hemlock and spruce boughs.

On this third pilgrimage to the land of Hiawatha, the weapons they used – a Winchester 30-30, a smokeless Marlin and a hammerless shotgun – produced eight deer, three bucks and five does. With deer populations nationwide extremely low, the Upper Peninsula of Michigan still remained the finest white-tailed deer hunting Mecca in America. On this deer hunt, another hunter, M. M. Clark (known as "the greenhorn"), listened to the editor's nightly, fireside readings of *The Song of Hiawatha:*

Dead he lay there in the forest,
By the ford across the river;
Beat his timid heart no longer,
But the heart of Hiawatha
Throbbed and shouted and exulted,
As he bore the red deer homeward,
And Lagoo and Nokomis
Hailed his coming with applauses.

On October 30, 1900, Shaffmaster, Bennett, Clark and P. A. Buck (another hunter from Bronson, known as "the jolly butcher and grocer") arrived at the Eckerman railroad station for the Fourth Annual Hunt. On the next day, they reached their reconstructed

The meat pole sags to its very limit as does the Silver Creek tarpaper shack. As the tarpaper pulls away from the shack, the deer camp boys add more rolls of tarpaper and indiscriminately hammer in more slants as needed to keep things afloat.

Courtesy Wegner's Deer & Deer Hunting Photo Collection.

logging camp office from the year before, a unique structure combining tarpaper with logs to form a tarpaper-log cabin combo. Firewood was quickly cut and beds of freshly cut hemlock and spruce boughs made to order. Their cabin Shaffmaster reported, "presents a genuine sporting appearance, with rifles, axes and belts and hunting clothing hung up in all manner of places." The 1900 Silver Creek Deer Camp sported a massive meat pole. In addition to venison they frequently dinned on oyster stew and beans.

On November 10, while still-hunting, Shaffmaster shot two bucks about fifteen minutes apart, downing both of them with neck shots. He paced the distances off at 60 and 80 yards. Two days later on Monday, November 12, in thick brush he shot another white-tailed buck, a massive ten-pointer that would eventually reign supreme in his antler collection back in Bronson. In the amber glow of the shack that night, the editor paid full tribute to his trophy:

"Walking carefully up to my game, I discovered to my delight it was a fine large ten-point buck with beautiful spreading antlers, and a bold handsome face and full, rounded neck. He was, indeed, a grand prize, and I could not help

Bringing whitetails back to the Silver Creek tarpaper – log cabin combo, circa 1900.

feeling a thrill of satisfied pride in realizing that I had killed the largest and noblest game in this country and in a place far remote from even a log road or hunters' trail." During the early years of the twentieth century Shaffmaster emerged as one of the early American antler collectors, along with Ernest Thompson Seton and Archibald Rutledge.

The rest of the hunters in camp were missing bucks and all complaining: "Away bounds the buck, flag up and heels cutting the air." They reported the lack of snow on the ground made deer hunting very difficult. Yet, before the Fourth Annual Hunt ended on November 30, some very fine bucks adorned the Silver Creek meat pole. And as usual the nighttime readings continued from *The Song of Hiawatha*:

Swift of foot was Hiawatha;
He could shoot an arrow from him,
And run forward with such fleetness
That the arrow fell behind him!
Strong of arm was Hiawatha;
He could shoot ten arrows upward,
Shoot them with such strength and swiftness
That the tenth had left the bowstring
Ere the first to earth had fallen!

One year later the editor and Clark Green, a prosperous farmer-sportsman, arrived at the platform of the little railroad station at Eckerman on October 28, 1901. This year they hunted farther to the north on Silver Creek and had to use a tent. By October 31, the hunters had their tent in place along the banks of Silver Creek, a creek Shaffmaster described in his diary as "a beautiful but small, clear stream flowing over a pure, white bed of sand, which trickles and murmurs day and night, winter and summer, and is only about forty feet from our tent. It is the finest and purest water I ever enjoyed in camp in Michigan."

On November 18, with no deer meat in camp after ten days of still-hunting, Shaffmaster was determined to bag some venison. Both hunters intensified their still-hunting efforts. On that day at 11:30 AM, the editor stopped near a large beech tree and watched and waited for ten minutes. Something impelled him to stay longer. As he was about to take a step forward, he caught a slight glance of a moving object to his left.

"A second glance and I saw it was a big buck, a royal old fellow with antlers like a rocking chair. I drew the old .30-30 Winchester down fine on his shoulder blade, held low and pressed the trigger. The noble buck dropped to the ground at the crack of the rifle."

After a tremendous amount of work getting this ten-point buck with an estimated live weight of 325 pounds back to camp, the distinguished editor posted the following menu on the center pole of the tent in the amber glow of the hanging lantern:

Venison Steak.
Cold Boiled Heart. Fried Bacon.
Fried Onions.
Potatoes with Jackets on.
Fresh White Bread. Buns.
Dairy Butter.
Hot Coffee—Rich and Black.
Fresh Milk and Cream.
Sugar. Clover Honey.
Raspberry Sauce.
Cucumber Pickles. Cold Baked Beans.
Spring Water from Silver Creek.
Crackers. Fried Cakes.

After finishing this hearty, venison meal, Shaffmaster said to Green, "I think we quit eating from exhaustion!" Many pipes and yarns followed as the fragrant blue smoke swirled up in graceful little clouds through the amber light of the lantern. As usual the editor entertained his guest with readings from Longfellow's *The Song of Hiawatha*. As the amber light dimmed and darkness descended in the tent the deer hunt that day ended most peacefully.

From the red deer's hide Nokomis
Made a cloak for Hiawatha,
From the red deer's flesh Nokomis
Made a banquet in his honor.
All the village came and feasted,
All the guests praised Hiawatha,
Called him Strong-Heart,
Soan-ge-taha!
Called him Loon-Heart,
Mahn-go-taysee!

The Silver Creek still-hunters often shot their Winchester barrels hot. On November 11, Green still-hunted an old logging road a mile north of their tent. He suddenly saw two bucks run across the road ahead of him. Shaffmaster documented the scene: "They were about six rods apart and going like a cyclone, but he pumped two shots out of his .40-82 cannon at them, just to augment their speed a little." Shaffmaster fondly admitted that the bucks rose from their beds and leaped into space in an amazing uncoiling manner – remaining virtually untouchable.

Before retiring for the night the editor would always step outside to gaze into the sky: "There is a beautiful crescent or half moon, which is surrounded by fleeting clouds, which float over airily, leaving flashes of bright moonlight which floods the forest around, glistening with its coat of snow and frost. All is still as death, and I withdraw to the tent where warmth and good cheer abound."

After more pipes and yarns and more stanzas from Longfellow, Green and the editor turned in for the last night's sleep in the Silver Creek deer camp of 1901:

He had mittens, Minjekahwun,
Magic mittens made of deerskin;
When upon his hand he wore them,
He could smite the rocks asunder,
He could grind them into powder.
He had moccasins enchanted,
Magic moccasins of deerskin;
When he bound them round his ankles,
When upon his feet he tied them,
At each stride a mile he measured!

One year later in 1902, after a hard and tedious two-day train ride, Clark, Green and Shaffmaster arrived at the Eckerman Railroad Station on November 4 for the sixth annual deer hunt along with 38 other deer hunters. Teamster McMullen's full load forced Green and Shaffmaster to walk almost thirteen miles before reaching Silver Creek. Upon arrival at their cherished deer camp at 1 AM on November 6, the editor wrote these words in the camp journal: "The old camp site looked natural as ever, and Silver Creek was babbling along as brightly and sparkling as ever. We drank from the ice cold stream again and oh, how good it seemed."

The first day in camp they spent repairing the leaking roof with tarpaper, building shelves in the tarpaper shack and constructing a large comfortable bed with freshly cut spruce and hemlock boughs plus baled hay. New canvas, woolen blankets, quilts and pillows created the effect of neatness and cleanliness. The weather remained very warm with constant rain. On November 11 he added this item to his deer camp journal:

"A hard rain and wind storm is raging with unabated fury tonight – the rain beats down on our tarpaper roof like the noise of roaring musketry, while the wind sweeps through the

"Venison for Supper."

forest swaying the tree tops and branches like reeds; how the moaning sounds roll along in billows of flying spray, as the heavy gusts strike the woods. But our cabin is snug and cozy, a fire snaps and crackles in the stove, while the savory smell of roasting venison floats up around us."

But nonetheless, Shaffmaster described as magical the effect of camp life on their systems: he felt like a boy again, who could eat as much as two ordinary men and sleep like a log and arise in the morning feeling rested even though he went to sleep very tired.

Despite the steady rain for days on end, the 1902 Silver Creek deer hunt remained very successful. By the time they broke camp on November 24, six deer, one black bear and a large timber wolf bent the meat pole to the very limits. During this particular hunt, Shaffmaster took many fine Kodak exposures of their adventures and both men took

time to read T. S. Van Dyke's article "Hunting The Virginia Deer," which appeared in the November 1902 issue of *Outing Magazine*. Both hunters agreed with Van Dyke that still-hunting is a science that demands a great deal of learning about the animal and its habitat and that it represents "the most charming excitement the land beyond the pavement has to offer," as Van Dyke so fondly put it.

On November 6, 1903, eight deer hunters from southern Michigan embarked upon the seventh annual deer hunt to the land of Hiawatha. On this spiritual pilgrimage eight gentlemen once again searched for the true meaning of Longfellow's *Song of Hiawatha*. First, there was C. C. Bennett, one of the pioneers of Branch County and an old-time sportsman, genial and overflowing with boyish enthusiasm, even though in his seventy-third year; P. A. Buck, the jolly butcher and grocer who dearly loved deer hunting stories; M.

M. Clark, the well-known hardware man and devoted deer hunter; Thomas Russell, a prosperous farmer and old-time deer hunter; Joseph Sager, another prosperous farmer and member of the younger generation of sportsmen; J. T. Pickhaver, the brawny blacksmith and experienced deer hunter, and his partner from Coldwater, Michigan, D. A. Buck, the efficient sheriff of Branch County; and lastly the author of Hunting in the Land of Hiawatha, A. D. Shaffmaster, the hunt master incarnate of the Silver Creek Deer Camp and editor and proprietor of the *Bronson Journal*.

After attaching a 14-foot tent to their tarpaper shack, they built a large bed to accommodate eight deer hunters. Although these die-hard still-hunters spent each day alone in their individual pursuit of whitetails, they anxiously awaited their return to the evening time camaraderie and the awesome supper

The Silver Creek deer hunters took their deer hunting seriously, as their expressions and well-loaded cartridge belts indicate, 1903.

of the Silver Creek Deer Camp. Noonday lunches frequently consisted of little more than limburger cheese and hickory nut cake. In his diary, Shaffmaster describes the warmth and coziness of their deer-hunting tent:

"As I write this tonight I can hear the northeastern wind beating the branches of the forest trees until they give out weird sounds—sounds of the night, those eerie rustlings of bush and leaf and twig. The lofty hemlocks sway with restless motion and the forest seems awaiting the swirling snow and the early presence of winter, but we are cozy and so warm, and the tent is aglow with light fragrant smoke, lazily curling from four pipes, while the boys indulge in a quiet game and ye editor writes and writes."

The 1903 deer season opened as usual on November 8 and luck came early, with Art Buck taking an eight-pointer early in the morning. That morning as he still-hunted an old logging road running towards the Tahquamenon Bay, a large buck sprang up and started off on a jump. Shaffmaster described the scene:

"Art got busy with his old .40-82 Winchester, and began pumping lead at the old fellow as he bounded along, his big body seeming a comparatively small mark as he dashed out and in among the brush, and under the dark shadows of towering hemlocks, but the aim was true, and the buck fell down to stay after the third shot."

The Silver Creek luck continued. On November 9, both Joe Sager and J. T. Pickhaver downed two bucks in good style. The editor also got an eight-pointer just at dark. Three days later Schaffmaster also got

Members of Deer foot Lodge and Shaffmaster's Silver Creek Deer Camp traveled many hours on trains and horse-drawn wagons to get to camp. Wegner's Deer & Deer Hunting Photo Collection.

another deer. On November 14, Art Buck shot another fine buck on a runway west of camp with a neck shot. Three days later the editor collected another antlerless deer. The limit at that time was five deer, either sex. On November 19, Buck and Pickhaver returned from a two-day hunt at another camp with a big buck, a royal old fellow with antlers like a rocking chair and three does.

With eleven days of the season still open, heavy snow forced the hunters to leave for the Eckerman Railroad Station. After boarding the train for the Straits of Mackinac,

Shaffmaster summed up the last annual pilgrimage to the land of Hiawatha in 1903: "In this, the concluding chapter of our Seventh Annual Hunt, it is worthy of mention that it was the general opinion expressed by the members of our party that we had all enjoyed a nice time in the woods and had been very successful in getting game, our party of eight having killed 12 deer, and a good amount of small game. No accident or sickness marred the event, and therefore we all voted the hunt to be a happy one, and to be recalled with pleasure in future years."

CUNNINGHAM'S
ΞR CAMP
AT LOST CREEK

I have seen the "blackened timber,"
I have camped beside the stream,
Rested on a couch of "feathers,"
Listened to the wild, weird scream
Of the night bird. Watched the eagle
Soaring over lake and heath,
Walked the "log jam at right angles
To the current" far beneath.
But no rhyme can paint the picture,
Neither can the learned in art;
It must be transferred from Nature
By the soul unto the heart.

– G. W. Cunningham.
"Deer Hunting in Wisconsin." Forest and Stream.
January 9, 1904.

Courtesy Wegner's Deer & Deer Hunting Postcard Collection.

During the mid-1890s, as Americans embarked upon their "Back to Nature" movement, a distinguished Hoosier deerslayer named George Washington Cunningham – a member of the prominent Cunningham family of Pennsylvania, manufacturers of the famed Cunningham piano – formed a Wisconsin deer hunting club near "Buckhorn Road" in the Northern Highland of Vilas County.

There he attempted to re-enact the Arcadian Myth of eating trout, venison and grouse while shooting noble white-tailed bucks to adorn the entryway of his plush residency back in Portland, Indiana. We learn from Cunningham (1853-1910) that while the poet and artist can assist us in understanding the true significance of deer hunting and camping out in primitive tents, we must allow Nature itself – as he alludes to it in his poem – to transfer the real meaning of these activities into our souls.

With whitetails virtually extinct in the Hoosier State by 1900, Cunningham (nicknamed "G. W.") and his crew, which eventually grew to fourteen gunners over the years – White, Gilmer, Winters, C. F. Bender, Proper, Lewis, Hearn, Baur, Dr. C. W. MacKey, George Hedrick, J. E. Spahr, John Sturgis, Journay and John Bishop – headed north on the Chicago, Milwaukee, & St. Paul Railroad with the great encouragement of this railroad company's promotional literature to chase deer near Plum Lake in Vilas County, Wisconsin, and on other occasions to travel to Draper as well.

Between 1895 and 1907 Cunningham wrote 16 detailed feature articles in the pages of *Forest and Stream*, the foremost American sportsmen's journal of its time, in which he documented these vintage Wisconsin deer hunts plus several forays into Michigan as well. Today these classic deer hunting stories provide us with one of the best historic records we have for early twentieth century Wisconsin deer hunting, especially in Vilas County.

During this period white-tailed deer exhibited a marked decline in numbers due to forest fires, logging, market hunting and, as Deputy Game Warden Mackie believed at the time, predation by wolf and lynx. The letters to the editors of the local newspapers indicated many Wisconsin deer hunters believed too many deer were also being taken by out-of-state residents whose license fees they insisted should be substantially increased.

The *Eagle River Democrat* reported in a pre-season report for 1895 that in the previous year 93 deer were shipped from Eagle River in one day and stated that nearly as many were shipped from Conover, State Line, Star Lake, Woodruff and Minocqua. The paper noted the railroad shipped 1000 deer out of the area, a figure that exceeded the number left alive during the 1894 deer season. The local natives in the backwoods' saloons blamed the foreign, redneck "army" of Illinoisans and Hoosiers for the scarcity of "their" deer. Indeed, the controversy between resident and non-resident deer hunters remained entrenched as early as 1894.

The fascinating story of Cunningham's legendary Wisconsin deer camp really begins in 1894, when the Chicago, Milwaukee, & St. Paul Railroad built its station in Plum Lake near the home of Orrin W. Sayner, the pioneer founding father of the Town of Plum Lake (1891), which rapidly became known thereafter as Sayner. Sayner, born in Indiana, soon emerged as one of the most popular and best known resort men in northern Wisconsin. In a portrait of him in the November 30, 1895 issue of *Forest and Stream* we see a tall, lean, handsome man with a thick mop of black hair and dashing black handlebar mustache who is dressed in a fringed buckskin jacket topped off with a black felt dress hat. He stands on the snow covered ice of Plum Lake with snowshoes in hand.

As postmaster, local teamster and proprietor of the Sayner Hotel, the social centerpiece for the deer hunters in that area at the time, "O. W." (as he was commonly called) greeted them at the railroad depot and took them on their merry way to their deer-hunting destinations via buckboards and sleighs in a most accommodating and congenial manner. He soon served as Cunningham's stage manager and huntmaster par excellence for more than a decade. Traveling on such special deer camp railroad cars as the Green Bay & Western 2490 to Sayner was indeed a unique experience! For this railroad car was a traveling deer camp itself with built in woodstove,

The Green Bay & Western 2490 railroad car was a traveling deer camp itself with built in woodstove, lanterns and sleeping quarters.

lanterns and sleeping quarters.

On October 27, 1895, Cunningham and five of his deer club partners arrived at the Sayner depot with massive deer-hunting trunks which contained more than 2000 pounds of supplies for the, twenty-day, either-sex Wisconsin deer season of 1895 (November 1-20). Their camp supplies consisted in two 10-oz. wall tents measuring 12′x16′, a sheet iron stove, two stew-pots, two frying pans, coffee pot, buckets, table ware, an axe, a hand saw, and a small cross-cut saw for sawing tree trunks – plus trunks full of rifles, ammunition, bedding and wearing apparel and all the food supplies and unique delicacies imaginable for a vigorous 20-day northern Wisconsin deer hunt. We know from an account dated July 27, 1895, that the boys at Lost Creek deer camp ate a lot of beans:

"Ere the last gray streaks of dawn had left the horizon, we had breakfasted, and to Reuben's question, 'What shall I cook for dinner?' the answer came, 'BEANS,' which brought from the veteran George the camp song: 'Beans for breakfast, beans for dinner, beans for supper – BEANS – BEANS – BEANS,' sung to the tune 'Martin'!"

With Mr. Sayner's assistance Cunningham and his five comrades loaded their supplies aboard a large wagon and a buckboard and headed 2.3 miles south from the depot for the banks of Lost Creek – a picturesque, romantic creek running between Lost Lake and Big St. Germaine Lake – a legendary piece of deer hunting country highly cherished by many readers of *Forest and Stream* including Cunningham and his crew. According to legend, Lost Creek received its name because it clearly did not seem to know where it was going. After studying it and hunting along its banks for a decade, G W. provided this description of it:

"It would be difficult to picture an imaginary creek whose turnings and windings

A familiar sight in Northern Wisconsin around Lost Creek: Deer hunters riding the buckboard to and from deer camp.

were more absurd. Its source and mouth are Lost Lake and Big St. Germaine Lake respectively. They are not over one and a half miles apart, but this erratic stream, albeit it has a swift current, must flow six to eight miles, most through marsh land and bordered with tamarack and other swamp brush, and does not go far out of its general course, either. These swamps furnish excellent hiding for deer, rabbits and grouse."

G. W.'s preferred method of hunting was to still-hunt in the Van Dyke tradition of stealth and good marksmanship. "The man who cannot glide through the forest from hill to hill, stump to stump, and walk logs like a cat, seeing deer before they see him, or should a deer break cover, bring it down with a repeating rifle before it gets out of range, should be content to keep camp." Cunningham readily acknowledged that he and his deer club members often still-hunted deer cover for up to nine square miles.

On November 1, the opening day of the 1895 deer season, while still-hunting in heavy cover along the banks of Lost Creek, G. W. came to the base of a ridge, on top of which stood a very large pine stump. As he silently approached the stump he walked up one of its massive roots. In doing so he gradually brought up his old Model 1886 to a ready and steady position as he stood erect. This is what he saw:

"A ten-point buck lying down forty-five steps facing me. What magnificent antlers, and how his eyes gleamed in the early morning light. He either thought himself undiscovered in that small depression behind a bunch of twigs, or remained transfixed with fear and surprise at the apparition before him, for he never blinked while I drew a bead on his right eye and fired. My aim was so true that the skin around his eye never broke."

And then traveling the rails from Fort Wayne to Chicago, Milwaukee, Green Bay and Sayner and then on to Lost Creek via buckboards and bobsleds with "O. W." for a total of more than 30 hours and 450 miles. They eventually slept in two small tents in the heart of Vilas County deer country with a wood stove hissing away at the end of the Harvest Moon. There the smell of sweet hemlock boughs, wood smoke and roasting venison loin literally bewitched

A full-time cook always presided at Cunningham's encampments.

the Cunningham tribe:

"The full measure of benefit derived from this mode of camping impresses itself on one during inclement weather. While the forest is bending to the blast and waves are lashing at the shores of Lost Lake, within the tents all is warmth and comfort."

The 1895 deer season permitted hunters to take any kind of deer and any number of deer. On the second day of that season G. W. shot a doe at 75 yards for camp meat with his .38-56 Winchester carbine. As the forest reverberated with the Winchester's report two of his club members – C. F. Bender and Dr. C. W. MacKey – soon arrived on the scene to assist in making a traveling meat pole from a small tree on which they lashed the carcass, referred to at the time as a "litter."

Although they tramped a long way, these two hunters made good headway toward camp as the third carried guns and moved forest debris as vividly portrayed in the popular photo by H. H. Bennett, Wisconsin's legendary photographer, dated circa 1895. It represents the traditional mode for moving deer within the forest at the time. These photos frequently got the caption "Venison on a Stick." After arriving back at their tent Cunningham & Company enjoyed freshly fried venison tenderloins in bacon and onions cooked on their woodstove with beans, beans and more beans.

During these early Wisconsin deer hunts a Green Bay & Western railroad car would frequently come to a screeching halt near the banks of Lost Creek, for F. A. Miller, the General Passenger Agent, informed the conductor and engineer to stop the train at the precise location where Cunningham & Company wanted to erect their deer camp site. Mr. Sayner, also informed about the precise location of departure, would be at the site for assistance. The club members jumped out, quickly unloaded their trunks and gear as the Green Bay & Western railroad car sped down the tracks for the Sayner depot with the whistle blowing a fond farewell!

During the first years of the twentieth century (1900-1905) deer hunters in Wisconsin experienced a whole host of changes and restrictions. In 1900 the Federal Lacey Act prohibited interstate commerce in venison. In 1901, the Wisconsin legislature prohibited deer hunting with dogs except in 16 southern counties. In 1902, legislation prohibited the sale of venison statewide. And in 1905, deer hunters could no longer use salt licks.

As the Chicago, Milwaukee & St. Paul Railroad train roared its way through Vilas County on November 8, 1902, and headed toward the little station of Sayner, Cunningham relaxed while reading the 1902 November issue of *The Outing Magazine,* edited by Caspar Whitney and published in New York. In that issue he read with great interest Van Dyke's feature article "Hunting the Virginia Deer" highlighted with the incredibly romantic line drawings by his friend Carl Rungius. As the train chugged along he periodically looked up at his deer club comrades – Charlie Bender and George Hedrick – sitting across from him and read out loud certain classic one-liners from the Apostle Van Dyke's deer hunting epistle; they sounded like bullets coming out of Van Dyke's classic Winchester 1873:

Hunting was always more of a charm than shooting, and game that knew how to get away was always my first choice.

Glossy curves of fur curl over the lofty logs. Almost always the head is well erect and all senses keen for danger.

There are fools among the wildest animals and the more one hunts deer the more apt one is to feel a painful suspicion that the greater part of success comes from stumbling over a fool.

Sometimes in rutting time a grand old buck may stop and stand like a stone statue within a few yards from you.

When deer hide it is because they know what you are and know you cannot see them.

Still-hunting makes the most charming excitement the land beyond the pavement has to offer, and is the main reason why thousands are crazy over still-hunting.

That last statement represents exactly why Cunningham, Bender and Hedrick stepped off the train at the Sayner station at 1:30 P.M. on Saturday, November 8, 1902 – to still-hunt whitetails along the banks of Lost Creek – well beyond the pavement of Portland, Indiana. In the wilds of Vilas County they would often tramp the wilderness chasing whitetails for six to eight miles a day; shoot rabbits for the pot with their Winchester rifles along the way and return to their tents for "fried mush and bean soup" when lacking deer meat; and indulge in a good hit of Hunter Baltimore Rye to cut the phlegm.

As avid readers of *Outing* they took the advertisements seriously in their favorite magazine. The November ad for their spirit of choice read as follows: "Two elements of pleasurable social life are health and hospitality. Hunter Baltimore Rye contributes to both as the physician's and the host's first choice because of its Sterling Quality and Superb Flavor." Indeed. Cunningham & Company agreed. It also seems likely that as committed readers of *Outing* they carried Elgin Watches and wore Dr. Deimel's (Linen Mesh) Underwear. Dr. Deimel told the boys in '02 to wear his genuine underwear and bag a buck, not a cold!

Immediately upon exiting the train and doing some preseason scouting they noted

7650. HUNTING IN THE ADIRONDACKS.

"Venison on a Stick." Deer hunting at the time became a muscular, manly, cultist affair with dignified pallbearers, 1916.

some very fundamental changes since their last deer hunt in the area. They found very little as they left it a year ago. "Where the big buck tore his way through the brush, crossed the railroad and landed in Plum Lake, which he swam in his escape from the hounds and rifle balls of Mr. Saltsic and his friends, we found a desolate wasteland in the south, some small empty buildings, a meadow of a couple of acres, then more downed timber and desolation down to the edge of the beautiful Plumb Lake. . . The forest, especially the pine, is about all gone." With the summer hotel and the lumber camps filling up with local hunters, they decided to use the station house as their headquarters for their first night.

Several days later the 20-day, two-deer-any-size-or-sex deer season opened. That Monday, November 11, dawned clear and very cold but with no tracking snow on the

ground. The die-hard still-hunters left their tents along the bank 30 feet distant from the creek and took to the mass of burned over, downed timber, brush, briers and old stubs with great gusto as they followed along Lost Creek near Big St. Germaine Lake. After a very tiresome day in which none of them even saw a deer, G.W. again penned another description of the uniqueness of Lost Creek: "Lost Creek plays hide and seek in a massive marsh, while high ridges border its boggy shores and patches of evergreens give color to its otherwise gloomy appearance."

In this somewhat gloomy setting with cloudy November skies several more days of rain persisted with more negative results for their still-hunts. "Grub low; no venison; no mail." Nevertheless, when Sunday the 17th dawned without deer meat, the boys sallied forth with even a greater sense of determination and drive, but yet another day of still-hunting on dry ground ended with a non-bending meat pole at the tent and more bean soup.

But then suddenly on Monday morning, November 18, Charlie Bender's Winchester .38-40 spoke. Bang! Bang! Bang! As the shots reverberated through the heavy brush he saw a rutting eight-pointer following a

Schlitz Beer comes to the American deer camp, 1903.

doe with his nose close to the ground collapse in his tracks on the third shot. An early lunch of deer brains followed. Later in the day George returned from Sayner with two pine squirrels, two loafs of bread and a peck of potatoes. A major banquet ensued that night served on a red-checkered oil cloth over a large oak door laid upon their storage trunk with authentic tableware to match. Long, involved and sometimes rather convoluted deer hunting tales and excuses unfolded under a clear, bright, starry sky to the sweet taste and aroma of roasting venison.

The highlight of the 1902 deer hunt, however, occurred on Wednesday, November 20, when George made a one-man drive for Cunningham early in the day. Shortly after the drive got underway G. W. spotted a doe running like a streak of lightning followed by a buck which dashed right out in front of him. Bang! went his Winchester .38-40 as the noble eight-pointer turned, took a few jumps, stopped a couple of seconds and fell over dead.

After field dressing the buck, Cunningham stood by the fallen quarry for no more than 15 minutes when this startling incident repeated

itself although from a somewhat different direction. This time a doe and a buck came past at "break-neck speed." The lever-action .38-40 now spoke three times and the buck – an awesome, wide-palmated 10-pointer – walked about 10 feet and dropped dead very near where the other dressed monarch lay: two bucks for the entryway back in Cunningham's Portland residence. Lacking supplies to make a "litter," they returned to camp. They then constructed a crude raft and finished the day by rafting the two bucks down Lost Creek into camp and onto the meat pole at the tent.

Cunningham closed his report about this hunt in the pages of *Forest and Stream* by deeming it as the most pleasant deer hunting trip to Lost Creek, albeit the most expensive of their annual deer hunting trips. He referred of course to the high $30 cost of the non-resident deer hunting license (30 times that of the resident license). Nevertheless, the 1902 Lost Creek deer hunt remained his most special hunt of those annual trips to the Vilas County (1895-1907). On that 1902 hunt 72,635 deer hunters bought a license and they took 3,352 deer based on railroad transportation estimat-

Courtesy Wegner's Deer & Deer Hunting Postcard Collection.

THIS IS THE WAY THEY HANG THEM UP AT NEW AUBURN, WIS.

This dignified deer camp near New Auburn with a bending meat pole resembled Cunningham's camp at Lost Creek.

ed information. In 1902, 293 non-residents purchased a deer hunting license and shipped 318 deer out of state. Two of them belonged to George Washington Cunningham, who considered all of his deer hunts to Lost Creek "a good, jolly, rough and tumble time!"

After a short train ride from Fort Wayne to Chicago, the hunters transferred to the Chicago, in November 1903, Milwaukee & St. Paul Railroad and found themselves crossing into Wisconsin near Kenosha en route for the small railroad station at Sayner. As the train sped along the rails, the threesome – they would be joined by Cunningham who stopped at the Chicago Sportsman's Show and other deer club members later for the Opening Day on November 11 – talked about the virtues of still-hunting whitetails.

At 1:06 PM on Friday November 7, they arrived at the Sayner depot and by nightfall, after a comfortable buckboard ride, securely resided in their tents along the banks of Lost Creek with three full days to scout and prepare their camping site before the Opening Day. All of their trunks and gear arrived safely, including their special rifles and several Stevens'

double-barreled hammerless shotguns. They looked forward to Opening Day for their ninth annual deer hunt.

It arrived with a cold westerly wind spitting particles of icy snow. According to Aldo Leopold's *Wisconsin Wildlife Chronology* the '03 deer hunt went on record as being a very cold affair. Indeed, several extremely cold days would keep the hunters in their tent that season. Cunningham arrived the night before Open Day and remained in his warm springy bed of cedar and hemlock boughs and woolen blankets as long as he could get away with it.

The tents faced an old timber railroad a few steps from where the Eagle River and Sayner wagon roads crossed Lost Creek. The snow continued for the next couples of days providing for excellent still hunting and one-man deer drives. By Saturday, November 21, due to ideal hunting conditions despite the cold temperatures, the four hunters had their limit of eight deer hanging from their Lost Creek meat pole – five bucks (one 10-pointer with a single shot from Doc's single shot Remington-Hepburn No. 3) and three does.

In 1904, Cunningham's clan began to read the deer hunting stories of Paulina Brandreth as more and more women deer hunters began to appear in the woods.

Their larder that season consisted of venison, smoked ham, potatoes, beans, canned goods, dried peaches, bread, crackers, meal, flour, butter, lard, coffee, tea, sugar, pepper, "Sault-evaporated cream," a few eggs and, of course, Old Hedrick's traditional, chronic corn mush which simmered for days on end on the wood-stove and got better with age.

The hunt ended that year on Saturday, November 21. The hunters rested on the following day and pulled into the Sayner railroad station aboard the Sayner buckboard on Monday afternoon during a blinding snowstorm. They took the 4:45 train for Chicago and arrived home in Portland at 10 PM, November 24, with two whitetails to the credit of each.

In the next installment of the adventures of Cunningham's deer camp published in the pages of *Forest and Stream,* G. W. acknowledged that Dr. MacKey became a good-natured tribulation every year in early January:

"The Doctor is the plague of my life. No sooner has he consumed his last bit of venison than he is ready for the next year's outing. The first thought he utters is how did the deer winter; the second, where we will locate? Then how many will be in the party, and how long will we stay? These are foundation stones for the building that goes on during the summer months, until by the first of October he has changed to, 'Have you heard from S?' By this time I am getting pretty well worked up, and if prevented from carrying out our plans (which seem to

Courtesy Adirondack Museum. Blue Mountain Lake, New York.

Paulina Brandreth at her deer stand in the Adirondacks with her cherished .40-65 Winchester.

grow just like mushrooms), something more serious would probably happen."

Their mushrooming plans for the '04 deer hunt quickly materialized and on November 8, G. W., Hedrick, Spahr, Dr. MacKey, Journay and Charlie Bender roared into the Fort Wayne railroad station with their 7-horse-power Runabout radiators steaming. By 10:30 PM that night they arrived in Chicago and boarded the Chicago, Milwaukee, & St. Paul train for Vilas County where Mr. Sayner would haul them to last year's campsite and furnish them

Legendary guide Reuben Cary with Paulina Brandreth's massive 13-pointer.

with a second woodstove, table, kerosene and a bale of straw. Their quarters that year along the shore of Lost Creek consisted in two connected 16'x12' tents with two wood stoves.

On Opening Day, November 11, they ate breakfast under kerosene-lamp light at 4:00 AM as 76,000 deer hunters took up their positions statewide. Daylight would not find Cunningham's tribe in bed on Opening Day! Nowhere on earth did hope bloom so eternally. After the party scattered in all directions to favorite deer stands, Spahr issued the first report with his giant .42-80 as a 5-pointer went to the meat pole for fresh liver, tenderloins, bacon and onions that night. The festive venison celebration continued in front of the wood stove that night with a touch of Hunter Whiskey, known for its "Absolute Purity, Faultless Quality and Exquisite Flavor," as the folks at the distillery in Baltimore, Maryland, insisted.

The deer season that year not only saw the emergence of women in the deer woods and at the meat poles but the appearance of their bylines and images in the deer hunting literature and sporting advertisements of the time. In the October 1, 1904 issue of *Forest and Stream* the 19-year-old Paulina Brandreth, an early, enthusiastic promoter of American white-tailed deer hunting, told Cunningham's crew "there is not a finer animal to shoot than a white-tailed buck weighing more than 200 pounds when in the short blue coat with freshly peeled antlers surmounting his graceful head."

By the close of the '04 deer hunt on November 30, several bucks matching that description hung form the Lost Creek meat pole. As the embers died in the woodstove that night, Cunningham read the poem "The Hunt of 1904" from the pages of the Man-I-Do-Wish Hunting Club's diary, a deer camp located nearby.

Cunningham's deer hunts usually ended in the Art Studio for final homage and respectful display.

On November 8, 1905, Cunningham & Company again arrived in the burned-over pine country of Lost Creek where their two sheet-iron woodstoves belched out heat and smoke as they burned split, pitch-pine stumps from an old chopping and ate porcupines ("porkers") and hedge hogs. As the stoves roared and the mush sizzled in the frying pans, anticipation of the Opening Day rose. While still lying on his boughs of hemlock G. W. planned his early morning tramp:

"I planned to make a circle, cross the creek and follow the wagon road down to Big St. Germain Lake, then turn up the Lost Lake road to the chopping south of the lake, then skirt the woods to the northwest, coming back to camp on the old timber railroad road which the boys dubbed Peggy. Peggy was an abandoned road, the bed of which was full of ties from which a good many spikes protruded, hence the name."

But that plan and the afternoon tramp as well both brought only tired legs for everyone. On the second morning with fresh snow on the ground Cunningham jumped a spike buck and managed to make a spectacular neck shot with his .38-56 Winchester Model 1886. That night the boys got their first taste of fresh venison steak served with boiled beans, fried bacon and onions and stewed peas.

Later at the woodstove near the lantern, as the full moon shined on the meat pool, they discussed Paulina Brandreth's "Days with Deer," just published in *Forest and Stream.* Her article dealt with her massive 13-pointer and expressed her profound adulation for the deer hunt:

"Those following out the desire to hunt deer find in it a wholesome, exhilarating pastime – one that gives rise to health, vigor, activity and numerous other virtues, including self-reliance . . . I hold toward it a feeling deeper seated than affection not merely for the sport it has afforded, but for the beauty of its environment: the serene sunsets, twilights and mystic moonlit nights witnessed there, when the

sublime creations of nature were made manifest no matter which way the eyes turned, and filled one with joy and inspiration."

After downing that magnificent buck with her cherished old .40-65 Winchester she wrote, "Under the silver radiance of a full moon we rode the buckboard into camp that evening, and the generous praise which was bestowed on the trophy filled the cup of satisfied elation to overflowing."

As the 1905 deer hunt ended, Cunningham & Company left for the train depot with seven whitetails aboard Sayner's buckboard. One year later on November 6, 1906, Bender, Spahr, Journay, Dr. MacKey and G. W. traveled farther west to Glidden, where through the courtesy of the management of the railroad they pitched their tents near an old lumber company building overlooking a small lake between Morse and Mellen. On the hunt one new product appeared in their tents – Grape-Nuts Cereal. Once again they took the ad seriously in their favorite magazine, *Outing:* "It's a matter of choice whether you will be strong, well and brainy. 'There's a Reason' for GRAPE-NUTS!"

With the aid of GRAPE-NUTS that year and Campbell's Tomato Soup at 10 cents a can, five hunters shot five deer; as they returned to Portland news spread quickly of how John Pettingill, the founding father of Iron River, shot a massive, 10-pointer with an estimated live weight of 477 pounds near the Cunningham campsite with his Winchester .38-56. They rode the rails back to Portland reading Horace Kephart's classic book *Camping and Woodcraft* and Maximilian Foster's essay "The Waiting Game: The Whitetail's Last Trail" in *Outing* while drinking Coca Cola in bottles for five cents a pop.

These early Wisconsin deer hunts were grandiose, romantic, and manly affairs played out in mainstream American culture under guidance and advice from none other than TR himself from the White House at 1600 Pennsylvania Avenue.

Cunningham and his clan ultimately dressed in black suits and ties as they traveled back and forth to Lost Creek via buckboards, bobsleds and the Old Milwaukee Road.

The Golden Age of American Illustration reigned supreme at the time. Such legendary artists as Frederic Remington, Philip R. Goodwin, Charlie Russell, Carl Rungius, N. C. Wyeth, Oliver Kemp and Hy S. Watson dazzled not only the Cunningham tribe but the deer hunting clan nationwide with dramatic deer and deer hunting scenes in lithographs, oils and watercolors. At the same time the classic sporting writers of the era – Stewart Edward White, Emerson Hough, Jack London, E. T. Seton, Paulina Brandreth and T. S. Van Dyke – enamored deer hunters with high-level prose and poetic descriptions of the deer hunt, the likes of which we have never seen since. And never will.

Cunningham and his boys ultimately dressed in black suits and ties as they traveled back and forth to Lost Creek via buckboards and the Old Milwaukee Road, looking like dignified pallbearers involved in a highly and holy cultivated affair of the North Woods – the All American White-Tailed Deer Camp. The hunt usually ended in the Art Studio for final homage and display – making the whole affair a cult activity to say the least.

*To evoke the deepest admiration it is
necessary to take a solitary walk
through the sun-dappled woods,
and walk until you jump a whitetail
and hear it snort as it springs away
with great leaps, then begin to gallop,
its flag-like white tail held high.
For to see a whitetail in the woods
is to see many things.
It is, for one, to see the very essence
of speed and gracefulness.
And it is to see a good deal
of this country's past history;
it is also to see an animal
that has survived all of mankind's
unwitting attempts to exterminate it.
The history represented by the whitetail
is more important
than most people realize.*

– Henry P. Bridges.
The Woodmont Story, 1953.

The most high-brow, utopian deer camp imaginable, the most exclusive deer-hunting and fishing club ever to appear in America, was undoubtedly the Woodmont Rod and Gun Club of

"Incident in Autumn." Painting by William Reusswig, 1953.

Henry P. Bridges, the Sage of Woodmont (1878-1957).

Hancock, Maryland, as Henry P. Bridges (1878-1957), the Secretary-Treasurer of the Club, suggests in his delightful book *The Woodmont Story* (1953), a widely sought-after volume of Americana.

During the late nineteenth century, the wilderness area of Western Maryland enticed elite urbanites to the deer woods for recreation and health. Numerous sporting clubs began to appear throughout America offering people a chance to match their deer hunting skills against wild nature. At the beginning of this so-called "wilderness craze," from 1870 to 1900, only the wealthy could afford hunting club memberships. While traveling through America at the time, the German sociologist Max Weber observed that one's affiliation with these distinguished sporting clubs, rather than one's accomplishments alone, placed one in a secure position within the urban, corporate world of America.

Situated on the Potomac River about ten

The Woodmont Club House, 1930.

Woodmont Rod and Gun Club—Clubhouse, near Berkeley Springs, W. Va., and Hancock, Md.

Courtesy Wegner's Deer & Deer hunting Postcard Collection.

miles west of Hancock in a valley between the Allegheny and Blue Ridge Mountains, this huge game conservation preserve of 3,500 acres sported a massive lodge popularly known as the Hunting Club of the Presidents. Between 1880 and 1957 it became an exclusive hunting club for rich and famous sport heroes, entertainers and six American Presidents: James Garfield, Chester Arthur, Grover Cleveland, Benjamin Harrison, Herbert Hoover and Franklin Delano Roosevelt. A large Presidential rocking chair at the lodge bears their names.

The lodge also hosted "Who's Who" of American government, leaders of twentieth-century industry, and notables such as Babe Ruth, Gene Tunney and Amos & Andy of radio fame. E. Lee LeCompte, a prominent Maryland State Conservation Commissioner and the first State Game Warden (1916-1945) and the legendary Dixie deerslayer Archibald Rutledge of the Hampton Plantation of South Carolina also dined and hunted white-tailed deer and turkeys at Woodmont. In 1995, the Maryland Department of Natural Resources purchased the club and now sublets it to the Izaak Walton League for a portion of the year and another portion for the public. In their press release the agency reported, "Once upon a time only for the famed, now happily ever after for all!"

The Club became well known for its classic venison recipe. Frederick Philip Stieff listed it with great distinction in his celebrated cook-book *Eat, Drink & Be Merry in Maryland* (1932), which included Edwin Tunis's snazzy illustration of the famous 100-plus-year-old Club; it seems highly likely that great cook-book of culinary lore as well as the famed *Derrydale Game Cook Book* (1937) by Master Chef Louis P. De Gouy resided in the kitchen area of the Clubhouse. The Club's proprietary venison recipe ran thus:

Venison

Get pure olive oil.
To one pint of olive oil grate four onions,
and beat up in a dish.
Get the skillet very hot, and put a little
butter in it to keep it from sticking.
Dip the venison steaks thoroughly
in the olive oil and onions.
Cook quickly and turn frequently,
searing the steaks medium to well done
according to how liked the best.
If a venison roast,
pour the olive oil and onions
over the roast as you start to roast it.
Baste it thoroughly while cooking.

– Woodmont Rod and Gun Club,
Washington County.

The elegant dining room at Woodmont with several full-mounted deer in attendance and classic sporting art hanging on the walls. George Cope's "Hunter's Paraphernalia." Oil on canvas, 1887.

Before introducing their cherished venison recipe in his cookbook, Stieff made these comments about the Club: "Few hunting clubs have as enviable a reputation as the Woodmont Rod and Gun Club. Founded many years ago by fighting Bob Evans it has flourished until now (1932); it is probably the best known in the country. Its limited roster of membership reads as though culled from the highest ratings of Dun or Bradstreet's and a Who's Who of National Sporting Life. Many Presidents have spent their days of relaxation there with rod and gun. Deer, wild turkey, ruffed grouse, imported pheasant, partridge, woodcock, wild duck and all upland game have served to make membership in this unusual club a coveted achievement to all lovers of good sport."

These wild game extravaganzas will never be seen again. In characterizing them, one observer, John Aldergrove, reported, "It is difficult to imagine a happier conjunction than the blending of the symbols when the arms of a sportsman are quartered with those of a cook. The tints of the autumnal woods reflected in the plumage of mature and lusty game are types of rich experiences and genial sentiments which flit about the sportsman's board and linger at his hearth with as gracious a fitness as that which diffuses a faint blush

through the russet of a well cooked mallard's breast, and with a zest equal to the relish which lurks within a woodcock's thigh."

The massive dining room at the Woodmont Club measuring 40 by 40 feet could accommodate 85 people or more. At the entrance, a life-size mounted white-tailed buck – the Monarch of Woodmont – stood in watch over the whole romantic affair. Below the ceiling laced with hand-hewn beams, the walls sported classic paintings of bears and deer and deer hunting scenes by great sporting artists such as J. J. Audubon, A. F. Tait and George Cope as well as photos of the club's distinguished members and their quarries, especially the wild turkey.

An Associated Press story during the 1950s described the first-floor interior of the Woodmont lodge:

"Two vast rooms are the heart of the lodge. Floors are covered with skins of animals, corners are filled with beautifully mounted specimens of animals and birds from the world over, some 600 all told, ranging in size from enormous moose heads hanging over equally enormous fireplaces to stuffed deer and squirrels. Dark wood walls and massively timbered ceilings carry the hunting lodge air, the ruggedness softened by great overstuffed leather chairs. Back of these two huge rooms are smaller rooms; a kitchen, the cold-storage room, bedrooms and small lounging rooms."

The whole menagerie of wildlife skins, stuffed animals and pelts represented the finest collection of mounted wildlife in the world at the time. The social centerpiece of this classic dining room, the massive stone fireplace called the "General Braddock Fireplace" (so named because it contained stone taken from the camp used by the British general during a winter he spent on the grounds of the present preserve) drew everyone's attention to the magnificent mounted moose above the mantelpiece.

The Club's grandiose venison dinners during the early years often began with words

Courtesy David P. Bridges.

During the early days, the membership hunted whitetails on horseback and the deer hunt took on the air of a rigorous military campaign.

of thanks from Oliver Goldsmith's poetical epistle "The Haunch of Venison" (1776):

"Thanks, my Lord, for your venison,
for finer or fatter
Never ranged on a forest
or smoked in a platter.
The haunch was a picture
for painters to study,
The fat was so white,
and the lean was so ruddy,
Though my stomach was sharp,
I could scare help regretting
To spoil such a delicate picture
by eating."

As the Bordeaux wine freely flowed, other sportsmen and men of letters rose to give toasts and quoted Sir Walter Scott (1771-1832):

"The Monarch saw the gambols flag,
And bade let loose a gallant stag,
Whose pride, the holiday to crown
Two favorite greyhounds should pull down,
That venison free, and Bordeaux wine,
Might serve the archery to dine."

Archibald Rutledge, known as "Old Flintlock," a close friend of Henry Bridges who served as the long-time Secretary/ Treasurer and Hunt Master and who the Maryland Conservationist called the "club's

(Left) Archibald Rutledge ("Old Flintlock") hung out at Woodmont and chased "the buck with the wide-branching horns!" (Right) "A Big One!" painting by artist J. G. Woods.

sparkplug," added choice poetical eloquence of his own while attending one of Woodmont's legendary stag parties. Standing in front of the "General Braddock Fireplace" he delivered this aristocratic, buckhorn epistle:

O it's not the bull moose of New Brunswick,
Or Wyoming's wapiti tall,
Or Canada's caribou tall,
Or the Kodiak bear
That I see and I hear
When I vision the forest of fall:

It's the buck with the wide-branching horns!
My stratagems wary he scorns,
My artifice wily he scorns.
He is haunting my dreams
Of the mountains and streams.

My evenings, my nights, and my morns,
The buck with the wide-branching horns!

When red is the reedland at sunrise,
And mallard and teal are in flight,
And gray goose and black-duck in flight,
Many men of good breed
Find the sport that they need,
But mine is a different delight:

It's the buck with the wide-branching horns!
His beauty the wildwood adorns,
His wonder the wildwood adorns.
He is haunting my dreams
Of the mountains and streams,
My evenings, my nights and my morns,
The buck with the wide-branching horns!

The Seal of the Club consisted of a stag's head with the motto "Protect and Enjoy." The elite membership loved to hunt the white-tailed deer and turkeys at Woodmont best of all, as member John J. Jackson's poem of December 1935 clearly reveals:

WOODMONT

We've hunted grouse in British Isles
And bear in Hudson Bay,
We've hunted pheasants, quail and duck
All through the U.S.A.

We've hunted stags in Scotland
Where heather hides the hare.
We've hunted, too, in India,
The tiger in its lair.

We've hunted boar in Germany,
We've trekked the caribou,
We've stalked the moose in Canada
And hunted lions too.

We've hunted sundry elephants
O'ver Africa's hot sands,
We've hunted other great big game
In many other lands.

But still the hunt we love the best,
For deer and turkeys grand,
Is Bridges' hunt at Woodmont Club
In the hills of Maryland.

As a result of a chance meeting in 1880 on a streetcar in Washington D.C. between Robert Lee Hill, an unknown Maryland mountaineer from Hancock, and Rear Admiral Robley Dunglison Evans, the Woodmont Rod and Gun Club came into existence. On the Fourth of July in 1881, the membership of twenty-five sportsmen celebrated the grand opening of their new clubhouse designed by Walker, an eminent builder of Washington, D.C. The distinguished membership arrived that day at noon in a special train car from Washington. A twenty-one gun salute from a howitzer with the Stars and Stripes waving in the breeze on a tall flagstaff greeted their arrival. The menu for the five o'clock dinner was printed on heavy white satin:

Soup
Mock Turtle
Fish
Boiled Rock – Lemon Sauce
Meats
Venison Roast. Roast Beef. Corned Beef.
Baked Ham. Roast Lamb.
Vegetables
Mashed Potatoes. Boiled Onions.
Peas, Raw Tomatoes. Baked Beans.
Salads
Cold Slaw. Lettuce. Shrimp.
Fruits. Nuts. Coffee. Cigars.

A special correspondent for *Forest and Stream*, writing under the pseudonym "Senex" (Latin for Old Man) reported that "the wines were extremely fine and in the greatest abundance." A. H. Evans, President of the Club, rose to the glorious occasion and gave the initial toast by quoting the Venison Verses written by Joseph Barber:

Daintily, daintily, graze the deer
On the autumn glade grass scented,
Royal their rest in the forest sere
On autumnal foliage tinted,
Sleek their skins, and their haunches round,
As they shake their antlers proudly,
Rampant with fatness they paw the ground
And snort in their coverts loudly.

Hurriedly, hurriedly, fly the deer
Through the wildwood thickets springing,
Merrily sounds the hunter's cheer
Through the wildwood arches ringing.

Crack! And down goes a lovely doe,
Marked out from the herd's confusion,
'Twas the crack of doom and
she found it so,
As she jumped to her last conclusion.

Daintily, daintily, on the air
An aroma rich is stealing,
Through the nasal flumes in a volume rare
It rolls to the seat of feeling.
A haunch, a haunch, from the doe of does,
That we shot the verse preceding,
Oh! Cut me a slice, for the Lord, He knows
That I love luxurious feeding.

Yes, cut me a slice where the loin and leg
Are each into each extended,
Let a piece of the white as firm as an egg,
With the rosy lean be blended.
Of jelly and gravy, give quantum suf.,
No, I thank you, no potato,
Let life be jolly, 'tis short enough,
And a fig for such muffs as Plato.

"Luxurious feeding" was indeed a major motif of the Woodmont Rod and Gun Club from the very beginning. As the vintage red wine flowed, General R. C. Drum soon followed with stanzas from T. S. Van Dyke's poem "A Dilettante Sportsman," which had just appeared in that great sporting journal of the day *The American Field:*

'Twas on a clear and frosty morn,
When loudly on the air were borne
Those weird and deeply thrilling sounds,
The clanging tones of clamorous hounds.
"How sweet," said he, "that music floats
And rolls in wild tumultuous notes;
Now ringing up the mountain's side,
Now waxing, waning, like the tide,
Or swinging loud across the dell
Like Pandemonium's carnival."

Hot bounds his blood in swift career,
When bursts the uproar still more near,
And hope and fear alternate play
With bounding joy and dark dismay.

As louder, nearer, bays the pack,
Cold shivers dance along his back;
From tip to toe his nerves all tingle,
All on his head each hair doth scramble;
He feels his heart erratic beat,
He nearly melts with inward heat,
And grasps with quivering hand the gun.

And now there comes an ominous sound
Of hoofs that fiercely spurn the ground,
Close followed by sudden crash,
As through the brush with headlong dash
There bursts in view a lordly buck.
"Ye God!" he chattered, "oh, what luck!
But oh! Ain't he a splendid sight!
Those spirit-eyes! How wildly bright!

What graceful form! What glossy vest!
What massive neck! What brawny chest!
What proud defiance seem to shed
Those antlers o'er his shapely head
How in the sun they flash and shine
From rugged base to polished tine!"

After chasing the polished tines of Woodmont's white-tailed bucks all say through the hills of Maryland during the early days of the twentieth century and tasting the exquisite white-tailed venison at the lodge after the hunt, one can now only imagine seeing the great Hunt Master Bridges, Rutledge and LeCompte standing in front of the George Washington Fireplace in the Great Room pontificating on the legendary bear and deer hunting exploits of Maryland's greatest deerslayer, Meshach Browning, who hunted deer, bear and turkeys just to the west of the Woodmont Rod and

Courtesy David P. Bridges.

The Great Room, where members collected memories and told tales around the Washington Fire Place.

Gun Club in Garrett County near the Deep Creek Lake area in western Maryland a half-century earlier.

At the Woodmont Club's library amidst deerskins and bearskins, in a big, black, over-stuffed leather chair, E. Lee LeCompte, the great promoter of Browning's classic autobiography, told the tale of Meshach Browning's vicious deer/man skirmish in the Youghiogheny River with his highly cherished deerhound "Gunner" in October of 1819.

With the 1928 edition of Browning's *Forty-Four Years of the Life of a Hunter* in hand, which Maryland's first State Game Warden edited and introduced, LeCompte shared the great hunting yarn with members of the Club and with Rutledge, another great admirer of Browning's deer and bear hunting prowess. It even seems likely that A. F. Tait's artistic reenactment of this great deer hunting adventure – "The Life of a Hunter: Catching a Tartar" (1861) – decorated the wall décor at the time of this yarn-spinning.

On a glorious October morning the 28-year-old Browning found himself on the west side of the Great Youghiogheny River. On reaching the river, he took off his buckskin pants and moccasins and waded across. After he had gone a short distance, he discovered the tracks of a very large buck searching out company in the heat of the rut. In several hours of tireless tracking, he soon encountered a massive ten-pointer. After Browning badly wounded the buck with a heavy charge of buckshot, his half-breed Greyhound "Gunner" took to the heels of the animal and drove him into the river, where the dog and the buck engaged in a desperate battle. Due to the river's deepness, neither hound nor deer could get a foothold.

Meshach left his gun on shore, as we see in A. F. Tait's popular oil on canvas, and

"How in the sun they flash and shine From rugged base to polished tine!"

quickly waded in with his "fighting" knife, a weapon with a ten-inch blade honed to a razor sharp edge and kept that way. The knife was a "Green River" made by E. Barnes and Son in Greenfield, Massachusetts, one of the best-known knifemakers of the era. When he reached the buck, he seized its antlers while Gunner floated helplessly downstream. A long scuffle ensued as the famed, masculine Maryland deerslayer and his wounded quarry floated downstream in deep water in an endless desperate attempt to end each other's life. With both of Browning's hands attached to his antlers, the buck threw his head from side to side. Browning's arms felt like they were being jerked from the sockets. In his chilling memoirs, Meshach described the outcome. LeCompte quoted the text:

"[Finally] when his strength was but little, I held fast to his upper horn with my left hand, and keeping my foot firmly on his lower horn, I pressed it to the bottom of three feet of water and, taking out my knife, when

The tales of Maryland's legendary deer hunter Meshach Browning, who shot as many as 26 deer in one day, often dominated the fireside storytelling at Woodmont. Illustration of Meshach and "Gunner" taking down "Old Bruin" by Charles Louis LaSalle, 1953. *Courtesy Outdoor Life / Wrights Reprints.*

his kicking was nearly over, I let his head come up high enough to be within reach, when at a single cut I laid open the one side of his neck, severing both blood vessels. This relieved me from one of the more difficult positions in which, during all my life, I had been placed."

It was not uncommon for Meshach to kill 26 deer in one day. On Meadow Mountain one day he killed two large black bears before breakfast. LeCompte reassured his attentive listeners in the Woodmont library that "few, if any of us, will ever have such sport as the hardy pioneer, Browning, enjoyed in search of his supply of winter meat, hunting bears armed with an old flintlock or at times only a knife, catching deer barehanded in the snow and lying out under the cold stars in his meager blanket."

"Old Flintlock," the Southern squire from the legendary Hampton Plantation, the studious-looking schoolmaster of English literature from the Mercersburg Academy, nodded his approval of LeCompte's remarks and added his own commentary on this adventurous escapade as well:

"This rugged wilderness hunter has managed

Meshach Browning and his cherished deerhound Gunner.
Dust jacket illustration, 1928. Illustrator unknown.

LeCompte also re-created the classic Browning/bear confrontation that stimulated a great deal of artwork over the past 150 years by such artists as A. F. Tait. Edward Stabler, Currier & Ives, Charles La Salle, Lee Teter, Wayne Hyde and others. This desperate fight with an enormous wounded black bear on Meadow Mountain on May 17, 1829, became a legendary tale told often at the Woodmont Rod and Gun Club. Theodore Roosevelt read, re-read and quoted Browning's classic account of it in his autobiography with great delight.

On that day in 1829, while bear hunting on Meadow Mountain with Gunner and another, younger deerhound, Browning suddenly encountered an enormous black bear pawing up leaves in search of acorns. After telling the hounds to stay, Meshach slowly pursued the bear. As he got into close position for a deadly shot, the hounds suddenly charged the bear, forcing Meshach to rush the shot. The sound of the bang resounded along the mountainside as the hounds sprang on Old Bruin like mad tigers.

The young, inexperienced hound attempted to seize the bear by its head, a move vividly portrayed in Charles La Salle's heroic 1953 illustration. Browning then fired a second shot, hitting the bear too far back from the vital organs. But the bear dropped to the ground as Meshach mounted Old Bruin and began stabbing him with his deadly Green River knife. After grotesquely groaning, sounding somewhat like a human being, the bear collapsed dead in its tracks.

During his lifetime Browning shot more than 2000 whitetails and 500 black bears in the western Maryland area near the Woodmont preserve, and the tales of these momentous big game hunts echoed throughout the halls of Woodmont, especially when LeCompte and Rutledge visited the club. Only one Woodmont member, Henry Bridges, ever downed a black bear on the club property. With a rifle shot well-placed behind the bear's front shoulder, he dropped a four hundred-

to preserve for us, as a part of our American heritage, not alone the record of his many adventures as a sportsman in the wilds of a primeval world, but has miraculously managed to savor his story with his simple yet felicitous descriptions of the birds, the game, the wild flowers, the stately forest, the silent glades, the bubbling crystal springs, the changes of the seasons, the reticent valleys retiring into mystery, the lonely mountains.

"And he mentions names that should be dear to us because they connote pioneer America and give appeal and authenticity to his work. He lets the light in on the fading past when he speaks of the Glades, Meadow Mountain, Little Crossings, Flintstone Creek, Indian Spring. Nor should we ever forget the valiant girl who gladly shared the pioneer's hardships, she who was always to Meshach Browning his Blooming Rose."

Before the night of yarn-spinning ended in front of the George Washington Fireplace,

"To see a whitetail in the woods is to see many things. It is, for one, to see the very essence of speed and gracefulness."

pound male and his hunting knife encountered its first bear blood. The membership of the club consumed the bear meat, and the bearskin gracefully rested on the floor of the clubhouse lounge for many years.

"To see a whitetail in the woods is to see many things," Henry P. Bridges, the active Secretary-Treasurer of the Club for more than 50 years, fondly reminded his fellow club members. "It is, for one, to see the very essence of speed and gracefulness. And it is to see a good deal of this country's past history, and it is also to see an animal that has survived all of mankind's unwitting attempts to exterminate it."

The legendary Woodmont deer hunts consisted primarily in deer drives under Bridges' skilled leadership with the assistance of Fillmore Bishop, woodsman and Woodmont deer hunting guide par excellence. On one of these drives Bishop, revealing his uncanny knowledge of white-tailed buck behavior, told Mrs. R. K. Mellon, the wife of Major General Richard K. Mellon to stand at a certain spot between two oak trees. "Keep your eyes on those trees. I'll drive a big buck between them for you," he told Mrs. Mellon. As the drive began, Fillmore bayed like a deerhound and unerringly drove a massive buck toward the gunner. As promised, a handsome buck soon turned up between the oak trees. Bang! Bang! went Mrs. Mellon's deluxe double barrel Parker shotgun loaded with slugs and the buck hit the turf, never to recover.

On December 15, 1920, Burt Knight of Fairmont, West Virginia, downed the largest whitetail ever taken on these deer drives: a 320-lb.-field-dressed 18-pointer whose pictures graced the walls of the clubhouse lounge for many years. In one photo of the clubhouse lounge we see an altar-like sideboard on which rests the "Monarch of the Glen." This fully-mounted, massive white-tailed buck stands there in regal splendor. Could it be the Knight buck? The whereabouts of that buck shot by Knight, however, remains unknown today.

The classic deer drives at Woodmont turned into great sporting events punctuated with that chronic malady, buck fever. In an article in *Outdoorsman Magazine,* Bridges describes a 1937 deer drive:

Courtesy David P. Bridges.

A morning's bag of whitetails at Woodmont. During the holidays, Bridges frequently sent the venison to the White House for presidential Christmas dinners. Standing, from left: G. Tyler Smith; John Kennedy; Judge Thad A. Cox; Dr. James A. Lyon; Dr. Walker A. Denny; ex-Congressman James T. Begg; and F. S. Henderson. Sitting, from left: Henry B. Mann; Ott Booth; Henry P. Bridges; Otis R. Johnson; and Dr. U. G. Jones.

"My companions were Congressman John Cooper of Youngstown and James T. Begg of Cleveland, Ohio, but only the latter had a license to shoot deer. The guide stationed Cooper and myself at points where deer were likely to pass when the drive got underway. We stood for perhaps an hour when there was a disturbance in the brush nearby and a big buck crossed in the open directly in front of us.

"From our vantage point we could see Mr. Begg taking careful aim, but before he pulled the trigger, the buck was out of sight. I looked at the Congressman but before I could say a word, there came sounds of a hurricane sweeping through the leaves and several deer appeared in the open place. This time our friend with the gun blazed away without stopping the hurried exit of the fleeing quarry. Mr. Begg turned around and looked at us for almost five minutes, too stunned, surprised or disgusted to utter a sound, but finally he did speak this one sentence, 'A whole trainload of deer and only one shot – a miss!' The deer hunting was

sporty and there was never a guarantee that the hunters could get their deer."

Bridges took a keen interest in world-class whitetails and played an instrumental role in crossbreeding Michigan and Wisconsin whitetails with Maryland deer. As Maryland deer reached near extermination in 1902, state officials prohibited deer hunting state-wide in Maryland. By the turn of the twentieth century, deer populations had been eliminated from all but the remote areas of western Maryland. Bridges and concerned sportsmen at the Woodmont Rod and Gun Club purchased 13 deer from Michigan in 1914 and again in 1933 bought 67 deer from Michigan and Wisconsin. When the Woodmont herd expanded to its limits of vegetation, Bridges released deer into Washington County.

As Bridges's grandson David Bridges notes in his book *The Bridges of Washington County* (2003), "Bridges's deer program at Woodmont was as productive as the turkey program. Trapping pens were located throughout the preserve, allowing for the easy capture of animals. The traps were baited with corn; when a deer entered, the doors fell shut behind it. Animals were crated and shipped on the Western Maryland railroad to buyers. Bridges himself went out into the preserve and shot the venison for the tables of Woodmont. By culling the herd Henry was able to leave the best animals for members and guests."

At Woodmont, Bridges shot hundreds of white-tailed deer with his Winchester .351 repeater rifle and with only one hand; he lost his left hand in a shooting accident. On one deer hunt he shot five deer with four shots, as one whitetail ran beside another. As he orchestrated the deer drives for his guests, he never ceased to amaze them with his incredible marksmanship despite his handicap. In December of 1935 he shot white-tailed venison for President Franklin Delano Roosevelt's Christmas table.

The Woodmont Rod and Club's innovative, historic efforts under Bridges's leadership to increase deer herd numbers and improve genetics as early as 1914 eventually resulted not only in the comeback of the Maryland deer herd but in some incredible Boone & Crockett Maryland bucks as well. We think of course of Bill Crutchfield's 26-pointer with a total, non-typical score of 268-4/8 inches taken in southern Charles County, Maryland, in 2006. And we also remember Kevin Miller's "Marsh Monster" taken on November 30, 2002, in a frost-covered alfalfa field in Kent County. The massive, twelve-point buck he got that day from his tree stand known as "The Hotel" netted a typical Boone & Crockett score of 194-0/8 inches with an inside spread of 22-2/8 inches.

Ultimately, Woodmont represented a unique deer camp paradise. Its majestic and rugged mountains and comfortable quarters seemed like a dream. Fine venison cuisine, warm beds, great fellowship and stimulating conversations in front of massive fireplaces all heightened the excitement. The hunters bonded in the deer woods and fine fellowship reigned supreme in the Clubhouse around the two massive solid wood tables in the dining hall. The Woodmont Rod and Gun Club remained an "Old English Style" hunting club in the romantic European tradition and was dedicated to the ideal of male bonding, a sentiment expressed by Edgar A. Guest's great poem "Out Fishing," which hung on the wall.

A feller isn't thinking mean, Out fishing,
His thoughts are Mostly good and clean,
Out fishing,
He doesn't knock his fellow-men,
Or harbor any grudges then;
A feller's at his finest when
Out fishing,
The rich are comrades to the poor,
Out fishing, All are brothers
of a common lure, Out fishing, The urchin,
with his pin and string,
Can chum with millionaire or king;
Vain pride is a forgotten thing,
Out fishing,
A feller gets a chance to dream,
Out fishing,
He learns the beauties of the stream,
Out fishing, And he can wash his soul in air,
That isn't foul with selfish care,
And relish plain and simple fare,
Out fishing,
A feller has not time for hate, Out fishing,
He isn't eager to be great, Out fishing,
He isn't thinking thoughts of self,
Or goods stacked high upon his shelf;
But he is always just himself, Out fishing.
A feller's glad to be a friend,
Out fishing,
A helping hand he'll always lend,
Out fishing,
The brotherhood of rod and line,
An' sky and stream always fine;
Men come real close to God's design,
Out fishing.

In reading these romantic lines one can still hear those quick-rhythmic mountain songs echoing through the hunting lodge: "Turkey in the Straw," "Coming Around the Mountain" and "Hagerstown Girl" as played by Woodmont's inimitable in-house mountain fiddler Harvey Van Gosen, who drank liquor "continuously and copiously" but who nevertheless played sweet mountain music on his so-called $50,000 genuine Stradivarius. Frequently as not, Van Gosen was accompanied by William Elkins on the accordion, a duo the likes of whom no American deer camp will ever hear again. They became the favorites of two American presidents and numerous notables, including many club members and guests.

Writing in the *Baltimore Morning Sun,* the legendary outdoor writer Tom McNally in his "Water and Woods" column described Woodmont as a "rod and gun paradise, a distant Land-of-Oz, where a tiny group of Lotus Eaters live in a world apart. It is a remnant of the age of sporting elegance." Indeed, Woodmont retained an aura of deer camp romance and emotional excitement; its classic deer hunting illustrations and paintings by Lynn Bogue Hunt, Bob Kuhn, Tom Beecham, Philip R. Goodwin, Carl Rungius and others stirred the deer-hunting imagination and heightened white-tailed buck fever, while Remington rifles and Core-Lokt Cartridges provided the deer hunters with a "sure cure for buck fever."

Many Woodmont deer hunters used Remingtons – "Fastest guns in the woods!" – including Babe Ruth, the Sultan of Swat, who deer hunted at the Woodmont Club and also starred in Remington gun ads. While I was growing up in the deer woods during the late 1950s, my dad gave me an old single barrel 12-gauge shotgun on unknown vintage

Fastest guns in the woods!

For game on the move, here are two rugged, dependable big-game rifles with repeat-shot speed and accuracy you can't beat anywhere.

The Remington Model 742. Its lightweight, automatic action is incredibly fast and accurate—lets you squeeze off five aimed shots in five seconds! And it's *the only automatic built to handle the powerful and versatile 30/06 cartridge.* Also in 6mm Rem., 280 Rem., 308 Win. New, de luxe grade features now include richer stock finish,

beautiful custom checkering, and a decorated grip cap.

The Remington Model 760 is the fastest hand-operated big-game rifle made. Well-balanced, accurate and light, with the extra dependability that makes Remington pump guns so popular. Power, too: five-shot capacity in 30/06, 280 Rem., 270 Win., 308 Win., 35 Rem. and six in 223 Rem. Same new, de luxe grade features as Model 742. Write for free Guns and Ammunition catalog to Dept. XC-11, Remington Arms Company, Inc.

Remington Arms Company, Inc., Bridgeport, Conn. 06602. In Canada: Remington Arms of Canada Limited, 36 Queen Elizabeth Blvd., Toronto, Ont. "Fair Trade retail prices in states having Fair Trade laws. Prices subject to change without notice.

Remington **DUPONT**

Model 742 Automatic Rifle, from $149.95*

Model 760 Pump-action Rifle, from $129.95*

Many Woodmont deer hunters used Remingtons – "Fastest guns in the woods!" – including Babe Ruth, the Sultan of Swat.

and a couple of slugs. But I soon acquired a Remington Model 742 semi-automatic and quickly learned one important lesson: no matter how many white-tailed deer hunts one makes or how many white-tailed bucks one downs, the deer hunter will forever remember the first trophy and what happened at deer camp after the hunt that day.

As I write the closing lines of this chapter I find myself reading *Deer Hunting with Jesus* (2007), in which Joe Bageant, in his excellent analysis of deer camp culture, describes in a most memorable way the aftermath of his first deer hunt in the fall of 1957 on the family farm in the southern uplands of Winchester, Virginia:

"Late in the day, after dressing the deer and hanging them on the back porch to chill,

One can just imagine Babe Ruth, who hunted at Woodmont, saying "Blackie, I'd have shot more bucks but I ran out of bumpers and fenders!" November 11, 1937.

we sat around the living-room woodstove, cleaned the guns, and talked about the day's hunt. To an eleven-year-old boy, the smell of gun oil and the stove's searing raw heat on the face, the polishing of blued steel and walnut, the clean raspy feel of the checkered gun grips, the warm laughter of the men, well . . . that's primal after-the hunt stuff so deep you can feel the sparks from Celtic yew log fires and the brush of bearskin leggings on your knees. It has been going on in this place and on the land for 250 years.

"The crack of distant rifle or the wild meat smell of a deer hanging under a porch light bulb on a snowy night still bewitches me with the same mountain-folk animism it did when I was a boy."

Things were different at Woodmont; it was indeed a very elaborate and elite affair, an exclusive escape into the wilds of nature. With the Western Maryland Railroad running tracks and private "hunting cars" just a few hundred yards from its idyllic setting, Washingtonians and Baltimoreans hunted white-tailed deer and turkeys in the hills of Maryland during the day and wined and dined in Washington that same evening. Those choosing to board at Woodmont enjoyed the festive board with classical hunting music such as Haydn's "The Hunt" Symphony playing in the background and with dinner conversation revolving around politics, popular culture and the emerging basic principles of wildlife – all played out in view of the magnificent Blue Ridge Mountains.

CAMP SURPRISE": MONARCH DEER VALLEY

James Dwyer, 1954. Courtesy of the Olin Corporation/Winfield Galleries LLC.

E very deer camp has a special mythic buck, a monarch of monumental proportions as we see in James Dwyer's "Deer Camp Surprise" that eludes the hunter with his mocking white-tailed adieu, and Rob's Deer Valley is no exception. But the 5-1/2-year-old Monarch of Deer Valley eventually went to the library wall for graceful display in April of 2006, but not without slipping through my fingers on many occasions "like the thread of a beautiful dream." Indeed, I missed him twice on one-woman drives in 2004 made by my wife Maren. Following T. S. Van Dyke's advice, I hunted this buck for three years to study him and studied him to hunt him in the true hunter-naturalist tradition. Over time I came to believe that he observed and studied me more than I studied and observed him.

One night in late August 2005, I passed through the tall foxtail grass of The Orchard on my compact Case International. I suddenly saw his rack fifteen yards to my right. I never

This 1954 promotional poster portrays the Winchester Model 70 as the All-American Deer Rifle. Indeed, nothing better defines our deer hunting culture and heritage than such classic rifles of deer camp as the Winchester Model 70. This Opening Day scenario remains engraved in the memories of millions of white-tailed deer hunters nationwide from all walks of life.

The Monarch of Deer Valley scraping in the orchard at 10:45 PM on November 4, 2005.

Rob Wegner.

flinched or changed the speed of the tractor as I approached him; he never moved. I believe he knew that I knew he was there as I went past him. On another occasion with the moon almost full, I suddenly came out of the marsh along the Blue Mounds Creek and stepped into an alfalfa field. And there he stood within twenty-five yards of me. As if he came out of nowhere! And was just there! That mass of velvet under the moonlight and his hasty retreat back into the morass of Roelke Swamp will remain etched in my memory forever.

While studying and hunting this buck I re-read the deer hunting stories of William Faulkner, especially his classic deer hunting tale "The Old People," which begins with that great one-liner: "At first there was nothing." It's what every writer and deer hunter confronts: the blank page, the unfocused gaze in the early morning darkness of November. Then suddenly the white-tailed buck materializes:

"Then the buck was there. He did not come into sight; he was just there, looking not like a ghost but as if all of light were condensed in him and he were the source of it, not only moving in it but disseminating it, already running, seen first as you always see the deer, in that split second after he has already seen you, already slanting away in that first soaring bound, the antlers even in that dim light looking like a small rocking-chair balanced on his head." In reading Faulkner's deer hunting stories one soon realizes that deer hunting for Faulkner became a form of writing and imaging. His brilliant tale of the white-tailed buck, the boy and the mentor is poetic, concrete, aphoristic and haunting.

I moved to The Uplands of Wisconsin's Iowa County in 1983 to study and pursue white-tailed deer. Over the years The Monarch of Deer Valley continued to haunt me and brought me into several close nerve-racking encounters only to slip away with grace and defiance while waving a farewell mockery to me, the former editor of *Deer & Deer Hunting* magazine, with his white flag blowing in the breeze – a bitter adieu to several failed still hunts in the heart of "The Uplands."

Iowa County lies within the Driftless Area of southwestern Wisconsin and is generally known as "The Uplands." Its rolling hills and lush, fertile valleys make it particularly beautiful when the oak leaves turn to the color of wine in October. When the autumn colors of the mixed hardwoods intermingle with the majestic rock formations and spectacular outcroppings, The Uplands serve as a refuge for the whitetail hunter's spirit as well as a refuge for his quarry, the white-tailed deer; I cannot conceive of these beautiful bluffs, steep slopes, hidden valleys and saturated meadows without whitetails.

This region not only presents one of the most picturesque arrays of landscapes in the state but during the 1980s produced more deer than any other county in the Badger State. You do not need to climb the observation towers at Blue Mounds or stand on the Mississippi River bluffs at Wyalusing State Park to see the splendid views of valley bottoms, steep, forested bluffs, and cropped fields dotted with dramatic numbers of white-tailed deer; this picturesque landscape with its dynamic population of whitetails seems to be almost everywhere. You see it as you travel through the Wyoming Valley to view Taliesin, the magnificent home of world-famous architect, Frank Lloyd Wright; you experience it as you travel through the wooded hillsides of oak, birch, aspen, and black cherry to New Glarus for the annual performance of Schiller's drama of Swiss patriotism, Wilhelm Tell. The intimacy of these secluded valleys filled with fox-colored deer eating alfalfa during the summer rivets itself into the mind of the deer hunter and heightens anticipation.

Yet, this beautiful landscape was once devoid of white-tailed deer. According to Aldo Leopold's *Game Survey of Wisconsin* (1931), man originally exterminated them as early as 1880. By then the deer population in The Uplands was virtually wiped out. In his *History of Wisconsin Deer* (1946), Ernie Swift, the director of the Conservation

Courtesy Wegner's Deer & Deer Hunting Photo Collection.

Pa, who could spit tobacco at great distances, always chased the big monarchs of "The Uplands" with pistol, knife, and hatchet and Remington rifle in hand. He always wore a tie. "And don't forget that, Kid!" he would always say.

Department during the late 1940s, compared the disappearing deer herd with a fading April snow bank. "As soon as the black prairie sod had been turned under and the mighty hardwoods burned away, the state's last big game animal was declared a public enemy for jumping stake-and-rider fences to nip off carrots and tender young wheat. Under the constant pressure of pioneer farming, the deer herds of southern Wisconsin faded away like an April snow bank."

Indeed, the deer seemed to vanish from The Uplands like the infamous Ghost of Ridgeway after one of his nocturnal raids on McKillip's Saloon – an infamous place in its own right on Old Military Road for deerslay-

Like Pa, Aunt Agnes was an Uplands buck hunter in her own right, who loved high-top leather boots, high-class Winchester rifles and hung out at McKillip's Saloon. When not there or in the deer woods she worked as a librarian. A Diana-like huntress by avocation. Circa, 1904.

ers with a rather soiled and dented reputation. By 1890, the very sight of white-tailed deer remained a neighborhood newsmaker; reporters gathered to study the track. For thirty-five years, the deer season in Iowa County remained closed. From 1907 to 1942, the guns stayed silent in The Uplands during the somber days of the November rut.

The story of that extermination and how the deer herd eventually recovered approximately 100 years later to the point that in 1984 man again instituted a "deer shoot" to annihilate the beast, represents a classic case history of a deer explosion. That story underscores the difficulties of managing a public resource on private property – a paradigm that is broken and in dire need of fixing as chronic deer mismanagement continues in Wisconsin.

These two still-hunting, green-horn dudes of The Uplands who preceded the author by about 107 years, look more like they're headed for McKillip's Saloon on Old Military Road near Ridgeway, Wisconsin, rather than to a legitimate deer hunt in Deer Valley on Farm #12.

In that 1984 deer season, gun hunters killed 12,308 deer in Management Unit 70A. Bow hunters killed 931 deer and the automobile eliminated 534 deer for a grand total of 13,773 deer – making The Uplands the leading deer-producing area in the state at the time. Today, almost two decades later, the white-tailed deer is again a neighborhood newsmaker in The Uplands with the outbreak of Chronic Wasting Disease, a disease with a low 1.3 percent rate of incidence overall that is symptomatic of a larger problem: deer overabundance and deer mismanagement that go unresolved.

As a result of this $30 million dollar-plus mismanaged fiasco and the impossible, unnecessary and irrational white-tailed deer "eradication" war that followed, 3-1/2-year-old bucks in 2002 safely moved on into the older age classes, becoming 5-1/2- and 6-1/2-year-old deer, because many deer hunters and landowners in The Uplands stopped hunting and/or chose to hunt elsewhere. As a result, The Monarch of Deer Valley acquired a longer lease on life and successfully negotiated crossing a busy Country Truck highway for 5-1/2 years, unlike many of his fallen cohorts.

In the fifth year of its life this buck taught me more about what makes a 5-1/2-year-old white-tailed buck tick than anything else I ever learned in more than thirty years of deer hunting and book reading. He took me into the insurmountable morass of Roelke Swamp and when I saw where he bedded there on numerous occasions I became convinced he was "unkillable" on a one-on-one. And after many failed one-woman drives and numerous still-hunts ad infinitum I reached the same conclusion and took solace in Archibald Rutledge's optimistic statement on deer-hunting failure with regard to his persistent chase of the elusive Black-Horn Buck:

"It is now many years since I first became acquainted with the Black-Horn Buck. Still he roams my plantation woods and in the summer helps himself to my peas and corn. And still I am privileged to love and admire him, for he has taught me that the natural world can develop a great personality. And whenever a hunting season passes without proving disastrous to him, I rejoice that his magnificent ebony crown is not drying out at some taxidermists, but is thrusting aside dewy pine boughs in the moonlight or, deep in a fragrant bed of ferns and sweet-bay, is affording the shy moonbeams something really mystic on which to sparkle."

In early December 2004, I found his left shed antler with twelve points – "a magnificent ebony crown" as Rutledge would have it. I easily found it in the open alfalfa field where he fed and bedded during the nighttime hours. But it took me another six weeks in which I logged over 60 hours to locate the right beam which sported eight points – making The Monarch of Deer Valley a 20-pointer at 4-1/2 years old with an estimated 20-inch inside spread. My friend and neighbor Mark Peck – a die-hard whitetail hunter – scored the sheds at 173-4/8 Boone and Crockett typical points.

The right beam I found high on an oak ridge in his bed overlooking the entire valley where he could see all of our human movements and activities. Drawing a straight line between the shed locations approximated 300 yards. At that site I found his tracks and deer beans amidst nine different beds in the snow. Finding the right beam that cold, crisp January day in 2005, brought greater joy and elation than taking possession of The Monarch of Deer Valley itself later in the year. I studied the trails coming and leaving his bedding site and later still-hunted that area but to no avail.

In his third and fourth years The Monarch

The author with the 21-point, 5-1/2-year-old Monarch of Deer Valley that scored 185-6/8 typical and his shed antlers from the previous year, which scored 173-4/8 Boone & Crocket.

of Deer Valley remained highly visible in the daylight hours. But as he entered his fifth year he became extraordinarily elusive and nocturnal. His core areas remained consistent and very small: Buck Hill, The Orchard, The Pines and Roelke Swamp. My sightings of this buck remain consistent with the current scientific findings of Professor Nancy Mathews, an Associate Professor in the Gaylord Nelson Institute for Environmental Studies at the University of Wisconsin - Madison and her Graduate Student Lesa Skuldt in the Department of Wildlife Ecology. In their radio-telemetry work on white-tailed deer movements in The Uplands they conclude that adult bucks maintain smaller home ranges of less than 1/2 to 1/3 square mile. His core area consisted of less than 120 acres. In that area he had everything he needed: alfalfa, apples, corn, acorns, spring water, a dense swamp, a thick pine plantation to winter in, and mates.

After a three-year hunt and after entering the author's dreams on a number of occasions, The Monarch of Deer Valley fell in November of 2005, scoring 185-6/8 Boone & Crockett gross typical points.

Mark Peck.

During the peak of the rut in 2005, I saw him make a mid-day, 100-yard beeline across the alfalfa field from Buck Hill to a spring-fed stream leading to the Blue Mounds Creek to drink water. His tracks at the base of a large cottonwood tree at the stream's bank indicated he did this watering maneuver frequently, but I only observed it once. In studying the runways crossing the stream throughout the valley it became apparent that all deer in the valley have definite and distinct places they prefer to water at. A general consensus of opinion among deer researchers indicates that deer have a daily requirement of about one and a half quarts of water per 100 pounds of body weight in winter and about two or three quarts of water per 100 pounds of body weight in summer.

His large tracks and large deer beans led me to Buck Hill, where I found his rubs on cedar trees with circumferences of eight to twelve inches. When I finally got a picture of him on the Cuddeback digital camera at 10:25 PM on November 4, 2005, we see him scraping in a very large scrape that completely surrounded an apple tree with several overhanging branches. That highly active communal scrape maintained a diameter of almost ten feet. In eight days with the camera

on during the first week of November, I got 213 deer photos, but only one photo (#192) of The Monarch of Deer Valley. Why? Was he being spooked by the flash? Was he the prime breeder buck? Or was he in the preservation mode? These questions go unanswered.

Every deer passing through this area engaged itself with this scraped deer turf. I once watched The Monarch approach this massive scrape at midday with my 60X Kowa TSN-822 spotting scope. With a southeast wind he traveled nose into the wind through a narrow, 75-yard long rectangular area of dense, heavy brush laced with stinging nettle and red sorrell of the buckwheat family. He spent a half hour traveling about 75 yards towards the scrape – frequently standing still for long periods of time. It was so thick I sometimes could only see a vague image of him – "a shadow lurking in a shadow," as Paulina Brandreth would say. He eventually stopped five feet from the scrape, stood still for several minutes and then quickly departed at around twelve noon – running cross wind toward another scrape I had seen him at earlier.

After many failed one-woman drives and even more unsuccessful still hunts, I returned to stand hunting as the rut intensified. The end came quickly and in a very humane fashion:

a neck shot at 75 yards with a Browning A-Bolt II Hunter in .270 WSM. That critical moment when the Red Gods smiled I will never forget; it was a gift from nature.

With clear skies and a prevailing southwesterly wind blowing into my 4'x6' homemade wooden shack placed in an elevated position overlooking an alfalfa field, a doe and her fawn slowly passed by traveling toward the east. As they passed by I turned toward the west and The Monarch of Deer Valley was suddenly there – as if he came out of nowhere. He was just there in the open.

That critical moment became primeval and changeless. What a romantic, fantastic moment – a Boone & Crockett buck moving pass providing me with a broadside shot in the heart of Deer Valley. I began to allow him to walk into the cross hairs. I looked to the left; the doe and her fawn stopped. The buck also stopped, but between two large walnut branches forcing me to try a neck shot. All three deer remained unaware of my presence. Bang! went the Browning 270 A-Bolt II with the WSM cartridge sending the bullet through the neck.

I field dressed him with my favorite deer-hunting knife: an A. G. Russell 8A given to me by Skip Braden. Mark Peck green-scored the 21-pointer with a 21-inch inside spread at 185-6/8 gross Boone & Crockett typical points.

When I returned without The Monarch of Deer Valley from Bill Hetzel's The "Alive Look" Taxidermy Shop in Bear Valley the next day I still saw all the ghost-like imagery of his magnificent escapes up Buck Hill and into the heart of Roelke Swamp and his flashy exits from The Orchard and dramatic dashes upslope into The Pines. The ebony-stained, heavily- beaded antlers weaving their way through the Goldenrod and Cocklebur along the alfalfa field will remain engrained in my mind forever.

The morning star still hung over The Orchard that morning as I returned from Bill Hetzel's Taxidermy Shop, but my deer mentor – The Monarch of Deer Valley – was gone; there was no more to be learned from this noble old boy in the hunter-naturalist tradition. He now existed only in my mind and memory. I knew there would be a replacement with his genes; but my eyes watered nonetheless as I drove up Deer Valley and passed all his old familiar intimate haunts and recreated in my mind all of his romantic, ghost-like imagery that so dazzled me with anticipation as I pushed the chase to the limits; for I already missed all the fun and suspense, the romance and excitement that he provided for me, my family and my deer-hunting friends.

He lived close to the household and my study windows in particular and all members of the household observed and talked about him for three delightful years. On many occasions we would see his ghost-like image pass by the sun room and disappear into the cedars and rock outcroppings of Buck Hill. His nighttime bedding frequently occurred within less than forty yards of my study window in the alfalfa field in the moonlight. I watched him on many moonlit nights chewing his cud in the alfalfa field with a smaller 12-pointer who frequently ran with him and most of the time in the up front position. The Monarch of Deer Valley became almost a permanent fixture of Deer Valley; he was always there for me to watch and study and think and to speculate about his behavior. He was always on my mind. He entered my dreams. On November 5, 2005 – one day after showing up on my Cuddeback digital – he became a standard icon on my computer desktop. As I watched him I could hear Archibald Rutledge saying,

It's the buck with the wide-branching horns!
His beauty the wildwood adorns,
His wonder the wildwood adorns.
He is haunting my dreams,
Of the mountains and streams,
My evenings, my nights and my morns,
The buck with the wide-branch horns!

This gallant mount, done thoughtfully and artistically by the master taxidermist Bill Hetzel from Bear Valley, Wisconsin, forms the centerpiece of the Wegner Deer & Deer Hunting Library at Deer Valley.

This gallant, old fellow genuinely distinguished himself as an unconventional individual in the deer woods and will ever remain so in my mind. "There are distinct individuals in nature," Archibald Rutledge tells us in his classic essay "The Black-Horn Buck," originally published in *Wildlife in the South* (1935), "creatures whose unconventional behavior is proof of their high intelligence. Most of them are superb solitaries. Now and then we encounter complete originals. So informal and arbitrary in their deep sagacity that the mere novelty of them is refreshing. And The Black-Horn Buck is of this type."

The Monarch of Deer Valley was and is in spirit also of this type and will always remain so in my memory. I will always continue my study of the whitetail, thanks to this noble buck. I will never forget his fancy footwork and sneaky maneuvers and all those mystic and romantic disappearances amidst the stone outcroppings of Buck Hill and The Stone Quarry followed and punctuated with the mocking buck snorts. His gallant mount done thoughtfully and artistically by the master taxidermist Bill Hetzel from Bear Valley, his 4-1/2 year-old sheds, his 3-1/2 year-old left antler shed and my digital picture of him scraping under the apple tree in The Orchard will remain the cherished centerpieces of the Wegner Deer & Deer Hunting Library at Deer Valley.

Two hunters "examine the shot" after a successful hunt in 1952.

John Arneson (seen here eating his daily banana) got "his" buck in Northwestern Wisconsin in 1959, the year the state unveiled the deer management unit registration system that is still used today.

In 1957, plaid culture and the meat pole continued to invade The Corner Drug Store in Atlanta, Michigan, where prizes were given each year for the first ten white-tailed bucks on the rack.

Deer Hunters gather for Sunday Mass in Northern Wisconsin in 1957.

CHAPTER 14

POSTCARDS FROM PLAID NATION

(Courtesy Wegner's Deer & Deer Hunting Postcard Collection)

"Something happens to a man when he sits before a fire. Strange stirrings take place within him, and a light comes into his eyes which were not there before. An open flame suddenly changes his environment to one of adventure and romance."

– Sigurd Olson,
"Campfires," The Singing Wilderness, 1956.

Oh, the romance and adventure of it all, those spectacular deer camp fires and tall tales with venison hanging from the meat poles! Deer hunters seem to argue about a lot

This vintage deer-camp postcard was sent from Northern Wisconsin to Chicago on January 2, 1957.

of things these days – from management techniques to equipment usage to hunting tactics – but most agree that deer hunting's greatest, most nostalgic decade was the 1950s.

Why were the '50s so great? Maybe it was because whitetail populations were first showing signs of rebounding from the devastating market hunting era. Or maybe it can be traced to the simple fact that life generally seemed so much less complicated that it is today.

In any event, here's a postcard tribute to the great hunters and deer camp memorabilia that made Plaid Nation one of white-tailed deer hunting's most beloved subcultures!

This young Diana dressed in red nailed a nice nine-pointer at Otter Lake, New York, in 1951 – the year New Yorkers shot 31,124 whitetails.

In 1952, the L. L. Cook Co. of Milwaukee, Wisconsin, highlighted this classic postcard showing a young girl with her dad's bow-killed yearling buck.

Humor was a constant theme in postcards from the plaid era. Most of us can relate to O. W. Reese's 1958 "The Only Buck I Saw All Year" scenario and the 1953 "Raw Deal" postcard. The theme was still alive in the 1970s, both in the Back 40 at most deer camps and in the popular "beer hunting" postcard of the era.

DEER CAMP
NOSTALGIA

In A Dusty, Rustic Old Cabin

We are in a dusty, rustic old cabin
Up in the brush,
We have porcupines gnawing at the door,
And a den of skunks under the floor.

Some of the boys are cussing about the heat,
Others are complaining of cold feet,
Some of the boys sleep in pajamas,
Others in their drawers.
All these thing don't make any difference
Everybody goes to bed and everybody
snores.

Some of the boys are killing deer that's been
Dead for twenty years or more,
Others are still fighting the First World War.

Some of the boys are sitting at the table,
Hollering fifteen two and fifteen four,
With part of the cards on the floor.

A few more rounds of Roses Four,
They would still be hollering
Fifteen two and fifteen four if
All the cards were on the floor.

There is the good cook standing
By the door, he says, "Boys you have
Time for just one hand more, then
Clear the table and put on the
Plates and get ready for your
T-Bone steaks, some of you like
Them rare, some like them well,
You will eat them the way I
Cook them or go plum to Helena."

Such is life in a dusty, rustic
Old Cabin up in the brush.

– Author Unknown

Courtesy Wisconsin Historical Society.

With high-quality deer meat, a classy black 1931 Chevy Coup, a Remington Model 8 Auto Loading rifle and a Remington Model 14 Slide-Action rifle, two Minnesota hunters arrive at Fire District Station #4.

Whether at the meat pole or resting against the bumper of the old Model A Ford Coupe with "Spiky" riding the fender, the Remington Model 8 reigned supreme during the first half of the twentieth century.

"Woodie" Wheaton's Grand Lake Brook Camp, 1945

Fred Bear with a Northern Wisconsin whitetail taken in 1941, the year he joined the fledgling Wisconsin Bowhunters Association.

The wariest, craftiest and the hardest game of all to hunt is the white-tailed deer of North America. I hunt deer because I love the entire process: the preparations, the excitement, and sustained suspense of trying to match my woods lore against the finely honed instincts of these creatures. On most days spent in the woods, I come home with an honestly earned feeling that something good has taken place. It makes no difference whether I got anything; it has to do with how the day was spent.

Life in the open is one of the finest rewards. I enjoy and become completely immersed in the high challenge and increased opportunity to become for a time a part of nature. Deer hunting is a classic exercise in freedom. It is a return to fundamentals that I instinctively feel are basic and right.

I have always tempered my hunting with respect for the game pursued. I see the animal not only as a target but as a living creature with more freedom than I will ever have. I take that life if I can, with regret as well as joy, and with the sure knowledge that nature's way of fang and claw or exposure and starvation are a far crueler fate than I bestow.

– Fred Bear,
"Thoughts on Hunting"

Fred Bear's Cameron Road Deer Camp at South Mountain, Pennsylvania, 1915, where Remingtons and Winchesters prevailed. The 14-year-old boy slept in the loft of the old line shack.

Fred Bear in the classic deer camp setting while hunting whitetails in Pennsylvania.

CHAPTER REFERENCES

"Going In"

Bangor & Aroostook Railroad. *In the Maine Woods*. Maine: Bangor, 1898-1930.

Cook, Robert W. *Chasing Danforth: A Wilderness Calling*. New Hampshire: Wilderness Books, 2005.

Cronk, Oscar E. *They Called Him "Wildcat."* Missouri: Pendleton Press, 2000.

Danforth, John S. *Hunting and Trapping on the Upper Magalloway River and Parmachenee Lake: First Winter in the Wilderness*. Boston: D. Lothrop & Company 1882.

Hunter, Julia A. & Earle G. Shettleworth, Jr. *Fly Rod Crosby: The Woman Who Marketed Maine*. Maine: Tilbury House/Maine State Museum, 2000.

Ives, Edward. *George Magoon and the Down East Game War: History, Folklore and the Law*. Chicago: University of Illinois Press, 1988.

Libby, Will T. *Libby's Camps: Headwaters Aroostook River in the State of Maine*. Maine: Brooklyn Eagle Press, n. d.

Lynch, V. E. *Thrilling Adventures: Guiding, Trapping, Big Game Hunting from the Rio Grande to the Wilds of Maine*. Maine: Privately printed, 1928.

Wilson, Donald A. *Maine's Hunting Past*. South Carolina: Arcadia Publishing, 2001.

Forest City Hunting Club

Banasiak, Chester F. *Deer in Maine*. Maine: Department of Inland Fisheries and Game. January, 1961.

Bangor & Aroostook Railroad. *In the Maine Woods*. Maine: Bangor, 1905, 1907-1912.

"Big Game Season in Maine." *The American Field*. 69(2): 26. January 11, 1908.

"Bring Back Many Deer: Members of Forest City Hunting Club Return from Trip to Maine Woods." *Cleveland Leader*. November 18, 1907.

"Deer Management: 1830-1977." *Maine Fish and Wildlife*. 26(3): 37. Fall 1984.

Fawcett, Joel S. "Days of Big Bucks and Market Hunting." In *The Maine Sportsman Book of Deer Hunting* edited by Harry Vanderweide (Maine: *The Maine Sportsman*, n. d. Pages, 94-100).

Hornaday, W. T. "The Caesar Head." *Outdoor Life*. 29(4): 333. April 1912.

Hunter, Julia A. & Earle G. Shettleworth, Jr. *Fly Rod Crosby: The Woman Who Marketed Maine*. Maine: Tilbury House/Maine State Museum, 2000.

Hutchins, Leonard. "Maine's Deer Hunting History." In *The Maine Sportsman Book of Deer Hunting* edited by Harry Vanderweide (Maine: *The Maine Sportsman*, n. d. Pages, 88-92.)

Illustrated Souvenir Book of the Original Buckhorn Saloon. Texas: San Antonio, c. 1901.

Ives, Edward. *George Magoon and the Down East Game War: History, Folklore and the Law*. Chicago: University of Illinois Press, 1988.

Libby, Will T. *Libby's Camps: Headwaters Aroostook River in the State of Maine*. Maine: Brooklyn Eagle Press, n. d.

Lynch, V. E. *Thrilling Adventures: Guiding, Trapping, Big Game Hunting from the Rio Grande to the Wilds of Maine*. Maine: Privately printed, 1928.

Maine Antler and Skull Trophy Club Records Publications. Maine: Maine Big Game Publications, 1979-2006. [Volumes 1-28.]

Maine Big Game Magazine. Maine: Dover-Foxcroft, 1997-1999. [Volumes 1-3.]

Maine Sportsman. Maine: Bangor Public Library. [Monthly]. 1893-1908. 799.M2843m.

Mann, Brandon W. *Factors Affecting the Harvest of Big Game in Northern Maine, 1894-1941*. Maine: University of Maine, 1996. Honors Thesis in Wildlife Ecology.

O'Connor, David. "Deer Camp: Maine Hunting Tradition." In *The Maine Sportsman Book of Deer Hunting* edited by Harry Vanderweide (Maine: *The Maine Sportsman*, n.d. Pages, 106-109.)

Perkins, Jack. *A Guide to Deer Hunting in Maine*. Maine: Twin City Printery, Inc., c. 1954.

Potter, Arthur G., et al. *The 1907 Hunt of the Forest City Hunting Club in the Wilds of Northern Maine*. Ohio: Privately printed 1907.

Remington, Thomas K. *The Legend of the Grey Ghost and Other Tales from the Maine Woods*. S. I.: 1st Books Library, 2003.

Smith, Edmund Ware. "Jake's Rangers Hunt the Whitetail." *Upriver & Down: Stories from the Maine Woods*. New York: Holt, Rinehart and Winston, 1965. Pages, 132-148.

Speck, Frank G. *Penobscot Man: The Life History of a Forest Tribe in Maine*. New York: Octagon Books, 1970.

Stanton, Don C. *A History of the White-Tailed Deer in Maine*. Maine: Department of Inland Fisheries and Game, 1963.

The Maine Atlas and Gazetteer. Maine: DeLorme, 1999. 22nd Edition.

Van Tassel, David D. (ed.) *The Encyclopedia of Cleveland History*. Indiana: Indiana University Press in association with Case Western Reserve University and the Western Reserve Historical Society, 1996.

Vanderweide, Harry. (ed.) *The Maine Sportsman Book of Deer Hunting*. Maine: *The Maine Sportsman*, n. d.

Vickery III, James B. "Jock Darling: The Notorious 'Outlaw' of the Maine Woods." *Maine History*. 41:3: 197-213. Fall/Winter 2002.

Warner, William S. The Origins of Maine's Game Laws." *Maine Fish and Wildlife*. 25(4): 4-7. Winter 1983-1984.

Wegner, Robert. *Wegner's Bibliography on Deer & Deer Hunting*. Wisconsin: St. Hubert's Press, 1992.

————. *Legendary Deer Camps*. Wisconsin: Krause Publications, 2001.

————. "Three Weeks to Remember: The 1907 Deer Hunt." *Hunt Club Digest*. Spring 2003. Pages, 44-47.

Weight, David E. *Words From the Woods: The Personal Narratives of Maine Deer Hunters*. Maine: University of Southern Maine, 1999. M.A. Thesis.

Wilson, Donald A. *Maine's Hunting Past*. South Carolina: Arcadia Publishing, 2001.

Wenzel, William. "About Lying." *Hunting and Fishing & Other Tall Tales*. Wisconsin: Privately printed 2005. Pages, v-vii.

White, E. B. "Coon Hunt." *One Man's Meat*. Maine: Tilbury House Publishers, 1997. Pages, 214-219.

Wilson, Donald A. *Maine's Hunting Past*. South Carolina: Arcadia Publishing, 2001.

"World-Record White-Tailed Deer Head." *Zoological Society Bulletin*. September 1911. P.132.

The Balladeer of Buck Mountain

Audubon, John James. "Deer Hunting." *The American Turf Register and Sporting Magazine*. 9(9): 421-425. September 1838.

Bailey, John Wendell. *The Mammals of Virginia*. Virginia: Williams Printing, 1946.

Bell, J. M. "Hunting the Fleet-Footed Deer in Virginia." *American Field*. 79(5): 98. February 1, 1913.

Brown, Douglas Summers. "Wilburn Waters: The Legendary Hermit-Hunter of White Top Mountain." *Virginia Cavalcade*. 27(1): 42-47. Summer 1977.

Butt, Lillian Stuart. "The Wilburn Waters Portrait." The Historical Society of Washington County, Virginia. Publication Series II, No. 15. August, 1978. Page, 20.

Camuto, Christopher. *Hunting from Home*. New York: W. W. Norton & Company, 2003.

Clark, David L. "Meeting with Wilburn Waters the Celebrated Hunter and Trapper of White Top Mountain." *The Roving Artist: A Biographical Sketch*. Virginia: Privately printed, 1895. Pages, 85-87.

Coale, Charles B. *The Life and Adventures of Wilburn Waters: The Famous Hunter and Trapper of White Top Mountain*. Tennessee: The Overmountain Press, 1994. (Paperback).

————. *The Life and Adventures of Wilburn Waters: The Famous Hunter and Trapper of White Top Mountain*. Virginia: G. W. Gray & Company, 1878.

————. "A Bear Hunt in the Iron Mountain." In Clarence Gohdes (ed.), *Hunting in the Old South: Original Narratives of the Hunters* (Louisiana: Louisiana State University Press, 1967, pages 165-170).

"Death of the Buck, The." *The Spirit of the Times*. 10(24): 277. August 15, 1840.

Detweiler, Frank I. (ed.) *Wilburn Waters: A Gathering of Materials from Unpublished Out of Print Sources*. Virginia: Privately printed, no date. Limited Edtion # 147. Wisconsin State Historical Society.

Goodridge, Wilson. *Smith County History and Traditions*. Tennessee: Kingsport Press, 1932.

Hallock, Charles. "Metaphysics of Deer Hunting." *Forest and Stream*. 1(8): 120. October 2, 1873.

Handley, Jr., Charles O. & Clyde P. Patton. *Wild Mammals of Virginia*. Virginia: Virginia Commission of Game and Inland Fisheries, 1947.

Mallison, Dallas. "Ashe Pioneer Was A Rugged Man." *Mount Airy News*, clipping dated 1959, in the North Carolina Clipping File through 1975, U. N. C. Library, Chapel Hill.

Mr. Chips. *A Hound Bays in Ellsworth*. New York: Vantage Press, 1991.

Parker, Wilbur F. "Sportsmanlike Deer-Hunting." *The American Sportsman*. 3(12): 184. December 20, 1873.

Perry, Charles & Joe Coggin. *Virginia's White-Tailed Deer*. Virginia: Virginia Commission of Game and Inland Fisheries, 1978.

Perry, Octavia J. *My Head's High from Proudness*. North Carolina: John F. Blair Publisher, 1963. (Novel about Wilburn Waters.)

Reeves, Jr., Hohn Henry. *The History and Development of Wildlife Conservation in Virginia: A Critical Review*. Virginia: Virginia Polytechnic Institute, Ph.D. Dissertation, 1960.

Schullery, Paul. "Wilburn Waters." *The Bear Hunter's Century*. New York: Dodd, Mead & Company, 1988. Pages, 47-62.

Street, A. B. "Floating for Deer." *The American Sportsman*. 2(3): 44. December 2, 1872.

Taylor, Jno. M. "Deer Hunting in Virginia." *Forest and Stream*. 5(12): 188. October 28, 1875.

Thomas, William S. "A Hunt After Deer in Old Virginia." *Hunting Big Game with Gun and Kodak*. New York & London: G. P. Putnam & Sons, 1906. Pages, 151-166.

Trimble, Ruth. "Wilburn Waters: A Man for His Time." *Appalachian Heritage*. 27 (Spring): 75-77. 1999.

T.T.P. "A Deer Hunt in Southwest Virginia." *Forest and Stream*. 15(15): 295. November 11, 1880.

Virginia Atlas & Gazetteer. Maine: DeLorme, 2003. 5th Edition.

Watson, Edward A. "Notes. [Nimrod Hall, VA]." *American Field*. 40(5): 101. July 29, 1893.

_____. "Some Notes on Deer at Nimrod Hall, Bath County." *American Field*. 56(22): 453. November 30, 1901.

Wegner, Robert. "The Balladeer from Buck Mountain." *Deer & Deer Hunting*. 28(3): 92-103. October 2004.

Worth, Thomas. "Deer Hunting on Long Island." *Harpers Weekly*. 17(880): 996, 998. November 8, 1873.

E. N. Woodcock's Camp

Bronner, Simon J. *Popularizing Pennsylvania: Henry W. Shoemaker and the Progressive Uses of Folklore and History*. Pennsylvania: Pennsylvania State University Press, 1996.

_____. (ed.) *Manly Traditions: The Folk Roots of American Masculinities*. Indiana: Indiana University Press, 2005.

_____. "This Is Why We Hunt: Social-Psychological Meanings of the Traditions and Rituals of Deer Camp." *Western Folklore*. 63(1/2): 11-50. Winter 2004.

Fegely, Tom. *A Guide to Hunting Pennsylvania Whitetails*. Wisconsin: Krause Publications, 2000. 2nd Edition.

Forbes, Stanley E. et al. *The White-Tailed Deer in Pennsylvania*. Pennsylvania: The Pennsylvania Game Commission, 1971.

Hough, Emerson. "Hunting the Deer." *Let Us Go Afield*. New York & London: D. Appleton and Company, 1916. Pages, 241-259.

Lyman, Robert Ray. "The White Deer." *History of Roulet, PA and Life of Burrel Lyman*. Pennsylvania: Potter County Historical Society, 1967.

McLellan, Isaac. *Poems of the Rod and Gun*. New York: Henry Thorpe, 1886.

Rinkus, Gregg. "E. N. Woodcock: Sage of Potter County." *Pennsylvania Game News*. 75(8): 8-12. August 2005.

Sajna, Mike. *Buck Fever: The Deer Hunting Tradition in Pennsylvania*. Pennsylvania: University of Pittsburgh Press, 1990.

Shoemaker, Henry W. *Pennsylvania Deer and Their Horns*. Pennsylvania: The Faust Printing Company, 1915.

_____. *Stories of Great Pennsylvania Hunters*. Pennsylvania: The Altoona Tribune Company, 1913.

Warren, Louis S. *The Hunter's Game: Poachers and Conservationists in Twentieth Century America*. Connecticut: Yale University Pres, 1997.

Wegner, Robert. "Black Forest Deerslayer: E. N. Woodcock." *Fur-Fish-Game*. 100(1): 14-18. January 2003.

Woodcock, E. N. *Fifty Years a Hunter and Trapper*. Ohio: A. R. Harding, Publisher, 1913.

_____. *Woodcock's Method of Trapping: The Fur Bearing Animals*. Pennsylvania: Privately printed, 1907.

The Echo Lake Deer Camp

Bersing, Otis S. *A Century of Wisconsin Deer*. Wisconsin: Wisconsin Conservation Department, 1966. 2nd Edition.

Bronner, Simon J. "This Is Why We Hunt: Social-Psychological Meanings of the Traditions and Rituals of Deer Camp." *Western Folklore* 63(1/2): 11-50. Winter, 2004.

Holand, Hjalmar. "H. C. ("Bert") Scofield." *History of Door County, Wisconsin, the County Beautiful*. Chicago: S. J. Clarke, 1917. Volume 2. Pages 36-38.

Railroad Map of Wisconsin, 1887. Prepared for the Railroad Commission by Allan D. Conover. Reproduced by the *Wisconsin Trails Magazine*.

Robertson, Jim. "Claim to Oldest Hunter Dies with 'Bert.'" (Unidentified newspaper clipping attached to Scofield's Hunting Log.)

Scofield, H. C. (Bert). *The Echo Lake Deer Hunting Log, 1904-1926*. Wisconsin: Privately printed, 1926. Wisconsin State Historical Society: Green Bay Area Research Center. WIHV00-A58.

_____. "A Taylor County Deer Hunt." Unpublished article. Wisconsin State Historical Society. No date. 3 pp. Edited by Robert Wegner

Swift, Ernest. *A History of Wisconsin Deer*. Wisconsin: Wisconsin Conservation Department, 1946. Publication #323.

Van Dyke, T. S. *The Still-Hunter*. Pennsylvania: Stackpole Books, 2004. 18th Edition. Foreword by Robert Wegner.

Wagener, Attorney W. E. Unpublished Letter to Walter E. Scott, Administrative Assistant Wisconsin Conservation Department. February 14, 1955.

Wegner, Robert. "Echo Lake Deer Camp, 1904-1913." *Wisconsin Outdoor Journal*/2005 Hunting Annual. 19(7): 54-59.

_____. "The Perkinsville Pirates, 1915-1926." *Wisconsin Outdoor Journal*. 21(1): 48-53. December/January 2007.

Wisconsin Atlas & Gazetteer. Maine: DeLorme Mapping Company, 1988.

The Minnisink Deer Camp

Bascom, W. P. "A Remarkable Case of Fighting Bucks with Locked Horns." *Forest and Stream*. 85(6): 333. June 1915.

Bell, Bob, Betsy Maugans and Bob Mitchell. *Pennsylvania Big Game Records, 1965-1986*. Pennsylvania: The Pennsylvania Game Commission, 1988.

Bonner, Simon J. "This is Why We Hunt: Social-Psychological Meanings of the Traditions and Rituals of Deer Camp." *Western Folklore*. 63(1/2): 11-50. Winter 2004.

Chandler, Roy. *A History of Hunting in Perry County*. Pennsylvania: Bacon and Freeman Publishers, 1974.

Fegely, Tom. *A Guide to Hunting Pennsylvania Whitetails*. Wisconsin: Krause Publications, 2000. 2nd Edition.

_____. "Deer Camps in Pennsylvania." In *The Great American Deer Camp* edited by Tom Carpenter. Minnesota: North American Hunting Club, 1999.

Forbes, Stanley E., et. al. *The White-tailed Deer in Pennsylvania*. Pennsylvania: The Pennsylvania Game Commission, 1971.

Froment, Frank L. *History of the Blooming Grove Hunting & Fishing Club, 1871-1999*. Pennsylvania: Blooming Grove Hunting & Fishing Club, 1999.

Frye, Bob. *Deer Wars: Science, Tradition, and the Battle over Managing Whitetails in Pennsylvania*. Pennsylvania: Pennsylvania State University Press, 2006.

Heller, Morris. *American Hunting and Fishing Books*. New Mexico: Nimrod and Piscator Press, 1997.

Henn, William F. *The Story of the River Road: Life Along the Delaware from Bushkill to Milford, Pike County, PA*. Pennsylvania: Privately printed, 1975.

Kosack, Joe. *The Pennsylvania Game Commission, 1895-1995: 100 Years of Wildlife Conservation*. Pennsylvania: The Pennsylvania Game Commission, 1995.

Pennsylvania Atlas & Gazetteer. Maine: DeLorme, 2001. 7th Edition.

Pennsylvania Game Commission. *The Pennsylvania Deer Problem*. Pennsylvania: Harrisburg, 1930. Bulletin #12.

Peterson, Buck. *Buck Peterson's Complete Guide to Deer Hunting*. California: Ten Speed Press, 2006.

Sajna, Mike. *Buck Fever: The Deer Hunting Tradition in Pennsylvania*. Pennsylvania: The University of Pittsburgh Press, 1990.

Shissler, Bryon P. *White-Tailed Deer Biology and Management in Pennsylvania*. Pennsylvania: Wildlife Managers, 1985.

Shoemaker, Henry W. *Pennsylvania Deer and Their Horns*. Pennsylvania: The Faust Printing Company, 1915.

Warren, Louis S. *The Hunter's Game: Poachers and Conservationists in Twentieth-Century America*. Connecticut: Yale University, 1997.

Wegner, Robert. *Wegner's Bibliography on Deer & Deer Hunting*. Wisconsin: St. Hubert's Press, 1992.

_____. *Legendary Deer Camps*. Wisconsin: Krause Publications, 2001.

_____. "The Minnisink Hunting and Fishing Club." *Pennsylvania Game News*. 73(8): 28-31. August 2002.

_____. "Bear in the Cumberland Valley." *Pennsylvania Game News*. 78(6): 18-23. June 2007.

Wolfe, Oliver Howard. *Back Log and Pine Knot*. Pennsylvania: Privately printed, 1916.

– Oliver Howard Wolfe, *Back Log and Pine Knot: A Chronicle of the Minnisink Hunting and Fishing Club, 1916*.

Bent's Camp

"A State of Escape." Wisconsin Public Television documentary film produced by Dave Erikson. 2002. 60 minutes. Contains film footage of Bent's Camp.

Anonymous. "Clow's Deer College." *Wisconsin Conservation Bulletin*. 3(12): 19-20. 1938.

Ashley, Steve. (ed.) *Wisconsin Trophy Records, 1840-2005*. Wisconsin: Wisconsin Buck and Bear Club, 2007. Volume 8.

Bent, Arthur J ("Dunny.") *Bent Trails: A Family History*. Pennsylvania: Privately printed, 1991.

Bent, Lucy Ann. *Our Bent Family in America, 1541-1993*. Michigan: Privately printed, 1994.

"Bent's Camp File Folder." Ashland Research Center. Northland SC-28.

"Bent's Camp Resort." www.bents-camp.com.

Bersing, Otis S. *A Century of Wisconsin Deer*. Wisconsin: Wisconsin Conservation Department, 1966.

Boone and Crockett Club. *Records of North American Whitetail Deer*. Montana: Boone & Crockett Club, 2003. 4th Edition.

_____. *A Whitetail Retrospective: Vintage Photos and Memorabilia from the Boone and Crockett Club Archives*. Montana: The Boone & Crockett Club, 2006.

Clow, W. E. Sr. "Half Century of Deer Hunting." *Wisconsin Conservation Bulletin*. 2(9): 10-ll. 1937.

_____. My 60 Years in the Cast Iron Pipe Business. Chicago: James B. Clow & Sons, 1938.

Conover. A. D. Railroad Map of Wisconsin. Reproduced by the Wisconsin Trails Magazine.

Coventry, Kim. *Classic Country Estates of Lake Forest: Architecture and Landscape Design, 1856-1940*. New York: W. W. Norton & Company, 2003.

Currey, J. Seymour. "Vilas County Notes, 1906." [Unpublished.] Information on Charles A. Bent and his family on Lake Mamie. 11 handwritten pages. Wisconsin State Historical Society. Madison, Wisconsin.

Dahlberg, Burton L. and Ralph C. Guettinger. *The White-Tailed Deer in Wisconsin*. Wisconsin: Wisconsin Conservation Department, 1956.

Flader, Susan L. *Thinking Like a Mountain: Aldo Leopold and the Evolution of an Ecological Attitude Toward Deer, Wolves and Forest.* Missouri: University of Missouri Press, 1974.

Kanish, Waube & "Dunny" Bent. "The Cisco Chain of Lakes." www.gogebic.org.

_____. "The Cisco Chain of Lakes from History and Memory." Pennsylvania: Privately printed, 1987.

Leonard John W., ed. *The Book of Chicagoans: A Biographical Dictionary of Leading Living Men of the City of Chicago.* Wisconsin: Brookhaven Press, 1999. Page 127.

Manierre, "Franny." The Story of the Clow Deer Hunt." Michigan: Privately printed, 1938.

Rosenberry, M. B. "A History of Deerfoot Lodge: Memories of Happy Hunting." Wisconsin: Privately printed, 1941.

Schorger, A. W. "The White-Tailed Deer in Early Wisconsin." Transactions of the Wisconsin Academy of Sciences. 42(1953): 197-247.

Swift, Ernest. *A History of Wisconsin Deer.* Wisconsin: Department of Conservation, 1946.

Wegner, Robert. *Wegner's Bibliography on Deer & Deer Hunting.* Wisconsin: St. Hubert's Press, 1992.

_____. *Legendary Deer Camps.* Wisconsin: Krause Publications, 2001.

_____. "Bent's Camp." *Wisconsin Outdoor Journal.* 17(8): 24-29. November 2003.

_____. "John Pettingill Killed a 477-Pound Buck in 1905: Iron River's Big Boy." *Wisconsin Outdoor Journal.* 16(8): 16-21. October/November 2002.

Wisconsin Atlas & Gazetteer. Maine: DeLorme Mapping Company, 1988.

Camp Comfort

Bartlett. Ilo. *Michigan Deer.* Michigan: Department of Conservation, 1950.

Bennett, Carl L., et al. *A History of Michigan Deer Hunting.* Michigan: Department of Conservation, 1966. Research and Development Report Number 85.

Brandreth, Paulina. "Hints on Deer Shooting." *Forest and Stream.* 63(14): 281-283. October 1, 1904.

_____. "Days with the Deer." *Forest and Stream.* 64(11): 213-214. March 18, 1905.

_____. "Days with the Deer." *Forest and Stream.* 64(12): 234-235. March 25, 1905.

Canfield. H. S. "Following Deer Trails in Northwestern Woods." *The Outing Magazine.* 45: 187-192. November 1904.

Daniels, Jeff. "Escanaba in da Moonlight." DVD. Monarch Home Videos, 2002.

Friedrich, Albert. "Illustrated Souvenir Book of the Original Buckhorn Saloon." Texas: Privately printed, circa, 1900.

Hemingway, Ernest. *The Nick Adams Stories.* New York: Schribner, 2003.

Henshaw, Thomas. *The History of Winchester Firearms, 1866-1992.* New Jersey: Winchester Press, 1993.

Long, William J. *Following the Deer.* Boston: Athenaeum press, 1901.

McGaffey, Ernest. "How They Hunt Deer in Arkansas." *Field and Stream.* November 1905. Pp. 648-652.

Michigan Atlas & Gazetteer. Maine: DeLorme, 2000.

Ozoga, John. "Camp Comfort." *Deer & Deer Hunting.* 22(4): 64-71. November 1998.

Petersen, Eugene T. *Hunters' Heritage: A History of Hunting in Michigan.* Michigan: Michigan United Conservation Clubs, 1979.

_____. *The History of Wildlife Conservation in Michigan, 1859-1921.* Michigan: University of Michigan, 1952. Ph. D. dissertation.

Reimann, Lewis C. *Incredible Seney.* Michigan: Northwoods Publisher, 1953.

Richmond, A. B. "Synopsis of the Hunt of 1900." Reprinted in Mert Cowley, *A Palace in the Popples: Part 2.* Wisconsin: Privately printed, 2006, pp. 58-62.

_____. "A Deer Hunt in the Snow." *Outdoor Life.* 7(4): Not paginated. April 1901.

_____. "A Hunt in Michigan." *Outdoor Life.* 14(6): 803-811. December 1904.

_____. "An Outing." *Outdoor Life.* 16(2): 629-634. August 1905.

_____. "In Michigan Woods in November." *Outdoor Life.* 20(3): 229-238. September 1907.

_____. "Boyhood Days." *Outdoor Life.* 24(1): 3-10. July 1909.

_____. "A Michigan Deer Hunt." *Outdoor Life.* 34(?): 434-440. November 1914.

Roosevelt, Theodore. *Outdoor Pastimes of an American Hunter.* New York: Charles Scribner's Sons, 1905.

Stein, John. *Big Rack IV: A History of Texas Trophy Whitetails.* Texas: Privately printed, 1993.

Verme, Louis J. *The Cusino Wildlife Research Station: A Historical Sketch.* Michigan: Department of Natural Resources, 1994.

Wister, Owen. *The Virginian.* New York: Oxford University Press, 1998.

Still House Inn

Bell, Bob; Betsy Maugans; and Bob Mitchell. *Pennsylvania Big Game Records, 1965-1986.* Pennsylvania: The Pennsylvania Game Commission, 1988.

Carlton, L. *A History of Hunting Trip in Sierra Madres, Northern Mexico.* Texas: Privately printed, 1922.

Fegely, Tom. *A Guide to Hunting Pennsylvania Whitetails.* Wisconsin: Krause Publications, 2000. Second Edition.

_____. "Deer Camps in Pennsylvania." In *The Great American Deer Camp* edited by Tom Carpenter. Minnesota: North American Hunting Club, 1999.

Forbes, Stanley E., et al. *The White-Tailed Deer In Pennsylvania.* Pennsylvania: The Pennsylvania Game Commission, 1971.

Frye, Bob. *Deer Wars: Science, Tradition, and the Battle Over Managing Whitetails in Pennsylvania.* Pennsylvania: Pennsylvania State University, 2006.

Kosack, Joe. *The Pennsylvania Game Commission, 1895-1995: 100 Years of Wildlife Conservation.* Pennsylvania: The Pennsylvania Game Commission, 1995.

Mc Donald, J. Scott & Karl V. Miller. "Pennsylvania White-Tailed Deer Restocking Records." *A History of White-Tailed Deer Restocking in the United States, 1878-2004.* Georgia: The Quality Deer Management Association, 2004. 2nd Edition. pp. 80-82.

Minehart, Charles D. as told to Louis Lester. *Meat on the Pole: A Story of the Orrstown Hunting Club.* Pennsylvania: Privately printed, 1948.

Pennsylvania Atlas & Gazetteer. Maine: DeLorme, 2001. 7th Edition.

Pennsylvania Game Commission. *The Pennsylvania Deer Problem.* Pennsylvania: Harrisburg, 1930. Bulletin #12.

Rutledge, Archibald. "The Master Wildwood Sport." *Forest and Stream.* 92(11): 483-485, 506-507. November 1922.

Sajna, Mike. *Buck Fever: The Deer Hunting Tradition in Pennsylvania.* Pennsylvania: The University of Pittsburgh Press, 1990.

Shissler, Bryon P. *White-Tailed Deer Biology and Management in Pennsylvania.* Pennsylvania: Wildlife Managers, 1985.

Shoemaker, Henry W. *Pennsylvania Deer and Their Horns.* Pennsylvania: The Faust Printing Company, 1915.

Warren, Louis S. *The Hunter's Game: Poachers and Conservationists in Twentieth-Century America.* Connecticut: Yale University, 1997.

Wegner, Robert. *Wegner's Bibliography on Deer & Deer Hunting.* Wisconsin: St. Hubert's Press, 1992.

_____. *Legendary Deer Camps.* Wisconsin: Krause Publication, 2001.

_____. "The Still House Inn: The Orrstown Hunting Club, 1897-1947." *Pennsylvania Game News.* 74(7): 10-14. July 2003.

The Silver Creek Camp

The American Field: The Sportsman's Journal. Chicago and New York. 1897-1903

Bartlett, I. H. *Michigan Deer.* Michigan: Michigan Department of Conservation, 1950.

Bennett, C. L., et., al. *A History of Michigan Deer Hunting.* Michigan: Michigan Department of Conservation, 1966.

Forest and Stream: A Journal of Outdoor Life, Travel, Nature, Study, Shooting, Fishing, Yachting. New York. 1897-1903.

"Good book of sports has been written by Allen Shaffmaster." [Review of *Hunting in the Land of Hiawatha.*] *The Courier.* Coldwater, Michigan. August 26, 1904. Page 1.

"Here's a Sporting Editor: Bronson Journal Man Becoming a Famous Hunter." *The Courier.* Coldwater, Michigan. May 20, 1903.

Longfellow, Henry Wadsworth. *The Song of Hiawatha.* London: J. M. Dent, 2002.

_____. *The Song of Hiawatha.* (Selections) Illustrated by Maragret Early. New York: Handprint Books, 2003. Juvenile poetry.

_____. *The Song of Hiawatha.* Massachusetts: David R. Godine, 2004. Illustrations by Frederic Remington.

Osborn, Chase S. *Northwoods Sketches.* Michigan: Historical Society of Michigan, 1949.

_____, and Stellanova Osborn. *Schoolcraft, Longfellow, Hiawatha.* Pennsylvania: Jaques Cattell Press, 1942.

Petersen, Eugene T. *Hunters' Heritage: A History of Hunting in Michigan.* Michigan: Michigan United Conservation Clubs, 1979.

Shaffmaster, A. D. *Hunting in the Land of Hiawatha.* Chicago: M. A. Donohue & Company, 1904.

_____. "Sport in Michigan." *Outdoor Life.* 13(5): Not paginated. May 1904.

_____. "Lost in the Big Elbow." *The National Sportsman.* May 1903.

Wegner, Robert. *Legendary Deer Camps.* Wisconsin: Krause Publications, 2001.

_____. *Wegner's Bibliography on Deer & Deer Hunting.* Wisconsin: St Hubert's Press, 1992.

_____. "The Silver Creek Deer Camp, 1897-1903." *Deer & Deer Hunting.* 26(2): 121-132. October 2002.

Cunningham's Deer Camp on Lost Creek

Brandreth, Pualina. "Hints on Deer Shooting." *Forest and Stream.* 63(14): 281-283. October, 1904.

_____. "Days with the Deer." *Forest and Stream.* 64(11): 213-214. March 18, 1905.

_____. "Days with the Deer." *Forest and Stream.* 64(12): 234-235. March 25, 1905.

Cunningham, G. W. "Still-Hunting Deer." *Forest and Stream.* 44(15): 287. April 13, 1895.

_____. "In a Michigan Camp." *Forest and Stream.* 45(4): 71. July 27, 1895.

_____. "About Non-Residents and Deer." *Forest and Stream.* 45(24): 515. December 14, 1895.

_____. "Still-Hunting Deer in Wisconsin." *Forest and Stream.* 49(21): 405-406. November 20, 1897.

_____. "Lake Superior Deer Hunting." *Forest and Stream.* 51(23): 447. December 3, 1898.

_____. "Lake Superior Deer Hunting – Continued." *Forest and Stream.* 51(24): 467. December 10, 1898.

_____. "Michigan Deer." *Forest and Stream.* 52(1): 10. January 7, 1899.

_____. "Michigan Deer." *Forest and Stream.* 52(6): 109. February 1, 1899.

_____. "In the Deer Woods." *Forest and Stream.* 53(18): 349. October 28, 1899.

_____. "Memories of Northeastern Wisconsin." *Forest and Stream.* 59(4): 67. July 20, 1902.

_____. "In Wisconsin Deer Woods." *Forest and Stream.* 60(8): 48-50. January 17, 1903.

_____. "Deer Hunting in Wisconsin." *Forest and Stream.* 62(2): 27-28. January 9, 1904.

_____. "Deer Hunting in Wisconsin." *Forest and Stream.* 64(5): 93-94. February 5, 1904.

_____. "Deer Hunting in Wisconsin – Continued." *Forest and Stream.* 64(6): 116-117. February 11, 1905.

_____. "Deer Hunting in Wisconsin – Continued." *Forest and Stream.* 65(17): 332. December 30, 1905.

_____. "Deer Hunting in Wisconsin." *Forest and Stream.* 68(7): 258. February 16, 1907.

Hornaday, William T. "The Deer Family." *The American Natural History.* Volume 2. New York: Charles Scribner's Sons, 1919. Pp. 55-121.

Leopold, Aldo. "Wisconsin Wildlife Chronology." *Wisconsin Conservation Bulletin.* 5(11): 1-15. November 1940.

Roosevelt, Theodore, T. S. Van Dyke, D. G. Elliot & A. J. Stone. *The Deer Family.* New York: The MacMillan Company, 1903.

Van Dyke, T. S. "Twentieth Century Deer Hunting." *Outing.* 45(1): 73-76. October 1904.

Wegner, Robert. "Iron River's Big Boy: John Pettingill Killed a 477-Pound Buck in 1906." *Wisconsin Outdoor Journal.* 16(8): 16-21. October/November 2002.

Wittemore, James O. "The Armored Buck of Toddy Pond." *Outing.* Volume 42. April – September 1903. Pp. 218-221.

Woodmont Rod and Gun Club

Ames, Kenneth L. *Death in the Dining Room & Other Tales of Victorian Culture.* Pennsylvania: Temple University Press, 1992.

Bageant, Joe. *Deer Hunting with Jesus.* New York: Crown Publishers, 2007.

Barber, Joseph. "Venison Verses." *The Field.* 4(10): 145. October 23, 1875.

Boggess, Hal. *Classic Hunting Collectibles.* Wisconsin: Krause Publications, 2005.

Bridges, David P. *The Bridges of Washington County: The Woodmont Rod & Gun Club,* Hancock, Maryland. Indiana: Bookman Publishing, 2003.

Bridges, Henry P. *The Woodmont Story: Hunting and Fishing and Raising Wild Turkeys in a Sportsman Paradise.* New York: A. S. Barnes and Company, 1953.

_____. [Title.] *Outdoorsman Magazine.* June, 1939. Pages 17-19.

Browning, Meshach. *Forty-Four Years of the Life of a Hunter.* Pennsylvania: Stackpole Books, 2006. [Classics of American Sport edited with an Introduction by Robert Wegner, Prologue by Archibald Rutledge and a Preface by E. Lee LeCompte].

_____. *Forty-Four Years the Life of a Hunter.* Philadelphia: J. B.Lippincott & Company, 1928, Introduction by E. Lee LeCompte.

"Case Study of the Woodmont Rod and Gun Club." *The Conservation Fund.* Virginia: Arlington, 2002.

E. S. "A Deer Hunt in Maryland." *Forest and Stream.* 11(25): 499-500. January 23, 1879.

"History of Maryland's Whitetail Harvest." *Deer Hunters' Almanac, 2006.* Wisconsin: F&W Publications, 2005. Page 154.

Glass, Bentley. [Review]. The Woodmont Story. *The Quarterly Review of Biology.* 30(4): 401 December 1955.

Goldsmith, Oliver. "The Haunch of Venison." London: G. Kearsly and J. Ridley, 1776.

LeCompte, E. Lee. "History of Conservation of the Natural Resources of Maryland 1785 to 1924." *Maryland Conservationist.* 1( ): 1924 p. 4.

_____. "Game Farms are Essential." *Maryland Conservationist.* 14(4): 13. 1938.

_____. "Inspection of Game Refuges in Western Maryland." *Maryland Conservationist.* 1( ): 15, Fall 1927.

_____. "The Propagation of Game in Captivity." *Maryland Conservationist.* 9(1): 18. 1932.

"Maryland." 21st Annual Meeting Southeast Deer Study Group, 1998. [Abstracts.] Page 49.

"Maryland White-Tailed Deer Restocking Records." In *A History of White-Tailed deer Restocking in the United States, 1878 to 2004,* edited by J. Scott McDonald and Karl V. Miller [University of Georgia, 2004). Pages 51-53.

McCluskey, Ross C. "Meshach Browning." *Outdoor Life.* 112(1): 32-33, 98, 100-101, 10, 110. July 1953.

McNally, Tom. "Woodmont and Its Master-Mind." *Baltimore Sun Magazine.* November 20, 1955. Page 13.

Ott, Cynthia. "A Sportsman's Paradise: The Woodmont Rod and Gun Club." *Maryland Historical Magazine.* 92(2): 219-237. Summer 1997.

Reiger, John F. *American Sportsmen and the Origins of Conservation.* Oregon: Oregon University Press, 2001. 3rd Edition.

Rutledge, Archibald. "Meshach Browning: Wilderness Hunter." (2-part article.) *Sports Afield.* 118(6): 48-49, 70-73. December 1947. 118(7): 54, 89-90. January 1948.

S. Powell Bridges Collection 1937-1992. East Tennessee State University Archives. Johnson City, TN. (A VHS videotape, produced in December 1993, contains views of the Woodmont Rod and Gun Club composed from 8mm and 16mm film originals.)

Sandt, Joshua L. "A Brief History of Deer in Maryland and the Northeast." www.arec.umd.edu.

Senex. "The Woodmont Rod and Gun Club." *Forest and Stream.* 16(24): 469. July 14, 1881.

Stieff, Frederick Philip. *Eat, Drink & be Merry in Maryland.* Maryland: The Johns Hopkins University Press, 1957.

"The History of White Tailed Deer Management in Maryland." www.dnr.state.md.us.

"The Hunt of 1937." (Portfolio of 52 8x10 black and white photos.) Washington County Library. Western Maryland Room. WMR975.291W.

"The Swamp Hunters' Club." [Maryland.] *Member Hunting Camps: A Gallery.* Minnesota: North American Outdoor Group, 1999. Pages 207-209.

"The Truth About Maryland's Deer Population."" www.marylandsportsmen.org.

"The Woodmont Rod and Gun Club." (Washington) *Evening Star.* April 28, 1883.

"The Woodmont Rod and Gun Club." (Washington) *Evening Star.* April 25, 1882.

"The Woodmont Rod and Gun Club. Its Organization – Description of Club-House, etc." *American Angler.* No. 17. October 21, 1882.

"The Woodmont Rod and Gun Club." *Shooting and Fishing: A Weekly Journal of the Rifle, Gun and Rod.* 10(8): 145. June 18, 1891.

"The Woodmont Rod and Gun Club: A Famous Shooting Preserve." *Maryland Conservationist.* 6(1): 1929.

""The Woodmont Rod and Gun Club." *Maryland Conservationist.* 13(2): 16. 1936.

Wegner, Robert. "Meshach Browning." *Legendary Deerslayers.* Wisconsin: Krause Publications, 2004. Pages 96-111.

_____. "Meshach Browning and his Famous Buck Fight." *Deer & Deer Hunting.* 23(3): 123-130. October 1999.

"Woodmont Rod & Gun Club a Great Asset to Western Maryland Sportsmen." *Maryland Conservationist.* 9(1): 20. 1932.

"$80,000 Woodmont Club, Finest in Trophies, Scene of Dinner Party." *Maryland Conservationist.* 8(2): 24. 1931.

Deer Camp Surprise

Devitt, Terry. "UW Study Shows Deer in CWD Zone Stick to Home." *Wisconsin Outdoor News.* November 4, 2005. 12(22): 7-8.

Faulkner, William. "The Old People." *Big Woods: The Hunting Stories of William Faulkner.* New York: Random House, 1955. Pp. 113-138.

Leopold, Aldo. *Report on a Game Survey of the North Central States.* Wisconsin: Sporting Arms and Ammunition Manufacturers' Institute, 1931.

Records of North American Big Game. 12th Edition. Montana: Boone & Crockett Club, 2005.

Rutledge, Archibald. "The Black-Horn Buck." *Wildlife in the South.* New York: Frederick A. Stokes Company, 1935. Pp. 79-83.

Swift, Ernest. *A History of Wisconsin Deer.* Wisconsin: Department of Conservation, 1946.

Van Dyke, T. S. *The Still-Hunter.* Foreword by Robert Wegner. Pennsylvania: Stackpole Books, 2004.

Wegner, Robert. "Deer Hunting in the Uplands." *Deer & Deer Hunting: Book 2.* Pennsylvania: Stackpole Books, 1987. Pp. 312-325.

_____. "The Monarch of Deer Valley." *Booners: The Journal of Monster Whitetails.* 3(1): 40-43. November 2006.

_____. "The Monarch of Deer Valley." *Deer & Deer Hunting.* 30(1): 81-82. September 2006.

Wisconsin Trophy Records: Volume 7, 1888-2000. Wisconsin: Wisconsin's Buck and Bear Club, Inc., 2002.

(This bibliography represents a continuation of "Wegner's Deer Camp Bibliography" in the author's *Legendary Deer Camps* (2001). It contains new items in addition to that list of more than 200 citations on American deer camps found since the publication of that book.)

Adler, Jeanne Winston. *Early Days in the Adirondacks: The Photographs of Seneca Ray Stoddard.* New York: Harry A. Abrams, Incorporated, 1997.

Anderson, Dennis. Deer Camp. *An Hour Before Dawn.* Minnesota: Voyageur Press, 1993. Pp. 49-54.

Anderson, Donald Jack. "New Look at the Old Deer Camp." *Field & Stream.* 74(11): 72-73, 160-164. March 1970.

Anonymous. "The 'Man-I-Do-Wish' Hunting Club. No Place." Privately Printed. No date. [Thirty-three unnumbered pages of text printed on one side only.] Organized in 1887.

Archibald, Robert R. *A Place to Remember: Using History to Build Community.* California: AltaMira Press, 1999.

Arlen, Alice "Libbys Camps." *Maine Sporting Camps.* Vermont: The Countryman Press, 2003. Pp. 192-196.

Bageant, Joe. "Valley of the Gun." *Deer Hunting with Jesus: Dispatches from America's Class War.* New York: Crown Publishers, 2007. Pp. 119-157.

Bailey, Jonathan. *Deer Camp.* [Handmade Book.] Vermont: Stony Brook, 1979.

Bailey, Tom. *The Grace that Keeps This World.* New York: Shaye Areheart Books, 2005.

Bain, Darrin. "The Cabin of Seven Shells." *Deer & Deer Hunting.* 26(6): 10-14. January 2003.

Barrows, William. *The General; or Twelve Nights in the Hunters' Camp: A Narrative of Real Life.* Massachusetts: Lee & Shepard, 1869.

Bestul, Scott. "Deer Club Dynamics." *Deer & Deer Hunting.* 30(6): 37-42. January 2007.

Bogdan, Robert. *Exposing the Wilderness: Early-Twentieth-Century Adirondack Postcard Photographers.* New York: Syracuse University, 1999.

Bonner, Simon J. *Popularizing Pennsylvania: Henry W. Shoemaker and the Progressive Uses of Folklore and History.* Pennsylvania: Pennsylvania State University Press, 1996.

_____. (ed.) *Manly Traditions: The Folk Roots of American Masculinities.* Indiana: Indiana University Press, 2005.

_____. "This is Why We Hunt: Social-Psychological Meanings of the Traditions and Rituals of Deer Camp." *Western Folklore.* 63(1/2): 11-50. Winter 2004.

Boyer, Dennis. "Deer Camp Dick." *Giants in the Land: Folk Tales & Legends of Wisconsin.* Wisconsin: Prairie Oak Press, 1997. Pp. 36-39.

Carden, Evan. "Where Everything is Made for Love: Double Gates Hunting Lodge." *The Thomasville Times.* Thomasville, AL. August 3, 2006.

Chandler, Roy F. "Deer Hunting Camps." *A History of Hunting in Perry County.* Pennsylvania: Bacon and Freeman Publishers, 1974. Pp. 145-149.

Chips, Mr. *A Hound Bays in Ellsworth.* New York: Vantage Press, 1991.

Collins, Erik. "She Belongs." *Deer & Deer Hunting.* 26(8): 10-12. June 2003.

Cook, Sam. "Deer Camp." *Camp Sights.* Minnesota: Pfeifer-Hamilton, 1993. Pp. 147-149.

Cowley, Mert ("The Jack Pine Poet.") *A Palace in the Popples: Part I.* Wisconsin: Privately printed, 2005.

_____. *A Palace in the Popples: Part II.* Wisconsin: Privately printed, 2006.

_____. *There's Daylight in the Swamps.* Wisconsin: Privately printed, 2002.

_____. *Dawn of the Deer Camp.* Wisconsin: Privately printed, 2001.

Creel, Mike. "Hunting Clubs." In *Carolina's Hunting Heritage* edited by John Culler (South Carolina, 1979), pp. 187-191.

Da Yoopers. "For Diehards Only." CD. Michigan: You Guys Inc., 1992.

_____. "Camp Fever." Tape cassette. Michigan: You Guys Inc., 1988.

Daniels, Jeff. "Escanaba In Da Moonlight." DVD. Monarch Home Video, 2002.

"Deer Camp Songs." CD. Kansas: Laughing Hyena, 1999.

"Deer Camp Special 2006." *Field & Stream.* 108(7): 64-74. November 2003.

Edwards, John. "Hunting Camps." *Pennsylvania Sportsman.* December 1985. Pp. 28-29.

Elinskas, Robert J. *A Deer Hunter's History Book: Twentieth-Century Woodland Adventures From Within and Around the Blue Ridge Wilderness Area.* New York: Privately printed, 2005.

"Family Deer Camp." Video. [Portrait of a NH deer camp.] 1-800-20NHPTV(64788).

Fegely, Tom. "Deer Camp Revisited: Palaces in the Popple." *Hunting Pennsylvania Whitetails.* Wisconsin: Krause Publications, 2000. 2nd Edition. Pp. 291-294.

Fears, J. Wayne. *Hunt Club Management Guide.* Maryland: Stoeger Publishing Company. 2003.

Fiduccia, Peter and Jay Cassell. *North America's Greatest Whitetail Lodges & Outfitters.* Wisconsin: Willow Creek Press, 2001.

Foster, Caroline. "If Walls Could Talk." *South Carolina Wildlife.* Pp. 14-19. November/December 2002.

Froment, Frank L. *History of the Blooming Grove Hunting and Fishing Club, 1871-1999.* Pennsylvania: Privately printed, 1999.

Gray, Mack H. III. "A Family Hunt Club." *Hunt Forever.* 2(2): 74-76. October/November 2004.

Gutschow, Gregg. "Search for the Perfect Deer Camp." In *Whitetail Wisdom,* North American Hunting Club, 1998. P.153.

Hallock, Charles. *Hallock's American Club List and Sportsman's Glossary.* New York: Forest and Stream Publishing Company, 1878.

Hampton, Walt. "Hunting Clubs: Deer Hunting's Saving Grace?" *Deer & Deer Hunting.* 26(8): 57-58. June 2003.

Hennessey, Tom. "The Camp." *Sportsman's Hunting Yearbook 2003.* Pp. 6-7, 81-82.

Hubley, Jack. "Deer Hunting is Much Easier Now." *Sunday News Lancaster.* November 22, 1998.

Hunter, Julia A. & Earle G. Shettleworth, Jr. *Fly Rod Crosby: The Woman who Marketed Maine.* Maine: Tilbury House Publishers, 2000.

Hurteau, Dave. "A Day in Deer Camp: At the End of a Maze of Logging Roads is the Entrance to Another World." *Field & Stream.* [Southern Edition.] CVIII(7): 64-71. November 2003.

Jolly, Tes Randle. "Dollarhide Days: Famous Southern Deer Camp Carries on Old Traditions." *Deer & Deer Hunting.* 28(8): 29-32. June 2005.

_____. "A Heavenly Deer Camp." *Deer & Deer Hunting.* 29(7): 40-46. March 2006.

Jones, Joe D. "Deer Camp or Corporation, Biz Basics the Same." *The Mississippi Business Journal.* 26(8): 4(2). February 23, 2004.

Jones, Robert F. "God Bless the Running Deer." *Game Journal.* 1(5): 64-76.

Kirk, Francis Marion. *A History of the St. John's Hunting Club.* South Carolina: Privately printed, 1950.

Lattimer, Dick. "Fred's Secret Hunting Camp." *I Remember Papa Bear.* Minnesota: IHunt Communications, 2005. Pp. 86-103.

Lindner, Bill. "Opening Day." *Deer & Deer Hunting.* 28(5): 26-33. December 2004.

"Log Creek Lodge: Memories, 1949-1984" DVD. Wisconsin: Hanna Production, 2005.

Mance, Dave III. "Good Deer Camps Never Die." *Field & Stream.* 111(8): 94-97. December/January 2007.

Marks, Stuart A. *Southern Hunting in Black and White: Nature, History, and Ritual in a Carolina Community.* New Jersey: Princeton University Press, 1994.

McKee, James "Mac." *His Steps My Path: A Collection of Deer Camp Stories.* Florida: Privately printed, 1997.

Miller, Peter. "Lessons from the Stalker." *Outdoor Life Deer Hunter's Yearbook, 1987.* New York: Times Mirror Magazine, Inc., 1986. Pp. 75-79.

Mills, Robert C. *Deer Camp: An American Tradition.* Michigan: Mills Publications, 2001.

Muth, Robert M. and Wesley V. Jamison. "On the Destiny of Deer Camps and Duck Blinds: The Rise of the Animal Rights Movement and the Future of Wildlife Conservation." *Wildlife Society Bulletin.* 28(4): 841-851. Winter 2000.

Nash, Roderick. "The Wilderness Cult." *Wilderness and the American Mind.* Connecticut: Yale University Press, 1982. 3rd Edition.

Nelson, Norman E. "Four Generations of a North Woods Deer Camp." *Deer & Deer Hunting.* 27(6): 45-51. January 2004.

Newman, Marvin G. "Last Hunt at Red Hills Lodge." *Deer & Deer Hunting.* 28(5): 103-104. December 2004.

North American Hunting Club. *Member Hunting Camps: A Gallery.* Minnesota: North American Outdoor Group, 1999.

_____. *Hunting Camp Almanac.* Minnesota: North American Outdoor Group, 1999.

_____. *The Great American Deer Camp.* Minnesota: North American Outdoor Group, 1999.

Olson, Sigurd F. "The Drive." *Spirit of the North: The Quotable Sigurd F. Olson.* Edited by David Backes. Minnesota: University of Minnesota Press, 2004. P. 45.

Palmer, Dave. "Ste. Genevieve County Deer Club Carrying on a Rich Tradition." *Missouri Conservationist.* 63(11): 32. November 2002.

Payne, Stephen Russell. "How We Got the Deer Camp. (And Why We're Not Going to Change It!")* Vermont Life.* LVII(1): 13-17, 22. Autumn 2002.

Peterson, Buck. *Buck Peterson's Complete Guide to Deer Hunting.* Toronto: Ten Speed Press, 2006. Revised Edition.

Randolph, John. "Hawk [Larry Benoit] Who Walks Hunting." *In Seasons of the Hunter* edited by Robert Elman and David Seybold (New York: Alfred A. Knopf, 1985, pp. 182-195.)

Reiger, John F. *American Sportsmen and the Origins of Conservation.* Oregon: Oregon State University Press, 2001. 3rd Revised and Expanded Edition.

Robbins, Chuck. "The 21 Club." *Deer 2001.* Pp. 36-31.

Schmitt, Peter J. *Back to Nature: The Arcadian Myth in Urban America.* New York: Oxford University Press, 1969.

_____. "Call of the Wild, the Arcadian Myth in Urban America, 1900-1930." University of Minnesota: Ph. D. Dissertation, 1966.

Sharp, Eric. "Ah, Deer Camp." *Outdoor Life.* 209(8): 15. November 2002.

Shorey, A. T. "On Closing Camp for the Winter." *New York State Conservationist.* 10(2): 16-17. October/November 1955.

Smith, Richard P. "Unusual Deer Camp." *Deer & Deer Hunting.* 9(6): 88-89. July/August 1986.

Speltz, M. G. "Camp 17." Minnesota: Privately printed, 1984. 28 pp.

_____. "Supplement #1 to the Camp 17 History." Minnesota: Privately printed, November 1984. 13 pp.

Steiner, Linda L. "Home Sweet Deer Camp." *Field & Stream.* CVI (9): 77. January 2002.

Strauch, Ileana. "The Last Deer Drivers." *The Double Gun Journal.* 12(1): 9-15. Spring 2001.

Sulllivan, Mark T. *The Purification Ceremony: A Novel of Suspense.* New York: Avon Books, 1997.

Swan, James. "Escanaba in Da Moonlight" Premieres, but . . ." www.james-swan.com.

The Legacy of Les C. Kouba. Minnesota: North Star Printing and Mailing, Inc., 1988.

Towsley, Bryce M. "The Benoits of Vermont: America's First Family of Deer Hunting." *Deer & Deer Hunting.* 20(5): 44-51. August 1997.

_____. *Big Bucks the Benoit Way.* Wisconsin: Krause Publications, 1998.

_____. *Benoit Bucks.* Wisconsin: Krause Publications, 2003.

Vaznis, Bill. "Death of the Deer Camp." *Deer & Deer Hunting.* 27(3): 130-137. October 2003.

Veine, Michael R. "Coming of Age at the Ten-Point Inn." *Deer & Deer Hunting.* 26(6): 60-64. January 2003.

Vroble, Jack, et. al. "Only in Deer Camp: True Stories & Dubious Legends from Whitetail Country." *Field & Stream.* [Southern Edition]. CVIII(7): 72. November 2003.

Walters, Kathyrn. "A Place Called Ralph." *Michigan Natural Resources.* November/December, 1986. Pp. 20-25.

Wegner, Robert. "Bear in the Cumberland Valley." *Pennsylvania Game News.* 78(6): 18-23. June 2007.

_____. *Legendary Deer Camps.* Wisconsin: Krause Publications, 2001.

_____. "Cult of the Whitetail: Part 1." *Deer & Deer Hunting.* 27(6): 22-28. January 2004.

_____. "Cult of the Whitetail: Part 2." *Deer & Deer Hunting.* 27(7): 44-48. March 2004.

_____. "Silver Creek Deer Camp." *Deer & Deer Hunting.* 26(2): 121-132. October 2002.

_____. "Ten Point Deer Club." *Deer & Deer Hunting.* 25(5): 28-34. December 2001.

_____. "The Leopold Deer Camp." *Deer & Deer Hunting.* 24(6): 64-69. January 2001.

_____. "William Faulkner: A Nobel Prize Winner in Deer Camp." *Deer & Deer Hunting.* 23(6): 35-40. January 2000.

_____. "The Bucks Camp." *Deer & Deer Hunting.* 24(5): 62-72. December 2000.

Wilson, Donald A. *Maine's Hunting Past.* South Carolina: Arcadia Publishing, 2003.

Wyman, Helen B. *Stories about Hunters and Hunting in Wisconsin and the North Country.* Wisconsin: University of Wisconsin—River Falls Press, 1987.

ACKNOWLEDGMENTS

Art Wheaton

Matt Libby

Remington Art Collection

Jennifer S. Bullins, Remington Arms Company, Inc.

Carol Luder, Fair Chase

Vicki Schrimpf, Winchester/Olin Corporation

Scott E. Schaefer, Winfield Galleries LLC

Earle Shettleworth, Maine Historic Preservation Commission

Lisa Stemen, Bent's Camp, Vilas County, Wisconsin

Paul Kennedy, Editorial Director, Krause Publications

Derrek Sigler, Editor, Krause Publications

Robert C. Mitchell, Editor, *Pennsylvania Game News*

Bob Sopchick

Lynn W. Wells

Alva Benjamin Wells

Wisconsin State Historical Society. Madison, Wisconsin

Minnesota Historical Society

University of Wisconsin – Madison, Department of Inter-Library Loan

The Adirondack Museum, Blue Mountain Lake, New York

Morgan Elmore, Librarian, Center for Research Libraries, Chicago, Illinois

Mitch Cox, Editor, *Fur-Fish-Game*

Paul Wait, Editor, *Wisconsin Outdoor Journal*

Dan Schmidt, Editor, *Deer & Deer Hunting*

Mert Cowley, "The Jack Pine Poet"

Jared Scofield, Sturgeon Bay, Wisconsin

Anne Jinkins. Door County Historical Society, Sturgeon Bay, Wisconsin

Historical Society of Washington County, Virginia, Inc. Abingdon, VA

Colby College Art Museum

Larry Huffman, Wildlife Images

Minnesota Historical Society

Professor Simon J. Bronner, Pennsylvania State University

The History Center and Archives at Ashland, Wisconsin

Michigan State Archive

Land O'Lakes Historical Society and Northern Waters Museum. Land O'Lakes, WI

Vilas County Historical Museum. Sayner, Wisconsin

Potter County Historical Society, Potter County, Pennsylvania

Nola Baker, Holbrook Heritage Room, Coldwater Public Library, Coldwater, Michigan

Archives of Appalachia, East Tennessee State University

Jill Craig, Western Maryland Room, Washington County Free Library, Hagerstown, Maryland

Robert Schwartz, Schwartz Gallery, New York, NY

Rod Crossman

Bob Kuhn

Casey Kuhn

Ken Callahan & Company Booksellers

Francis Lee Jacques Art Center, Aitkin, Minnesota

Library of Congress, Washington D. C.

Steve Ashley, Wisconsin Buck & Bear Club

Jack Reanau, Boone & Crockett Club

Fred Bear

Dennis Atkinson, Phillips Historical Society, Phillips, Maine

David Rhines, Sumner, WA

Superior Views, Marquette, Michigan

A. Aubrey Bodine Image Gallery

David P. Bridges

Mark Peck

Paul Birling

Tom Nelsen

Dan Shideler

ABOUT THE AUTHOR

A smiling former editor of *Deer & Deer Hunting* poses with his 11-pointer weighing 247 pounds field dressed (321.1 pounds live weight). October 1982.

In 1979, Robert Wegner received his Ph.D. from the University of Wisconsin - Madison where he was trained as a cultural historian. After studying at various locations in West Germany and a short-term teaching career at the University of Wisconsin, he became the editor and co-owner of *Deer & Deer Hunting* magazine. After the magazine was sold to Krause Publications in 1992, he became a free-lance writer specializing in the cultural history of white-tailed deer and deer hunting.

His award-winning work has appeared in such magazines as *Hunt Club Digest, Wisconsin Sportsman, Pennsylvania Game News, Michigan Sportsman, Fur-Fish-Game, Quality Whitetails, Whitetail Hunting Strategies, Wisconsin Outdoor Journal* and many others. His landmark book trilogy, *Deer & Deer Hunting,* has sold more than 100,000 copies. Fred Bear referred to this three-volume work as "a classic in American hunting literature."

Legendary Deer Camps (2001), part of The Classics Series from *Deer & Deer Hunting* magazine, won the 2003 Excellence in Craft Award from the Outdoor Writers' Association of America. In his review of the book, Dr. James Swan, author of *In Defense of Hunting,* writes: "Weaving together his love of deer hunting with his professional training as a historian, he has become the dean of the history of deer hunting in the United States."

In reviewing the second volume of this trilogy, *Legendary Deerslayers* (2004), for the magazine *Sporting Classics,* historian Dr. James Casada calls the book "a must for the avid deer hunter. By telling us where we have been in the sport as viewed through the eyes of deerslayers par excellence, it provides a fuller understanding of how we got to where we are today and where we might be going as hunters. Add this book to your shelves or coffee table, and as you do so, I'm sure you will join me in tendering a vote of thanks to Wegner for his stellar efforts in probing, then perpetuating, our rich deer-hunting legacy."

Wegner resides in Deer Valley, a secluded land filled with whitetails and wild turkeys in the heart of "The Uplands," in Southwestern Wisconsin with his wife, Maren, and daughter, Serena. As the former editor and co-owner of *Deer & Deer Hunting,* Wegner continues to contribute feature articles to that magazine and others as well. He also serves as an editor for Stackpole Books' Classics of American Sport and is finishing a book tentatively titled *Romancing the Whitetail,* 1900-1975. Wegner has studied, observed and hunted whitetails for more than 40 years.

He is a Charter Member in The Human Dimensions of Wildlife Study Group, a Charter Life Member of the Quality Deer Management Association and a former member of their Board of Advisors. He also serves as the Vice President of The Uplands Branch of the Quality Deer Management Association. Wegner has been an active member of the Outdoor Writers Association of America, Inc., since 1981.

Also By The Author:
Deer & Deer Hunting, Book 1
Deer & Deer Hunting, Book 2
Deer & Deer Hunting, Book 3
Wegner's Bibliography on Deer & Deer Hunting
Legendary Deer Camps
Legendary Deerslayers
Romancing the Whitetail (forthcoming)

As Editor:
Paulina Brandreth, *Trails of Enchantment*
George Mattis, *Whitetail*
T. S. Van Dyke, *The Still Hunter*
Friedrich Gerstaecker, *Wild Sports*
Archibald Rutledge, *Those Were the Days*
Meshach Browning, *Forty-Four Years the Life of a Hunter*
Philip Tome, *Pioneer Life, or Thirty Years a Hunter*

MORE HUNTING HERITAGE AND HOW-TOS

Bowhunting Forests & Deep Woods
by Greg Miller
Go deep with this exciting and informative guide to big woods hunting from champion bowhunter Greg Miller.
Hardcover • 6 x 9 • 240 pages 140 b&w photos
Item# BFDW • $24.95

Strategies for Whitetail
by Charles J. Alsheimer
Explore 200 brilliant photos from the field and reliable facts about rutting behavior, growth patterns, quality deer management, while you enjoy insights about the culture of hunters.
Softcover • 8-¼ x 10-⅞ 192 pages • 200 color photos
Item# WTLDD • $24.99

Mapping Trophy Bucks
Using Topographic Maps to Find Deer
by Brad Herndon
Learn how to use topographical maps to effectively implement sound terrain hunting strategies, to read deer movement, and to use the weather to your advantage.
Softcover • 8-¼ x 10-⅞ 192 pages • 150 color photos
Item# TRTT • $24.99

Trophy Bucks in Any Weather
How to Use Weather to Predict Deer Behavior
by Dan Carlson
This go-to guide for new and experienced hunters delivers biological and weather factors, including barometric pressure, fronts and air masses to predict deer behavior.
Softcover • 6 x 9 • 272 pages • 200+ color photos
Item# Z1781 • $21.99

Whitetail Wisdom
A Proven 12-Step Guide to Scouting Less and Hunting More
by Daniel E. Schmidt
If you're like many deer hunters, one of the biggest problems is finding time to get in the woods. Now, there's a book that offers easy and effective tips to make the time, and the best use of it.
Softcover • 6 x 9 • 224 pages • 110+ b&w photos • 8-page color section
Item# FTWH • $19.99

Krause Publications
P.O. Box 5009,
Iola, WI 54945-5009
www.krausebooks.com

Order directly from the publisher by calling **800-258-0929** M-F 8 am – 5 pm
Online at **www.krausebooks.com** or from booksellers nationwide.
Please reference offer **OTB8** with all direct-to publisher orders.